A group of eminent religio[us]
explores the position of reli[gion in the]
age of science

Religion Ponders Science

Religion Ponders Science

Edited by DR. EDWIN P. BOOTH

APPLETON-CENTURY
New York

Copyright © 1964 by Meredith Publishing Company

All rights reserved. No part of this book in excess of five hundred words may be reproduced in any form without permission in writing from the publisher.

First edition

Affiliate of
MEREDITH PRESS
Des Moines & New York

Library of Congress Catalogue Card Number: 64-12457

MANUFACTURED IN THE UNITED STATES OF AMERICA FOR MEREDITH PRESS

VAN REES PRESS • NEW YORK

HUGH STEPHENS LIBRARY
STEPHENS COLLEGE
COLUMBIA, MISSOURI

BL
240.2
.B66

Contents

v

89358

Introduction

by EDWIN PRINCE BOOTH

Boston University

THIS IS A COMPANION VOLUME to one published four years ago, edited by Dr. Harlow Shapley, entitled *Science Ponders Religion*. This one is entitled *Religion Ponders Science*, and each person who was asked to contribute a chapter to this book has been left completely free to express his own convictions. Yet there were major questions asked by the editor of the book. Science has in the past fifty years made such contributions to human life that the men who offer us leadership in religion must be answerable to the problems raised in this new advance of science. The editor of this book wrote to many men whose lives have been spent in the leadership of religion, asking them questions similar to the following:

How has the new scientific information influenced your attitude on religion?

Do you fear the new insights into the nature of time that the sciences set before us?

Do you fear the new understandings of the soul that the psychological sciences now make clear to us?

Does the difference in the knowledge of the physical world, its immensity, its intricacy, its apparent timelessness, have any effect on your understanding of the nature and the work of God in this universe?

In what way has the new understanding of human motivation brought to us by the scientists contributed to your thought concerning sin and guilt, which have so long been a part of the theological understanding?

In what other ways are the great issues of theology affected for you by the tremendous fields of knowledge uncovered and about to be uncovered by the scientists?

There is no unity in the book in the sense of a definite intellectual or theological proposition. The unity of the book consists in the data from the experience of leaders in religion, which is set before us.

No single writer in this book has been asked by the editor to set forth or defend any position other than that to which his mind is led by the questions asked him. There is a wide representation. There are men from the liberal and the conservative branches of Christianity. There is a great Hindu thinker, now the Vice-President of India, and there is a very prominent and eloquent representative of Judaism, in Temple Israel of Boston. There are philosophers, scientists, preachers, and teachers of the Christian tradition. There is also the testimony of one who has spent his life in the practice of law. This last pleases me considerably, since I remember Gandhi's great statement that the purpose of law is "to bring together them that are rent asunder." It is true that there is no Catholic representative here, but the editor has had correspondence with the President of Notre Dame and with Father Courtnay Murray. Both have expressed deep concern with the issues here discussed and both have written widely on the subject. The attitude of the Catholic Church is well known in her doctrinal statements, and Father Hesburg and Father Murray are both doing valiant service in our time to explain and modernize the values conserved in Catholic dogma. Just this year (1963), Boston College, a Jesuit institution, devoted its Centennial observance to inquiring about the "Knowledge Explosion" in our world. The absence of a Catholic chapter in this book therefore should be understood not as any refusal of co-operation but as an indication that the vantage point from which these questions are surveyed has not yet been made sufficiently universal for Catholics and Protestants to address themselves to the problem in the same book. This does not mean that a Catholic thinker is unaware of these grave issues, but on the contrary it means that Catholic thinkers are so aware of them that patience and considerable discussion is necessary before statements can be printed. Nevertheless the editor of this book, himself a liberal Protestant, believes that his own position is best set forth, when all things are considered, in the writings of the late great Jesuit scientist, Pierre Teilhard de Chardin.

By *religion* I mean the area of life that encompasses the individual and the whole, the particle and the total, the particular and the universal. This is the area of "ultimate concern," in Professor Tillich's words, the "attitude toward the Determiner of Destiny," in James Bissett Pratt's words.

By *science* I mean the area of life that encompasses the knowledge of man and his environment in all its manifold presentations, by the individual, who is also part of the whole.

Religion can be pure, i.e., unapplied, or it can be historic and exist in a definite applied form. Such applied forms are our historic churches and our theologies.

Science may be pure, i.e., knowledge of the laws, or it may be applied. The applied forms are technological structures in history, comparable to historic churches.

Between the applied forms there must be tension, since they are relative, but in the pure forms there is opportunity for understanding more and more the interdependence and the essential unity.

Writing for myself, I must say that in my opinion every concept of applied traditional Christian theology must be surrendered in the form in which our fathers stated it. The values those forms encased must be recaptured and reset in a modern vocabulary. Let me illustrate by suggesting that the Ten Commandments of Moses as they appear in the Old Testament are not pure guides for the human race. When these commandments were set forth, they were only for a section of the human race, and they were protective devices for the perpetuation of that segment of humanity in its historic evolution. As such they have nobly performed their function. But the evolutional view of the universe, rather than the protective view of the universe in which God has as his favorite one race thereof, requires totally new commandments. I suggest, for example, that the commandments under which humanity might live for the next one thousand years could better be stated somewhat as follows:

I. Thou shalt survive. This is the law of food. Each individual in the total universe must receive sustenance.

II. Thou shalt reproduce. This is the law that secures the survival of the species, just as law number one secures the survival of the individual. This means that reproduction of one's own kind receives a universal mandate.

III. Thou shalt communicate. This is the law of community. Nothing lives alone, be it plant, animal, particle of physics, or human being. The law of community is written into the evolutional process, and it must be obeyed.

IV. Thou shalt be thyself. This is an advanced stage in the evolutional process, but it heralds the introduction of self-respect and honor and integrity into the historical stream. There is an abiding truth in "egoism." Egocentrism is not a "predicament," as Toynbee says, but an amazing stage in evolution.

V. Thou shalt think. This has become a most serious problem. To what extent has the human mind a right to investigate the properties of the environment in which it lives? This law means that regardless of all circumstances the mind has appeared in the evolutional process for the purpose of thinking, and it can do no other. We must proceed in our investigations on all fronts.

VI. Thou shalt reverence. This is the law that gives birth to the religious conscience. Here I may be misunderstood, but I plead for serious consideration. In particle physics the particle, which is the basis of the physical structure, gets its reality and has its vitality constituted in its relation to all other particles in the combination with which the universe is made. In the same sense I maintain that each individual person must by nature reverence the whole of which he is a part. This is a kind of homesickness that gives religion its quiet beauty. The greater and the more immense and the more intricate the universe becomes, the more am I reverential toward it. I mean in all seriousness that the attitude the individual has toward the universal that gives him his life and sustains him in his individuality is the religious attitude. Therefore every advance in the sciences increases the depth of the religious mood.

These six laws I suggest should supplant the so-called Decalogue of Moses, which in itself was but a historic incident in mankind's long evolution. In the light of these new laws we could make a totally new ethic, in which race prejudice, child of the chosen-people complex, could disappear before the far nobler concept that no people is chosen but that all people are God's. These laws of evolution can sustain a world culture.

Writing as a Christian, however, I see no way to improve, under Science's instruction, the deep intensities of the Beatitudes and the Parables of Jesus. I do not mean this as exclusively Christian, for I believe that in the non-Christian religions there are also these tremendous central essences of spirituality. As the Christian creeds of Nicaea and Trent and the Christian theologies of Luther and Calvin must disappear into the mists of the past, so too must the structures of the non-Christian religions. But all of them—the tremendous spirituality of Hinduism, the deep anguish of the mystery religions in their cry for immortality, the protective devices of the "medicine man" religions of primitive peoples, the high and exceptionally fine ethics of Confucianism, the longing for immortal consolation of Buddhism, the social uplift of Islam, and above all the deep effort of Christian theologians to describe the nature of God's dealing with the universe—these all must surrender their historic forms of expression and be willing to be recast in the totally new and currently clear expression of unity that we now find between science and religion. Those who say that the issue between science and religion is solved do not understand of what they speak. This issue may never be solved, for all dogmatic statements of the religionist and of the scientist must fade quietly into the background before the birth of unity can be achieved. All creeds, all dogmas, all affirmations of eternal validity must moderate themselves, and a quiet, gentle humility must possess us all as we face the immensity and the majesty and the intricacy of the works of nature to which we belong. As a Christian I call the central essence of this unbelievable beauty "God," and so I say that the works of the world are the works of God. There is no conceivable discovery of science that could frighten me or move me from this final affirmation of filial devotion to that world to which I belong and to Him who I think is its moving spirit.

Read these chapters in quietness. Thoughtful men are here trying to match in value-judgments, and religious devotion, what they discover in intellectual cognition.

Religion Ponders Science

CHAPTER I

Religion and the Consciousness-Expanding Substances

by WALTER HOUSTON CLARK

Andover Newton Theological School

DURING WORLD WAR II a Swiss biochemist [1] was working on a drug derived from a mold. Suddenly, without any warning, he was afflicted with weakness of the joints and other strange sensations. Accustomed to the effects of drugs, he immediately assumed that he had ingested something sufficiently different to warrant investigation. Further research identified the new substance, which he then tried on himself in minute quantities. The resulting psychological symptoms convinced him that he had discovered a powerful new drug, later to be named lysergic acid, ordinarily referred to as *LSD-25*. Thus was revived the modern interest in what are variously called the "hallucigenic," "psychotomimetic," or "psychedelic" drugs, depending partly on whether the scientist wishes to emphasize the fact that these drugs often stimulate (1) hallucinations, (2) temporary psychotic states, or (3) the expansion of one's consciousness. Most likely and most creative of these results seems to be the expansion of one's consciousness, for there have been

[1] Dr. Albert Hofman of Sandoz Laboratories in Basel.

3

cases where the ingestion of the drugs have released artistic, religious, and other creative capacities that the subjects have never dreamed they had.

Allied to LSD is the drug mescaline, derived from the cactus plant and in unrefined form known as peyote, and also a drug derived from a Mexican mushroom, known as psilocybin. Of the three, LSD is the most powerful, but they are all similar in chemical structure and in the physiological and psychological effects when taken in corresponding dosages. The question to which I intend to address myself in this paper is whether an artificial substance, discovered and produced in a laboratory, can mediate a religious experience. We are used to organ music, preaching, stained-glass windows, hymn singing, fasting, solitude, and other such artificial stimuli performing this function. But can science produce it, much as it produces, let us say, an atomic bomb or a simulated lightning bolt? I think I can best discuss the subject by giving first of all a kind of personal testimonial, or in other words by describing experiments on myself with these new substances.

It is very difficult to make another understand what the experience is like, unless he has had it himself. Consequently, when it was suggested to the members of a seminar discussing the religious implications of the drugs that some of us might like to ingest them and report to the group, I was one of a number to volunteer. Accordingly six of our group, four men and two wives, assembled at the home of one of us one day about noon under the direction and care of two others who had ingested the drugs, understood their effect, and were used to administering them. A psychiatric physician was on call nearby, as a precaution, though it was not anticipated that he would be needed. It was understood that temporary psychotic symptoms might be encountered, but that they could be expected to clear up as the intoxicating substance was eliminated from the body. One who has presided over more than 1,500 ingestions of these drugs, many by dangerous convicts, has told me that he has yet in his experience to encounter a psychosis of this type with any permanence. Conceivably a latent psychosis might be and occasionally has been activated by these substances in an already unstable personality. We were pretty well aware of these facts. Furthermore, we noted that the experienced members of the gathering were not worried. I myself had perfect confidence and was looking forward to what I expected to be merely a very interesting experience.

Each of us took, in a glass of milk, the tiny dosage of 125/1,000,000th of a gram of LSD-25 and waited for results. Except to indicate that bizarre and dramatic results were evident with all of us, I will confine my narrative to myself. At no time did I feel I had lost touch with reality, nor did I become frightened about myself, though I had moments of uneasiness with respect to some of the others and spent some time in taking care of their needs as well as I could. The uneasiness I might have spared myself, for all of us recovered and, in varying degrees, felt our session had been creative and productive, with one possible exception.

My first awareness of change came in a feeling of weakness of the joints and slight loss of muscular control in my legs and in my speech. Shortly after this, when I closed my eyes, I became aware of colored visions of considerable beauty. The amazing part of these visions was that they had meaning, in some indescribable way, more precise and clear than any meaning I had ever in my life experienced. For the most part they concerned myself, my attitudes and conduct, with an almost terrifying objectivity. It was not that I had not lived a reasonably respectable life. In fact, many of my friends look on me as too much of a puritan. But the visions seemed to search out and spotlight chinks in my moral armor and faults in my attitudes of which my dull inward eyes had been at best only dimly aware. So cogent and clear were these awarenesses that they carried far beyond the session to effect such changes in my attitudes and behavior as to constitute what I felt as a kind of moral bath.

Not having been a conspicuous sinner before, I doubt that casual acquaintances noticed any change in me. But members of my family can testify to my words, while, from the perspective of some eight months, I can look back on what seems to me to have been a notable strengthening and integrating influence on my personality and character comparable to what many would call a conversion experience. It is amazing to me that while I could have written the day before a very clear account of my moral and ethical values, the latter could never have affected my inner moral and ethical life with the precision, keenness, and cogency as did my visions. This influence was effected with a curious mixture of a feeling on the one hand that none of this was new but all was I, but never so intensely; at the same time that, on the other, there seemed to be released a power I had never experienced before that seemed to come from outside of me. I seemed like a moral athlete in that certain desirable attitudes, difficult before, now seemed easy. We say "I know I ought not do this," or "I know it is unchristian to hate A——," or "If I keep on with this attitude I will get into trouble"; but usually these reflections make little difference in our thoughts or conduct. "What I would not do, that I do; and that which I would do, that do I not." But with LSD, not just during the session but afterward, too, I seemed to have an experience that was at least similar to the psychological experience of Saint Paul when he said, "Yet not I but Christ that worketh in me." There were moments when I seemed to be able even to "love my enemies."

Another notable feature of the session was the depth of the sense of fellowship with certain of the participants. The experience had been awesome and even terrifying to some. Certainly the awe had been shared by all. Such could be looked on only as a notable adventure of what most of us felt had great spiritual depth. The process of sharing this depth seemed to bring us into a relationship of mutual concern, responsibility, friendship, and even love. Years of close friendship seemed to have been compressed into those few hours. We wished to continue our relationship.

Many who ingest these psychedelic substances have what seem to be mystical experiences. Despite the fact that I was hoping for and even expecting this event, I was disappointed in that only peripherally did I seem to have experiences that paralleled those of the mystics. Nevertheless my visions certainly had their mystical aspects. On the other hand, at one point in a vision, I seemed to be on a desolate strand of beach confronted with a vast expanse of mingled water, mist, sky, and vapor. This limitless cloudscape seemed to symbolize eternity, and, without seeing my companions in the vision, I knew that we were all there together. This suggested the mystical as did another feature of the experience.

Mystics, it is well known, have great difficulty in describing their experience to others who have not had it. They often compare their frustration to that of one faced with the problem of describing exactly what the experience of sight is to those who are born blind. In writing this account I am having something of the same type of frustration, for any words, no matter how vivid and cogent, seem pale compared to the reality of the experience itself. In these ways, at least, whether the experience was mystical or not, I felt I had come into a better understanding of the mystics.

In this connection perhaps I should mention an experience on another occasion when I experimented with psilocybin. W. T. Stace distinguishes between two kinds of mystical experience, the *introvertive* and *extrovertive* types.[2] In introvertive mystical experience the mystic perceives everything as part of a unity in which the distinction between objects appears lost. This is common in the great mystics. In the extrovertive type distinctions remain, but the subject senses a unity

[2] *Mysticism and Philosophy* (Philadelphia: Lippincott, 1960).

nevertheless, particularly between himself and the object. On this occasion a rose had been placed on a table in front of me. During the session, as I contemplated the rose, a strange immediate understanding of the life of the rose built itself up within me until I felt, at least in some partial sense, one with the flower itself. I assume that this approximated extrovertive mysticism and perhaps approached the pantheistic experience which, for some reason, is so excoriated by theologians who presumably have never had it. It deepened my insight into the genius of poets such as Wordsworth, Tennyson, and William Blake.

But perhaps the most rewarding aspect of the session came not that afternoon but afterward. This was the enrichment of my understanding of Biblical language, religious symbolism, and theological formulations. It immensely fertilized insights into my field of the psychology of religion together with the stimulations of many hypotheses the testing of which would require several lifetimes. In this sense it enlivened my intellectual life.

Among the Biblical passages illuminated by the experience might be mentioned "eye hath not seen nor ear heard . . . the things which God hath prepared," "ye must be born again," and "the Kingdom of God is within you," as well as events such as the account of the visions of Ezekiel, Moses taking off his shoes before the burning bush, the conversion of St. Paul, and the punishments of Job. Also the creedal reference to descent into hell is clearer inasmuch as the session seemed in some respects similar to such a descent. Certainly I encountered the hell of self-judgment at the same time that in a certain sense there was a rebirth and resurrection, too, as the result of this judgment. While all these references seem egoistic and are in a high degree inexact, for there is no way of knowing how closely identical were my experiences with those of the great originals in the Bible, nevertheless I am continually coming across passages in spiritual reading of many types with a kind of awakening. I can say, "If the writer was having an experience something like mine, then what he says makes sense." Certainly this was the case as I reread Plato's passages describing the Cave of Illusion in the Seventh Book of *The Republic*, while the *mysterium tremendum* of Rudolph Otto became experientially credible. In similar fashion the lines of Francis Thompson took on more color:

> Not where the wheeling systems darken
> And our benumbed conceiving soars!—
> The drift of pinions, would we hearken,
> Beats at our own clay-shuttered doors.

Also, as I sang the second verse of Clifford Bax's hymn, "Turn back, O man!"

> Earth might be fair, and all men glad and wise.
> Age after age their tragic empires rise
> Built while they dream, and in that dreaming weep.
> Would man but wake from out his haunted sleep,
> Earth might be fair, and all men glad and wise.

I suddenly knew with cogency what before I had only dimly sensed, namely, that the "haunted sleep" is no other than the commonplace, sensible, everyday world of money, power, and the demands of physical living that to the man in the street seems so real and anything but "haunted."

These benefits that I have been discussing are largely subjective. It would be difficult to establish their authenticity scientifically, and the reader must be convinced by my "testimony" or not at all. But the session seems to have introduced me to a new dimension of life. It is not as if I learned anything new that I had not known before. But as I read back over some of my writing done previous to the session, I possess a new standard of judgment. I am amazed at how authentic some of it seems to be in light of what I have learned. On the other hand, there are indeed passages that I would change or delete, for I now seem to have dispelled the ignorance in which they were conceived. But the chief difference between before and after is that before, my knowledge seems to have been largely rational, logical, and intellectual, while now the freshness of illumination seems to have dispelled at least some part of the mists before my eyes. It seems to have been a gift that has been given.

Not everyone who takes the drug calls the result a religious experience. How then did mine seem to be so? Though it contained nothing specifically theological, nor did I feel that I had encountered God, yet the whole impressed itself on me as profoundly religious for these reasons: (1) I felt I had come in contact with another, unearthly realm that pointed to Eternity and the Beyond. (2) I had undergone a conversion experience that to some degree seemed to integrate and change me. (3) I had had the beginning of an experience of fellowship that greatly surpassed in depth what is usually called fellowship among the churches. (4) Finally my sensitivities were greatly expanded in capacity to comprehend and understand religious language and the religious mind.

Doubtless some readers will be disposed to test for themselves such a dramatic outcome by trying it themselves. The psychedelic substances are nothing to be ingested lightly, and certain cautions should be kept in mind and pondered before one decides to engage in experimentation—for we cannot say that we have yet firmly advanced from the experimental stage in our knowledge of them. The drugs are not yet on the market and are available only to qualified investigators. Furthermore, the classification "drug" harrows up many grounds for trepidation in the minds of the uninitiated. It is a term with many unsavory connotations. Actually we should ask not whether a substance ought to be classed as a drug, but what its effects are and under what conditions it may be on the one hand useful and on the other dangerous.

The first apprehension is whether or not the drugs are

habit-forming. Personally I would say that my particular encounter with LSD was about as likely to become habit-forming as going to the dentist. It is something to be repeated only
for reasons of great weight. Yet many find the sessions, especially with mescaline or psilocybin, very pleasurable. Anything pleasurable may become a habit. Though experts differ,
it seems that the likelihood of addiction is either very low or
altogether absent. From this point of view, nicotine and alcohol, two exceedingly popular and eminently fashionable drugs
in Western culture, seem to be much more dangerous addic-
tive agents as well as being much more harmful in their effect
on the physical structure. A friend who has ingested psy-
chedelics more than seventy-five times reports no harmful
effects, and claims that lower dosages are sufficient now for
comparable results.

So far the literature reports few or no physical side effects
that endure. However, people with weak hearts, high blood
pressure, or diseased livers are advised to be very careful in
using these substances. Their ingestion may be accompanied
by nausea and sometimes vomiting, while the excitement may
make sleep difficult the first night after, and can leave one
with a headache. Very occasionally psychotic symptoms have
lasted from a few days to a few months. It seems likely that
such effects may be due to improper screening or clumsy
administration. However, this fact is enough to give experimenters pause and to ask themselves whether the possible gains
are worth the risks.[3] My own conclusion is that they very defi-
nitely are. But one is never justified in using the substances for
fun or mere adventure. Careful preparation, skillful and experienced administration, and the responsible following up and

[3] For a readable account of the effects of these and other drugs on
the mind by an authority, see Robert De Ropp, *Drugs and the Mind* (New
York: Grove Press, 1960 [paper]). Sandoz Laboratories is said to have a
library of over two thousand studies of the effects of the psychedelic
drugs on animals and men. However, it should be said that experts differ
as to how dangerous they may be.

implementation of insights received would seem the minimum requirements for any use of the substances that might pretend to be religious.

The most important of these cautions is that the substances be taken under the direction of a doctor or other skilled person who has had firsthand experience with the drugs himself. Anxiety, panic, delusions, or other psychotic symptoms may be present with the larger doses, and it is important that the administrator be someone who knows that such eventuation is often to be expected and will wear off in time—usually six to eight hours, though they may linger longer. Furthermore the presence of one or more self-possessed and experienced administrators will greatly enhance the value of the experience. It may be fought, controlled, and resisted, but if so, the results are likely to be unpleasant. On the other hand, the subject retains command of his thought processes and to a considerable degree may decide about that on which he wishes to fix his attention. The religious person may choose religious values, the artist may utilize artistic objects, while the musician may wish to listen to music. The background of the person himself, his essential nature, and the immediate environment all constitute potent determiners of the result. This often involves considerable enhancement of self-knowledge.

Particularly LSD and psilocybin have been used in therapy, the former successfully, it is reported, with compulsive and obsessive neurotics and the latter with alcoholics and convicts. Results so far are promising, though there are differences within the medical fraternity as to the ultimate value of the substances. The best use, however, seems to be had with normal subjects, where extreme neurotics and psychotics have been screened out. It is with such people that religious and artistic results are to be expected, though they are by no means sure.[4]

[4] See S. M. Unger, "Mescaline, LSD, Psilocybin and Personality Change," *Psychiatry*, May, 1963.

When I judge from my own experience and that of others whom I have observed and talked with, I receive the impression that the psychedelic drugs release powerful forces from the unconscious, which may come into evidence for the first time with effectiveness and cogency. Because these forces often include repressed anxieties and conflicts, they explain the temporary psychoses often in evidence. But given a healthy liver, the organ that has the function of eliminating poisons or changing them into the normal chemicals of body chemistry, and since the higher intellectual processes seem unimpaired, the subject may sort out the products of his awesome experience. Delusions, hallucinations, and panic anxiety he can dismiss from his mind, for on recovery he sees them for what they are. They may even teach him much about himself. On the other hand, the very shock of such an amazingly new experience seems to jar the subject loose from old attitudes and values. Ingrained habits are superseded in an afternoon. If the mind approves the new ways, the individual may then settle down to the arduous and joyous task of consolidating his insights. He thus becomes "born again."

We may ask whether there is any reason why the more malignant aspects of the unconscious should not take over in place of those that are more creative. Logically there seems to be no reason why this should not happen. The only answer I, a neurological layman, can give is that as a result of some thirty to forty administrations I have observed directly, this has not happened. Whenever a significant change occurs, and this is not seldom, the idealistic, artistic, and mystical religious forces seem to be strengthened. It is as if these were sleeping within most people—perhaps everyone. Once having realized the actuality of one's higher possibilities, the ordinary transactions of what we call the actual and the real become as shadows in comparison. It is then that the world of the intangible becomes the real. Eternity, infinity, compassion, understanding, love, the immortality of the good, brotherhood, unity,

and the awesome but joyful encounter with the living God
become the solid realities one may encounter that seem so
much more substantial and satisfying than the so-called hard-
headed realities of everyday life. The latter then become the
miserable shadows in the murky corners of Plato's cave. Then
indeed we see that "We are such stuff as dreams are made on."
One has the feeling that at last he has found himself, and in
rejecting what Francis Bacon called the Idols of the Market
and withdrawing from the service of those things his neighbor
so greatly values, he serves his neighbor best by showing him
what human nature can be. The drugs are simply a device,
supplied by modern science, for opening windows into oneself
as well as onto the vastnesses of history. Shafts of light give
increased understanding of Socrates, Buddha, Francis of Assisi,
Meister Eckhart, Mohandas Gandhi, Moses, and Jesus of
Nazareth.

We may ask just what use religion may make of these
awe-producing substances. At this point it is hazardous to
make any exact predictions, for as yet there is much more
that we need to know. I will venture the suggestion that in
the psychedelic drugs we have the possibility of coming close
to creating religious experiences—or reasonable facsimiles
thereof—under near-laboratory conditions.

Furthermore the psychologist of religion or other religious scholar may participate himself in the experience he is
studying if he has the hardihood to ingest the substances himself. This may seem like a violation of scientific objectivity,
but it is no more so than the acts of a Margaret Mead, who
participated in the culture of Samoa at the same time she was
studying it. The one who knows religion best is not necessarily he who knows the least about it from the warmth of
his own experience. At any rate, this was not the theory of
the greatest of psychologists of religion, William James, who
did everything he could to share with sympathetic and actual participation in the experiences of those about whom

he was writing in his *Varieties,* including experimentation with drugs. We cannot say that indiscriminate experimentation with every new drug that comes down the road is to be advised. Anyone that insisted on it would not live long. But the evidence seems to be that psychedelic drugs, while not without their dangers, are relatively safe, certainly as compared with nicotine and alcohol.[5] They ought to be made available under proper safeguards for those qualified religious people who may wish to experiment and explore their values for the religious life. The enterprising religious scholar driven by the desire to probe the secrets of the religious life as well as religious pioneers will want to proceed in this area with a cautious boldness. No two people will have the same experience, nor will everyone necessarily feel it to be religious. But it is hardly likely to be boring, while many, like me, will be astounded, amazed, and grateful.

Another religious use of these substances lies in the field of the conversion and reformation of convicts. At least one such project is now in process, and there have been at least some spectacular conversions of hardened criminals, which at least warrants the characterization of "promising." [6] The application of the drugs, in these cases also, must be made skillfully and joined with a larger program of group therapy, support, and proper follow-up. In such cases the drug experience is no different from conversions brought about by other means. It is not impossible that the churches may learn from this program whether or not the drugs deserve wider use in any way as part of the program of organized religion. Here it may be noted that Catholic cults in the Southwest, whose members

---

[5] The most comprehensive survey to date indicates the incidence of psychosis lasting more than forty-eight hours following directly on the ingestion of these substances to be less than one in a thousand. See Sidney Cohen, "Lysergic Acid Diethylamide: Side Effects and Complications," *Journal of Nervous and Mental Disease,* January, 1960.

[6] See T. Leary and W. H. Clark, "Religious Implications of Consciousness Expanding Drugs," *Religious Education,* May–June, 1962.

trace their culture back to the old Indian culture of Mexico and the times of the Aztecs, make regular use of peyote in their religious ceremonies, apparently with beneficial results.[7] However, it should be said that, like other kinds of conversions, a "drug-induced conversion" also needs to be followed up by action. Otherwise sessions may become little more than parlor games.

In summary may I say that my own experiences with the consciousness-expanding substances together with what reading and inquiry I have been able to carry on lead me to believe that religion should welcome the pursuit of research on these drugs by science. It should assist those scientists who are interested in what light religion may throw on the interpretation of the consciousness-expanding experiences. Certainly one cannot say that these drugs *produce* religious experience, but apparently in some people they tend to release religious potentialities—perhaps the essential potentialities of the religious man. As in all such areas, the Church should proceed with deliberation and with caution. But it can hardly turn its face completely away from the religious implications of these awesome and astounding substances.[8]

[7] See J. S. Slotkin, *The Peyote Religion* (Glencoe, Illinois: The Free Press, 1956).

[8] For further information see Aldous Huxley, *Doors of Perception* (New York: Harper, 1954); and H. A. Abramson (ed.), *The Use of LSD in Psychotherapy* (New York: Josiah Macy Foundation, 1960).

CHAPTER 2

When Scientific Success Makes Religion Necessary

by BISHOP FRANCIS GERALD ENSLEY

The Methodist Church, Iowa Area

SCIENCE IS THE dominant human fact of our time. How it has reduced the volume of pain and disease! How it has liberated man from the muscular drudgery that was once indispensable to bare existence! How it has added to the days of our years! Perhaps three-fourths of the people now living on this earth would not now be alive, except for the technology developed in the last three hundred years. For they would have died, or they would never have been born because their forebears would have succumbed to the hazards of primitive life had not science interposed.

Its psychological and cultural effects have been as pervasive as its vital consequences extensive. The powers science has placed in human hands have inflated men's self-assurance, so that the race has vaulted to adolescence in a generation. By abolishing distance and banishing walls of isolation science has dissolved ancient cultures and forced the politician and economist to reckon in global terms. By psychological techniques, as well as drugs, man possesses the power to re-create himself. Professor Herbert Butterfield of Cambridge University, a distinguished historian of science, is within the truth when he declares that the scientific revolution of the modern world "outshines everything since the rise of Christianity and reduces the Renaissance and Reformation to the rank of mere episodes, mere internal displacements within the system of medieval Christendom." [1]

What is to be the influence of the march of science on religion and its intellectual servant, theology? There are three distinguishable alternatives:

1. That the primacy of science will make no essential difference to religion. This view has advocates within both the scientific and theological camps. When Einstein was once asked what effect the theory of relativity would have on religion, it is recorded that he answered, "None. Relativity is a purely scientific theory, and has nothing to do with religion." For this view science is concerned with the structure and ongoing processes of the natural world: it has no decisive bearing on our dogmas about the supernatural. In the ranks of Barthian theology on the other side of the science-religion boundary are those who insist that the natural world is "off limits." Theology must confine itself to an exposition of the world of the Biblical revelation. Religion can get along very satisfactorily, thank you, without taking the results of the laboratory into account.

There is truth in this position. Certainly the things science teaches about the space-time world do not belong to the marrow of Christian belief. What the scientist discovers about nature does not become normative for religion, any more than the Bible is an authority on nuclear physics. Surely we would agree that many of those whom we would rate first in religious devotion are last in scientific knowledge. While the circles of

[1] Herbert Butterfield, *The Origins of Modern Science* (New York, 1951), p. viii.

science and theology may intersect, the center of each lies beyond the compass of the other.

Yet in history no department of human endeavor has succeeded in living to itself. The effects of science upon religion may be long delayed—it was 1822 before "the sun received the formal sanction of the Papacy to become the center of the planetary system" [2]—but they register. Charles Darwin tells his readers ingenuously in the *Origin of Species* that he sees no reason for thinking that his theory was antithetical to religion. Strictly speaking, his judgment is true. Nothing in the doctrine of evolution refutes the logic of theism. But Christianity has yet to recover from the psychological damage wrought by a doctrine that in the common mind did away with the need of a Creator, impugned the Scripture, and ascribed to man an animal origin. Of course, the friends of religion inflicted some of the deepest wounds. When the hour came for the Faith to meet the challenge of the new anthropology with intellectual candor, its response was what Borden P. Bowne once called "a volley of shudders." At any rate, history knows no instance where a revolution of thought in one segment of experience has not brought about thoroughgoing changes in every other. Is it conceivable that Christianity can have meaning for men today without defining its attitude to the forces that more than any others are determining human existence?

The reason is evident. We may distinguish two disciplines such as science and religion academically, but Man is the subject of them both. The more he matures the more he endeavors to integrate his life, which means that his scientific and religious interests must adjust to each other in the interests of his own sanity and practical effectiveness. Further, not only is Man one, but Truth is one. A proposition cannot be true religiously and false scientifically, or the converse. Still further, with regard to nature, since Christianity holds the physical world to be a creation of God, the theologian and the scientist are making judgments about the same object. They employ different categories, to be sure, but they deal with the same reality. Theology cannot stop its ears to what the scientist is saying about the world it counts as belonging to its God.

2. Science will increasingly confirm and sustain religious belief. Unquestionably many of the teachings of contemporary science are favorable to faith in God. Science presents us with a law-abiding universe. The processes of nature are orderly, and order is one of the first marks of Mind. Science increasingly discloses the world to be a dynamic order. Energy is its ultimate, which fits well with religion's doctrine of a *living* God. The newer physics with its doctrine of indeterminacy has removed the most serious barrier to theistic belief, the notion of the world as an absolute mechanism. The biological sciences have brought evidences of adaptation to attention— the manifold adjustments of organs to bodily welfare and of the organism to its environment for its survival. Certainly it seems as if the parts operate for ends of the whole. And purpose is a religious as well as a quasi-biological category.

But the support science gives to religion is limited. Certain well-selected deliverances of science are apologetic weapons of *those already convinced*. Many of those who have written on the relations of science and religion were already practicing Christians. The number of scientists, however, who have been brought to religious faith by the persuasions of scientific fact are few indeed.

Immanuel Kant came to the study of teleology with probably as many predispositions in its favor as any thinker of the modern period. He acknowledged that the attempt to rise from the order and majesty of nature to an all-perfect Creator deserves ever to be named with respect. But while it moved him to one of his rare enthusiasms, it did not convince. We cannot demonstrate the existence of a necessary cause from the contingent phenomena of nature. Further, the physico-teleological argument is from analogy: the fact that a human artist requires thought and will for the creation of human products does not prove that the unknown cause of the wonders and majesty of the world is intellect and will. To go beyond Kant (though in the direction of his thought), the scientific argument fails religion at the point of its greatest need. The distinctive teaching of the Judeo-Christian tradition is that God is not just a Cosmic Intelligence but a Redeemer. He is one who has taken the salvation of men from sin and the moral government of the universe upon his shoulder. It is difficult to see how any discovery of physical science can possibly further Christianity at this point.

Again, religion encompasses considerably more than a theory of nature. The core of Christianity is commitment. The test of faith is obedience. "Hereby we know that we know him, if we keep his commandments. He that saith, I know him, and keepeth not his commandments, is a liar, and the truth is not in him" (I John 2:3-4). It is not easy to perceive how scientific advance can promote religious devotion. Indeed, as we shall see below, science may even put hindrances in the way.

3. There is another view, energetically supported in some quarters, that science is destined to reduce the significance of religion, perhaps to the point of destroying it. For science seems to damage religious faith at several points: The new astronomy makes it difficult to believe in the haunting concern of God for the individual, so precious to the Christian. When the nearest galaxy of stars is 750,000 light-years away and the earth itself is lost in the cosmic spaces, how can we believe that God numbers the hairs of our human heads? Further, the scientific account of the evolutionary process certainly subverts confidence in the literal infallibility of the Bible, and most Christian believers are Fundamen-

talists. The scientific mood of tentativeness, too—of waiting until the facts are in and acting provisionally—is not easily compatible with religious commitment. Science assumes a fact to be "guilty"—suspect—until it has proved itself innocent; faith, like the ideal of American jurisprudence, assumes the "innocence" of religious facts—their being what they purport to be—until their invalidity is demonstrated. There is a wide gulf fixed between these two attitudes. Further, scientific technology has supplied so many of the goods of life formerly assured by religious faith. What need is there longer to pray for health when we have antibiotics? What call is there for priests when we have psychiatrists? And if, as the logical positivists have been telling us, the only propositions that have meaning and are capable of verification are the scientific, religion is left without intellectual footing.

To announce the demise of religion for these considerations would be foolhardy to the extreme. Doubtless utilitarian religion is doomed—religion that uses faith as an auxiliary to health and worldly profit—simply because science in this area brews more potent magic. Science will make the going harder for superstition. But that science will displace the higher cosmic faiths is hardly supported by the evidence. The end of religion has often been predicted, but it has been "unconscionably long a-dying," even when aided and abetted by persecution. There is nothing in the teaching of science today that has not been expounded in principle by the skeptics of the ages. Hume said about everything that is to be said validly against religion. Yet some of the mightiest revivals of religion —the Methodist in England and the Great Awakening in the United States—have occurred since Hume's critique appeared.

The heart of religion is man's ultimate concern for values. It is hardly likely that he will lose interest in the fate of the things he prizes. Where a man's treasure is, there will his intellect, emotions, and will be also. Does the world have a meaning, so that life is worth living? Are human beings of priceless value, so that men are worth loving? Is our universe favorably disposed toward the higher goods, so that a man may give his life for righteousness' sake, confident that he is not spending it in vain? And when a man grovels and his conscience shames him, can he count on help from the nature of things as he struggles to get on his feet again? Is there anything envisaged in the advance of science that can possibly dampen the interest or shrink the relevance of such concerns as these for the human race?

Only in the light of an affirmative answer to these ultimate queries—which are religious—does science have a *bona fide* claim to human recognition. Religion will not be destroyed by science. The whole is greater than the part: indeed, if men relinquish their cosmic concern, they will carry their science into the limbo with them.

The direct meaning of science for religion is ambiguous. To the already convinced it offers confirmation. For the religious ends it supplies unsurpassed means. But science cannot be a basis for religion; a "scientific" theology is a vain hope. The dominant mood of scientific technology is irreligious: its aim is to impose its will on the world rather than the surrender of will characteristic of religion. The long-time effect of science will be to purge faith of superstition and magic. But science as such will never be either the chief patron or final executioner of religion.

We have been discussing the direct bearing of science on religion, an equivocal phrase. The most decisive consequences in the days ahead will be indirect. In my judgment *they will present religion with its greatest opportunity*. One does not need to be a Hegelian to recognize that the history of man's spiritual development tends to be dialectical. Man does not march straightforwardly to a clearly envisaged goal, but rather as a skater does, first a stroke to the right, then, when it loses its momentum, a shift of weight and a thrust to the left, and so on. The human race tends to lay hold of a notion and ride it relentlessly to its ultimate conclusions. But in the process of universalizing the idea it brings to light its self-contradictions. It collides with some of the abiding intuitions of the race. It reveals its practical sterility, not to mention its positive perils. Men's enthusiasm becomes tempered, and they seek for alternatives, or at least other conceptions with which to supplement it. This is the natural biography of human interests, and it is not likely that science will prove an exception. For the immediate future I predict that science will increasingly dominate the world. But as it extends its sovereignty, its intrinsic deficiencies as a way of life will become more and more perceptible and call for the complementing that religion alone can supply.

What are the inherent limitations of science? I mention only two, but they are basic.

First of all, science is unable to invest life with meaning, and in a number of respects. (1) Science cannot by its nature endow man with a worthful conception of himself. To begin with, its ideal is one of objectivity. Its interest is in the universal objects of common experience. Its goal is to reduce phenomena to laws or statistical generalizations. It is not interested particularly in the individuality that I prize and that marks me off from all other men. It leaves the feelings out of account, the warm and vital part of a human being, regarding them as subjective and to be distrusted. The scientist sets his snare for the publicly observable, for that reducible to motion in space, for that amenable to enumeration. In so doing, he passes by that which I am introspectively sure is the most significant part of me.

The outcome of the scientific approach is to depreciate man. Astronomy proclaims his microscopic size. Biology claims that he had animals, if not for parents, at least for first cousins, in the long evolutionary series. Chemistry affirms that he is a compound of hydrogen, oxygen, carbon, and other elements, of the same essential stuff as sticks and stones. Psychology teaches the equivalence of the species: that every basic feature of human nature can be studied without essential loss in the rat and the dog. It we add to the theoretical degradation of science the fact that it has supplied the weapons whereby the human race can be liquidated, the indignity is complete.

If this seems like a caricature and one is convinced that the human race will not proceed to the extreme of nullifying itself, the proper retort is that the sanity-restoring influences will not come from the logic of science. They will be due to the admission of non-scientific considerations, especially to the human values associated with the Judeo-Christian tradition. The more consistently science works out the implications of those disciplines in which it has enjoyed its greatest success—in the domain of physical nature—the less worthful the individual will seem.

(2) Science cannot supply knowledge of the whole of life. Assuming experimental verification to be the distinguishing mark of scientific inquiry, what possible experiment can be performed that will prove a hypothesis about the universe as a whole? What possible prediction can be submitted about the totality of things that a specific test will confirm? It is generally conceded now that the conceptual scheme which accommodates all known optical phenomena satisfactorily is one in which a corpuscular picture of light fits one set of experiments while a wave theory accounts for others, and it is highly probable that no experiment can ever be devised that will resolve the dilemma![3] If experiment cannot determine which of two theories of light—the corpuscular or the undulatory—is valid, what promise is there of science offering an authentic word on the nature of things entire, of which light is but an item?

[3] Dr. Conant discusses this point at some length in his *Science and Common Sense* (New Haven: Yale University Press, 1951), pp. 28-31.

It is noteworthy that John Dewey, perhaps the most enthusiastic champion of experimental method in modern cultural history, confessed in his well-known Common Faith that "the limited world of our observation and reflection becomes the Universe only through imaginative expression. It cannot be apprehended in [scientific] knowledge nor realized in reflection." [4]

This means that without knowledge of the whole we are bereft of any basic guidance for the ordering of our lives. Without knowledge of the meaning of the universe I can neither know what I myself am nor what I ought to be doing, since the part is understood only in the light of the whole. The late Dean Christian Gauss of Princeton observed a generation ago that there were three questions to which an intelligent man of our own time can find no answer but which an equally intelligent man of A.D. 1300 would have answered promptly and with assurance: What is the purpose of your civilization? Where is it going? Who should direct it? Our modern uncertainty is of a piece with the fact that we are looking increasingly to science for guidance in life, a discipline which by the very nature of its limitations cannot guide.

(3) Science cannot give a truly meaningful *explanation* of any subject of inquiry. That is, science is unable to answer the mind's question *Why*, which is quite as legitimate as *What* and *How*. Science is unable to explain for two reasons—it eschews both value and causation.

To take the first, one has not given a meaningful account of any phenomenon until one has related it to a value. A problem is left open so far as thought is concerned until a purpose is found or a value that justifies. Only then can thought rest. To employ the illustration William Temple offers in his Gifford Lectures,[5] if a plank lies across a stream and human beings did not place it there, it calls for much

---

[4] *A Common Faith* (New Haven: Yale University Press, 1934), pp. 18–19.
[5] *Nature, Man, and God* (London, 1934), p. 132.

explanation. But if men laid it down to form a bridge, whereby they could cross dry-shod, no further explanation is needed.

Science, however, abstracts from purpose and value. Of course, it presupposes the worth of its own inquiry and aims at solving a problem, but it is unconcerned with what ought to be. It is content to describe what is, and no judgment of *ought* can be derived from a judgment of fact, any more than the converse, the affirmation of what is on the basis of what we judge ought to be. Science is satisfied to affirm that event B was preceded by A and followed by C. It is not interested in whether Z, the terminus of the series, is of sufficient value to justify the series, nor in whether the series occurred for the sake of Z, nor, indeed, in why the series took place at all.

Science abstracts from real causation as well as value. To understand *why*, the mind must know not only the value for which a thing is done but the agent that produced it. It is not sufficient to know that a plank across a stream is valuable as a means to a dry crossing. The explanation is not complete till we know a person put it there for such an end. In addition to the final cause, to employ philosophic terminology, there must be also an efficient cause.

But science is not concerned with efficient causation. Its major interest is in functional correlation of facts and in statistical generalization. In contemporary physical theory, so far as a layman can make it out, the laws of intra-atomic activity are only statistical approximations drawn from the behavior of countless numbers of quanta. So far as the individual transitions are concerned, they are undetermined and lawless, governed by the laws of "chance"; in their overall statistical behavior they approximate lawfulness. According to the principles of indeterminism not only are we unable to describe exactly what happens, but there are no laws of explanation. In the degree, therefore, that the scientific attitude becomes the goal of intellectual endeavor, the less interest in and capacity there will be for basic understanding.

In the second place, science is not only unable to invest life with meaning for the reasons given, but it is impotent to cure when perverse meanings have taken possession. It is inadequate to the problem of moral evil.

Every scheme for human betterment collides and often founders on the fact that something in man resists the good. Sin, as religion calls this fatal flaw, has many facets—selfishness, sensuality, rebellion, faithlessness, pride. It is the specter at every feast. Man is not equipped for his earthly pilgrimage until he is armed against the evil in his own nature, which casts its dark shadow upon all his achievements.

But the scientific mentality, such a magnificent ally in the war against external foes, is practically helpless in the conquest of the inner man. To begin with, as we have seen, it abstracts from value. Science takes for its vocation the ordering of experience rather than its reshaping. It is concerned, too, with those aspects of man capable of external observation. Man's conduct of his own affairs has fallen tragically below his conquest of nature. It has not perceived the worm in the wood, because, as Reinhold Niebuhr has been saying for a generation, modernity's analysis of the human predicament is too superficial, thinking that a prudent self-interest or a balance of social forces will meet man's crucial need for redemption. Further, far from being the redeemer of man, science conspires in his destruction. Dr. Oppenheimer tells us that when the first atomic bomb exploded on the Nevada flats, he could think of only two lines from the *Bhagavad-Gita* to express his feeling, "I am become death, the shatterer of worlds."

Science has enabled man to control nature, but who is to control the Controller? Eschewing value, it can supply no authentic authority by which to live. It can build a bomb but not prevent its annihilative use. It has no power to enlist moral enthusiasm, to motivate. Men may die because $E = mc^2$, but hardly for the sake of it. The scientific intellectual is under the illusion that if men know the truth they will do the good, a proposition honored more in the breach than the observance. Sin does not yield to enlightenment. Further, the scientific mind is too tentative, too willing to experiment, too conscious of limits and qualifications to give the firm leadership a baffled race requires.

The world, like Lady Macbeth, needs the divine as well as the physician, for only religion offers man redemption from his sins in any serious way. Crane Brinton is not a professional advocate of Christianity, yet in his illuminating survey of Western morals he says, anent scientific rationalism—the quasi-religious faith of the modern world—"The religion of the Enlightened has a long and unpredictable way to go before it can face the facts of life as effectively as does Christianity, rich with two thousand years of experience of saints and sinners, good and evil, in all their protean—and by no means equal—forms." [6]

To sum up: The real influence of science upon religion in the days ahead will not be positive but negative, a revelation of its own deficiency and a corresponding need for the values represented by religion. As science becomes scientism—the dogma that science is sufficient for our requirements—it will unconsciously provide a new apologetic for religion in the modern world. For science is inadequate as a way of life. A scientific culture will eventually fall upon its own sword. A society cannot survive in which power is stressed above control, facts take precedence over value, when, to use Thoreau's pithy expression, means are improved to unimproved ends. It is no reproach to science to say that because of its limitations it is self-defeating. Prayer is self-defeating, too—without the complement of work! The moral of scientific success is

[6] *A History of Western Morals* (New York: Harcourt, Brace and Co., 1959), p. 462.

not less respect for its mighty achievement but a greater awareness that science must be supplemented by those values that by its very nature it cannot heed.

To fulfill its vocation, and to capitalize on its opportunity in our time, religion must offer an interpretation of life that is (1) meaningful, (2) true, and (3) historical. It must be "meaningful" in the sense that it makes a difference to the values that matter most. It must fulfill such validly human desires as the desire for explanation—children of chaos, we want an account of the world that makes sense; the desire for comfort, to feel that one is not an orphan in the universe; the desire for guidance, a frame of reference within which a person may place not only his life but each day's needs; the desire for redemption—a second chance and succor when the world has been too much for us. In short, religion must fill the value-vacuum created by an increasingly scientific culture.

Unless religion can supply the spiritual vitamins for which a scientific culture starves, it has little prospect of survival. The Middle Ages had a principle of parsimony called "Occam's Razor," which affirmed that what can be well explained on one ground is not to be explained again on another. There is a parallel Razor at work in the practical sphere: What can be done easily and effectively by science will not be turned over to religion. But, conversely, in the measure that religion supplies essential meanings beyond the power of science to give, men will beat a path to faith's door.

Secondly, religion in a scientific age must lay claim to truth. It must be congruous with the conditions of knowledge. It must not insist on special favors, such as appeal to authorities not vouchsafed to ordinary rational men. It must be willing to supply reasons for its faith and to submit its doctrines to criticism. Every world-faith claims to be true; it cannot abandon the claim and have standing in the eyes of men. Just as science claims to be true, so religion must be true. This does not mean religion must be scientific, but only that it does not contradict scientifically established conclusions and that its own results are coherent and capable of logical support and practical verification.

Appeal to truth means a reversal of some recently dominant trends in theology. "Christian existentialism" has given the impression sometimes that since life calls for decision, we may choose whatever we want, whether logically unsound or not. And not seldom the prevailing Biblicism has been guilty of the sort of theological brainwashing Professor John C. Bennett has complained of, which quietly substitutes the question, Is it Biblical? for the question, Is it true?[7] Theology must, rather, appeal to the same basic criteria of objectivity—coerciveness, system, and publicity—as other disciplines.

In order to justify its claim to truth, theology is not required to "prove" the existence of God. Epistemologically speaking, God is an Axiom rather than an Object. He is not a Person toward whom perception is directed, but the presupposition of experience. To employ Professor Hocking's apt figure, God is not another entity to be enumerated along with the other characters on the projection screen; he is the Projector, the light of all our seeing, without which there would be no vision at all. In reading Professor Shapley's *Science Ponders Religion,* one has the impression that many scientists reject God because they do not find him among the phenomena with which they deal. Because his presence cannot be verified scientifically, he is ruled out. Before dismissing God on these grounds, the scientist might verify his own premise of the reliability of nature, the notion that all instances of the same phenomenon P are determined in the same way by a set of conditions Q. What particular experiment can possibly prove a universal proposition? The orderliness of nature is an axiom presupposed by all experiments, as God is the Reality whom the theist takes for granted.

---

[7] John C. Bennett, "How My Mind Has Changed," *The Christian Century,* December 23, 1959, p. 1,500.

Finally, religion must be historical. When men speak, they do not use language in general, though speech has a generic structure. They speak a particular tongue—English, French, or German. Religious faith is historical, and for much the same reason. An artificial religion is about as consequential as Esperanto. To count as a living force, religious faith must be continuous with a historical tradition and be embodied in a cult and community. While God exists, we believe, as the ground of nature, the witness of the physical universe is ambiguous and incomplete (for Christians) until it is conjoined with the disclosure of the divine Reality set forth in the Bible, the history of the Church, and the personal encounter of mystic experience in every age. Only a faith rooted in such a historic inheritance is likely to be virile enough to contend successfully with the anti-religious forces of our time.

A religion relevant to human values, consistent with the conditions of truth-finding, and continuous with an established historical tradition, can supply a complement to science with sufficient weight to redeem its misproportions and to offer the spiritual direction upon which their mutual survival depends.

CHAPTER 3

A Possible Partnership Between Science and Religion

by SOPHIA LYON FAHS

Columbia University

SCIENCE AND RELIGION are both thriving in America, yet each seemingly is content to remain quite independent and ignorant of the other's basic assumptions. This is in marked contrast to the violent conflicts that off and on have characterized their history during the past three hundred years.

What is the meaning of this recent change in the relationship between these two parts of our Western culture? Is it because the major issues between the two groups have been resolved? Is it because as a generation we have decided that these two parts of our personal and group living can and should be kept apart, that they truly belong on two different levels of experience that need not affect each other? Or is this apparent indifference in reality an emotionally motivated withdrawal in order to escape a serious crisis?

I have come tentatively to the conclusion that this recent seemingly cold peacefulness is more a symptom of emotional instability than a sign of achieved harmony. Our society can be likened to a divided personality. In part it is very religious, and in part it is very scientific, but seldom is it truly both at the same time in the same person. The high values that humanity has gained through its centuries of religious development are felt to be too valuable to be risked in an open and frank encounter; on the other hand, the resources with which the sciences have blessed humanity are too much enjoyed to be relinquished. The two parties may be wise in continuing their inarticulate withdrawal from each other until they can feel they have gotten their bearings and understand themselves. But how long can this division last? And at what cost is it being maintained?

The Historical Roots of Our Emotions

Let us examine briefly some of the historical roots out of which these emotions have grown—the scientist's rather common lack of respect for religion on the one hand, and the religionist's fears of the destructive strength of the sciences. Does our generation still suffer from the hurt of the emotional wounds received by our ancestors during the acrimonious debates, imprisonments, and martyrdoms of former centuries so that it still shrinks from reasonableness? The answer, I believe, is that we do.

Let me touch briefly only on the emotional effects of the discoveries of Newton and Darwin, as symbols, of the warfare between science and theology during the past three hundred years. It was not Newton's discoveries of the law of gravity and of the nature of light that in themselves were resisted by religion; it was rather the mechanical, mathematically determined, overall conceptualization that his discoveries implied. This was in flat contradiction to the Biblical assumptions that a personal Deity was directing all movements, and that he could and would change the usual regularities when special needs arose. The strong emotional resistance was not because Newton had taken Deity away entirely, but that the scientist had made God merely the first cause, the one who had started the clock going and then had left it to continue in its mechanical way.

Then about two hundred years later the storm was increased because of the Darwinian theory of evolution, with its negative pronouncements regarding man's unique place in the story of creation. As evidence has accumulated, the literal interpreters of the Bible story of creation in the first six days of time have had to make adjustments. By admitting the ancient tales as either myth or allegory, yet holding what is still thought to be importantly true, the story of evolution can now be taught in our schools. That man is not so distinct from other animals as was once thought seems still to be difficult for many to accept. But the idea that struck the most serious blow to Western religions has been the notion that the whole process of evolution has been one of chance, combined with a tooth-and-claw struggle for survival between the so-called fit and unfit. Both Newton and Darwin confirmed a picture of the universe and its history as impersonal. On the one hand it seems chaotic and its history a matter of chance happenings, or on the other hand it seems to be wholly determined and mechanistic. It was not strange that religious people with a backward look to the past for their guidance were impelled to fight these positions and that some of their children to the third and fourth generations are still left prejudiced and resentful against science and fear it as an enemy.

Some Basic Changes in Modern Science

Scientists today, however, have significantly changed their understanding of the fundamental nature of the universe and of their interpretation of the processes of evolution from those which both Newton and Darwin propounded. They have found that the universe, although quite dependable and law abiding, is not as much like a machine as scientists even a generation ago thought. Nor is evolution now being explained merely on the basis of chance. Recent discoveries have been changing the whole emotional color of their picture of reality, and scientists are now daring to philosophize openly about it. Dr. Richard Feynman [1] of the California Institute of Technology wonders why poets are not singing songs in appreciation of this newly found universe and artists are not painting it. He concludes that the average man is not really scientific. He has instead merely accepted the gadgets and inventions and techniques of science without being aware of its new philosophy.

What then is this new philosophy that the modern scientists are trying to express regarding the universe and man? As one quite illiterate in the language of science, I hesitate to try to put into words my understanding of what they are now saying; but I must attempt it with the plea that I be corrected if I have falsely interpreted their general philosophy.

The universe, as I understand the scientists, for most practical purposes is a universe of law and order, but the order is not quite what it was once supposed to be. It now seems more like the order found in a living organism than like the order found in a machine. There is much more uncertainty in scientific thought than even a few years ago. The ultramicroscopic parts within the nucleus of the atom appear at present to be in disorder, and Nature's immensities cannot be measured except in statistical averages. As Dr. R. G. H. Siu writes: "Nature's secrets are matters of probability." [2] The relativity of all human thinking is recognized.

In addition, the universe begins to seem psychosomatic, a combination of mind and matter. It is both material and non-

[1] "The Value of Science," *Engineering and Science*, Vol. XIX, December, 1955.
[2] *The Tao of Science* (Cambridge and New York: Mass. Institute of Science Press and John Wiley and Sons, 1957).

material. It is both invisible and intangible energy and measurable mass. Yet there seems to be an all-pervading and all-encompassing unity. Atoms are found in the minutest forms of both inorganic and organic life. Scientists declare there is evidence that they are in the galaxies of suns and planets as far as telescopes can trace them; yet all these atoms share one pattern in common, that of units of energy-mass revolving around their centers. Scientists see all things bound together, yet held apart in a wondrous order—a harmony of dancing, flying forms. Yet within the order indeterminacy is found. Beneath the stability, unceasing restlessness.

It is within this kind of universe that the scientists tell us "we live and move and have our being." Is this unceasing energy alive? Many are suggesting this amazing thought. Is it conscious in varying measures in different parts, as we are conscious in varying degrees throughout our bodies? At present scientists differ in their answers. The English language has not yet the words needed to express the new thinking. The fact that all use a word primarily applicable to life—namely *energy* rather than the word power, which is primarily applicable to machines—is in itself provocative.

There are some other challenging generalizations on which all seem to agree. One of these is that all human beings share the essence of life with all plants and animals. We are blood relatives of all creatures living through the billions of years before us. They have passed on to us their genes. In some inscrutable way they have created the patterns that have formed us.

Furthermore this evolutionary process, at least as many biologists and geneticists are now describing it, is not simply a succession of the chance mixing of genes. Instead, many are saying that evolution is due to some kind of creative interaction between environment and genetic endowment. And just what is a gene, beyond being a piece of matter in a tiny chain called a chromosome? No scientist can as yet explain.

There are men such as Weston Le Barre [3] who are describing evolution as a long series of plant and animal "inventions," beginning with the lowest forms of single-celled plants. Dr. Le Barre even describes the little green Volvox as the one that made life's *"first moral invention,"* by uniting a group of single cells into one organism and making them divide up responsibility for the work of living. To this tiny Volvox the size of a small grain of sand, he and others ascribe the invention of real sex and real death.

Who among us is imaginatively able to grasp the possible meaning to be found even in one of the great discoveries of modern zoology, namely, that we are all blood relatives, from the least to the greatest living creatures? It is indeed an *Immense Journey*, as Dr. Loren Eiseley wisely names it, through which our living chains of genes have survived to become our creators. This feeling of relatedness suggests something not entirely unlike Dr. Albert Schweitzer's "reverence for life."

Dr. Joseph Wood Krutch in his book, *The Great Chain of Life*,[4] expresses more than even his poetic writing can put into words. No longer can one appropriately speak of a protozoan as "a simple blob of protoplasm," for, as he says, "without stomachs they digest; without lungs they take in oxygen; without kidneys they secrete uric acid; and without bladders they collect it in pockets from which it is finally expelled." "Simple indeed," he exclaims. "If the first living things really were like them, then the sudden appearance of a protozoan was a phenomenon almost as astonishing as the sudden appearance of an elephant would have been."

The universe, as modern science sees it, is no longer the great material mechanism it was once thought to be. As a Scottish divine once said, "Nature isn't as natural as it looks." We as humans, along with all our blood relatives, seem to be living not in a wholly dead universe, but within a surpassingly

---

[3] *The Human Animal* (Chicago: Univ. of Chicago Press, 1955), pp. 8–9.
[4] *The Great Chain of Life* (Boston: Houghton, Mifflin, 1956), p. 5.

organic, living body that seems to be guided or con-
ed from within by something akin to Mind or Spirit.
hy should man seek to gain supernatural power when
nergy beyond all man's greatest dreaming is still here waiting
for man's discovery and use?

Such a conception of the natural universe is a far cry
from that of Newton and Darwin. It is even further removed
from the picture of the universe glimpsed by the writers of
the Psalms, or by Jesus or Buddha or Mohammed. As we compare this with the universe of the Judeo-Christian Bible, a
half-domed dwelling made primarily for man with a God of
glory watching from above through the clouds, what a contrast! An expanding unplumbed universe with billions of
earths and suns, swinging majestically within their gigantic
spinning galaxies, spread over uncounted light-years of space!

What must such a change in the modern scientist's picture of the universe do eventually to an intelligent man's (or
even to an intelligent child's) belief regarding Divinity? Will
the word *God* suffice to symbolize this unifying, vitalizing,
universal, cosmic *Mind* or *Imagination* or *Heart?* God within
rather than God above or below or outside all these universes
—God, changing, developing, experimenting, growing? Is man
imaginative enough or courageous enough to try to stretch
his thoughts to encompass such immensities on the one hand,
and such microscopic mysteries as genes on the other hand?

To millions for whom God has meant an intimate, personal, supernatural guide and loving Father, such a cosmic
conception of God seems impossible to accept. It is too great,
and fearsome, and even distasteful sometimes, since it must
somehow include what we call evil as well as what we call
good. Humanity has never before been faced with such an
awesome and tremendous challenge. It is not strange that we
should find ourselves inarticulate and timid.

Four Major Patterns of Religious Withdrawal

As I have been trying to interpret the trends in attitudes and modes of thought that I have observed and experienced even within myself, I find four major religious patterns which may be regarded as those of withdrawal.

The first is represented by those to whom religion is primarily an inheritance to be preserved, not because it is actually one's personal philosophy for living, but because it is thought of as an inherited obligation to be perpetuated in ceremonies, rituals, and by the teaching of ethical principles. For this group, religion is not basically the result of intellectual affirmation or of personal choice. It is the result of an inherited and promoted culture. To change one's religion in the light of any of the new insights of science would be for these as drastic a step as to change one's ancestry. Their orientation is to the past, and loyalty to it has priority. For such, religion and science belong in two separate categories.

A second group is represented by those who decry a natural God as being no God or a natural religion as being pagan. This group emphasizes God's supernatural character. The natural world is too full of evil and too neutral to human values to be the manifestation of Divinity. God and Nature are two entirely different and separate realities. It is only occasionally that such a supernatural Divinity breaks through out of its heavenly realm in order to save humanity from its tragic predicament. The primary motive for enduring the present tragedies of this temporary life on earth is to be found in the hope of release into another existence of an entirely different sort. For such as these also, life can be divided into two parts, the natural and the supernatural. Thus any real challenge through a frank dialogue between science and religion can at least be postponed.

A third group is able to avoid the disturbing need to reconstruct its religion because of a deeper understanding of science, not by positing a supernatural world where all wrongs will be righted, but by limiting the area of experience with which religion deals to the area of human relations. This group starts with the assumption that the natural sciences have as yet found no evidence in the cosmos of a "God who cares"—a God who lends sanction to human values. For these Divinity cannot be seen in non-human nature. For these, religion is concerned primarily with the achievement of human values. In this venture they believe that the Universe is neutral and even sometimes destructive. Whatever divine values there are must be achieved by man. Although this group can accept realistically the new insights of science, their religion is not at all influenced by changes in cosmology or metaphysics in general. They would confine their religious partnership with science to those scientific disciplines dealing with human nature and human affairs.

Finally there is a fourth group for whom religion represents primarily idealism. For them, God is a reality quite different from the kind of reality the scientists talk of. For them God is either an abstraction or a personification of their highest ideals. God is perfection—in love, beauty, and truth. God lives in the real world of conscience, and in the dream world of hopes and longings. Humanity has been given glimpses of these ideals in the lives of certain very great personalities, such as Jesus and Buddha and others. These men are said to incarnate a perfection that has not yet been revealed in others. Such a point of view separates religion from the realism of science, not by putting religion into a supernatural world, but by making it equivalent to the highest human ideals.

These then are four quite distinct typical points of view represented in religion today. It would be unfair to say that these ways of thinking have been adopted consciously because of a fear of the consequences of new scientific discoveries, yet it seems evident that when such attitudes or beliefs are adopted, any need for a thoroughgoing encounter with modern science is lessened. The first group has assumed that its religion will not change. For the second group, the natural world is temporal, and only through the "grace" of a supernatural God can its evils be overcome. For the third group, religion concerns human values only, so that cosmic values are at least secondary. And the fourth group makes religion the pursuit of their highest ideals. Thus for many, at least, religion and science have not needed to enter upon any frank and full interchange of insights and thinking.

If this general analysis is at all in accordance with the modern situation in religion, then it is to be expected that its dialogue with science is most likely first to become a fruitful interchange when it speaks with those sciences that deal with human affairs, such as psychology and psychiatry, sociology, and anthropology. There are at present increasing evidences of mutual interest between these groups, yet there are evidences also of extreme caution on both sides.

In these interchanges it is the scientists who have taken the initiative. Without asking permission of the religionists, the psychiatrists and psychologists have entered the sanctuary of the human spirit, where until modern times the priests and clergy have been the private confidants and have long been given the prestige of social acceptance. Almost a rivalry for the opportunity to save sick souls has arisen. While religionists had long assumed that they knew how evil human nature is and that they have found the only way of salvation, the psychiatrists and psychotherapists began studying concrete samples of humanity from the youngest to the oldest, both the mentally sick and the normal. These scientists of human nature have learned how to find repressed, unconscious fears and longings, and hatreds and loves in dreams commonly forgotten and supposed to be silly. They have begun to experiment with new ways to salvation.

As a result these doctors of the mind are challenging

some of the most common patterns of thinking and practice among clergy and religious educators that have been assumed for many years to be good. They have discovered through experimentation the near futility of condemnation and punishment in reforming character. They have discovered the dangers involved in trying to induce emotions either by command or rebuke. They have also discovered the healing power of inner understanding.

Even the time-honored practice of holding up ideal personalities for emulation is being questioned. They have found that the strain for perfection when taken too seriously may break a personality apart. Some psychiatrists are of the opinion that as many, if not more, neuroses are being caused by this too serious struggling after perfection and the feelings of guilt that develop because of failure than are produced by any natural compulsions to do evil. Those who think they have succeeded are prone to become arrogant, tending to despise those of lesser attainments; while those who realize the extent of their failure despise themselves and tend to feel resentful toward those who seem to have been more successful. Traditionally Christianity has reduced these unduly strong feelings of pride and guilt by offering a supernatural Saviour as the only hope. But in a scientific age, such a Saviour will become increasingly difficult to accept.

Dr. John Mac Murray of England has written in his *Idealism Against Religion*,[5] "It is my belief that . . . idealism is a disease of the spirit which infects its marrow, and as it spreads it blinds us to the reality of the religious life, and shuts us up in the world of our sick fantasies. The disease has had a long course; in our time it has reached its climax. Our Christianity is very sick and can not recover until it is cured of idealism.

"If it were cured of idealism, religion would be about this world, and not about another world. . . . Its beliefs would be

[5] London: Lindsey Press, 1944, pp. 6, 18.

drawn *from* experience; they would arise in our contact with fact, and they would grow with the growth of experience and be tested and retested and remade as experience demanded. They would not be fixed, dogmatic or authoritarian. Instead of thinking about religious things we should think ordinary things in a religious way. Instead of living a spiritual life which is separate from and in opposition to our material life, we should live our ordinary life spiritually."

The new science of anthropology also is bringing refreshing wisdom from studies of primitive peoples. The anthropologists are not merely increasing our knowledge of our earliest ancestors and informing us of the nature of the beginnings of science and religion in human experiences. They are expanding our respect for our unlettered forebears. They are awakening us to realize some of our forgotten natural potentials for spontaneous religious response to our still mysterious universe.

Modern religion needs the help of all the sciences in order to achieve an integrating, dynamic philosophy for living that will include a new cosmology and physics and zoology, as well as a new psychology and new understandings of races and cultures, past and present. The achievement of such a dynamic, unifying philosophy for living has not only become urgent. It now seems more possible than ever before. In recent years there has been an impressive increase in conviction among scientists that man should contemplate with reverence and wonder a Total Oneness for which the word *God* has stood. Loren Eiseley calls it "a mysterious principle known as 'organization' which leaves all other mysteries concerned with life stale and insignificant in comparison." [6] Multitudes of mobile, living designs—different, yet alike—bound together, yet not too rigidly, in a creative interdependence within a Cosmic Organism. Surely in such a universe there can be no question that is irrelevant to a modern man's religion. "The God of Humanity" in such an age must be, as Harlow Shapley says,

6 *The Immense Journey* (New York: Random House, 1957), p. 26.

"God of Gravity and God of Hydrogen Atoms." [7] To this we would add God of animals and of man, God of continuing creation, God of experimentation, God of the evolutionary process, and God of "moral inventions."

If then as scientists and as religionists, we can honestly share such an all-embracing common purpose to find meanings in our present existence in this universe that will augment our courage and vitalize our better potentials, our next question is this: *Do* we realize what such a point of view involves by way of changing our attitudes and our methods of promoting our concerns, especially among the younger generation? Can we be congenial with science in our ways of developing religion? From this point on I shall write as an educator.

Can We Be Comrades in Our Basic Processes?

A satisfactory answer to this question involves more profound changes in attitudes and in procedures than most educators, ministers, and scientists realize. I am venturing to make live proposals regarding changes in common ways of religious development that seem to be of crucial importance, yet so very difficult to practice, and still so seldom attempted, that they deserve much more amplification than is possible here.

The major issue to be faced, which is the root from which the other proposals I am going to make have grown, is this: Can vital religion, in an age of rapidly changing understandings of the nature of the total Cosmos in which we are participating and creating members, continue to be regarded mainly as a cultural gift from the past—a systematized set of ethical codes, ritual practices, and profound truths made known to a few divinely appointed prophets or saviors for mankind? Or must we recognize that we are *living in a new age when religions must change* as the sciences are changing? And that in a democratic world *each person is to a degree responsible for work-*

[7] "Coming to Terms With the Cosmos," *The Saturday Review*, 1958.

ing out his own vitalizing philosophy for living, building it primarily on his own "direct relations with the universe," and only secondarily using the thoughts and experiences of his contemporaries, his elders, and his ancestors to expand, correct, and enrich his own?

1. Since this issue is most dramatically illustrated in the first steps taken by young children, my first proposal calls for a turn-about-face in our common ways of first introducing children to religious values. So far as I know, among all the so-called great religions of the world, children are commonly first introduced to religion *by being told how to think and act.* The great stories from the past are rehearsed, the young are taught to participate in the accepted religious ceremonies, and codes of conduct are taught. In short, religion usually has come to young children as a cultural gift and as an instruction sheet. Ancient scriptures, written three thousand, two thousand, fifteen hundred years ago, have been presented as guides, while the child's own experiences with the book of nature immediately open before him are disregarded because it is assumed that the small child is incapable of thinking his way through into religious values. Traditionally religious teachers have kept their faces turned toward the past and prided themselves in their loyalty to the "faith of the fathers," while scientists, on the other hand, keep their faces turned toward what is still undiscovered and pride themselves in thinking differently from their predecessors. If science and religion are to be sincere partners, we must at least face in the same direction.

For teachers of religion this involves a profound change in attitude, as well as in techniques, which most ecclesiastical organizations feel impelled to resist. It means our finding rich values in the incomplete phases of the process—in questioning as well as in answering, in not knowing as well as in knowing, in being agnostic as well as in believing, in being imperfect as well as perfect. It means *making religious nurture an experimental process for the growing child, an adventure of his own in discovering and in changing* in order to make possible further discoverings.

We need then to learn how to encourage the little child's earliest curiosities about his world by answering him little by little, by identifying with him in his surprises and in his experiences of wondering awe. We need to learn how to companion him in his first experiences with baby animals and growing flowers and with his own bodily parts. We need to stand with him with empathy as he ponders on the rainstorm and the new-fallen snow, on the thunder and lightning and the dark. We need to share sympathetically with him in his special moments of awe before the mystery of birth and death, and his early wondering about his sleeping and dreaming. We need to make room for great experiences at night under the stars and with the moon. What are they? How far away? Who made them? It was out of just such universal experiences that primitive man first became sensitive to the indescribable, invisible, all-pervading Reality we name God.

To give young children words before they have had the kinds of experiences that can put legitimate meaning into those words may not always be harmful, but it is always dangerous. The more important the word, and the more certainly its thought is affirmed, the more difficult it will be for the child to discard it later if he has misunderstood its meaning or if he finds later that what he is learning contradicts its meaning.

For adults to acquire so drastic a change in attitude and for children to learn to find their basic security in the processes of searching and questioning calls for far more than a mere simplification of the language by which religion has been taught. It calls for a dealing with the child's present before introducing him to the great persons of the past. Instead of indoctrination in the "faith of the fathers" it means sensitizing the child to his own opportunities for adventure and learning in his own world of wonder and surprise. Religious books for

children in our Western world should no longer be equated
with Bible-story books.

Each religious culture seems to have been afraid to let
its children have their own firsthand immediate and temporar-
ily uninterpreted relations with the universe—a right that Emerson said was every child's birthright. Most parents and
religious teachers feel they must begin at once to mold their
children into little Christians, or Jews, or Moslems, or Buddhists before the children have a chance to feel religiously in
their own natural and universal ways. The sciences have developed a universalism while religions have remained paro-
chial. This is because from first to last, with both old and
young, they have stood for the processes of direct observation
and experimentation with the natural cosmic and human
phenomena around and within. If in religion we are to become
rich partners with the sciences, we need also to explore existence with a freshness of inquiry and with the expectation of
profound change. If we are to approach religious development in the scientific spirit, we need to learn how to begin
where children can themselves become involved in the processes of discovery.

2. A second significant change relates to all records of
past experience, whether found in the Bible of our own culture
or in any others. In an age of science, all *Bibles should be
studied not as sacred books* set apart from all others, *but as
the literary deposits of human experiences* of men of long ago.
We should study these scriptures not to find *The Truth*, or
the stories of men of God in order to become like them, or
to find great principles or commandments to be obeyed. We
should go to these scriptures in order to enrich and expand
our own short-lived experiences through imagining the experiences of other humans under different circumstances and in
different times. The study of such historical records should be
postponed until children have grown mature enough to be able
to imagine ancient conditions, until they can distinguish be-

tween myth and legend and accurate and biased or falsified history. It is not the Bibles themselves that call for reverence; nor do the persons portrayed need to be ideal; nor their beliefs and ethical values acceptable to us, but to study such ancient records with profit requires a critical and imaginative understanding of the total milieu in which these historic people lived. Such a revision in the common procedures in religious nurture would call for a postponement of the use of the Bibles of Christians and Jews until children are old enough to be historically minded; and when the study is begun, it would call for a supplementing of the text itself with whatever any of the historical sciences might yield to bring the past truthfully and vividly to life. This has proved to be a hard saying, and most children's Bible-story books have been written by authors who seem unaware of the issues.

3. *Not just one Bible alone can suffice* if religion is to become universal in its outlook along with science. The Bibles of all the world's great religions have now been translated into the languages of the West. Stories of the founders of all of them are available. Myths of creation and of floods have been gathered from many races. We now know that the Hebrews were not more religious than many other peoples. Nor were they more ethical or the first to believe in one God. Indeed, the values in one religion cannot be appreciated until they are compared with those of another. So in an age of science the curricula of our religious schools should become non-sectarian. First, children should have their own present opportunities to discover the nature of the universe and the life of which they are a part. And then to enrich these discoveries of their own, they should be given opportunities to live imaginatively with people of the past who represent different kinds of religious philosophies, and yet who were human like themselves, also searching for deeper understanding and striving for something good still unachieved.

4. In the realm of personality development and human relations, we need to learn from the psychological sciences a *deeper understanding of the functioning of the primary emotions* such as those of love and hate, of courage and fear, of freedom and dependency, self-respect and shame. Instead of seeking to control behavior by means of codes and rules, by principles and idealizations, we need to learn how to *respect the original spontaneous emotions of children*, to feed them the nourishment they are calling for, and to help the child to channel these emotions in his own way for the fulfillment of his own basic desires for love and achievement. Instead of the usual abstractions, admonitions on the duty of love and kindness and unselfishness, etc., we need to look upon the *child's everyday living* from his point of view, as *a series of problems and experimentations*. If we are to encourage in him the attitude of an open seeking for what is good, we need to help him examine his problems, and to begin to analyze the varied concerns they involve for him and for others. This kind of experimenting with living together can begin perhaps most dramatically, although very simply, at a very early age, even at two years. A much more spontaneous and alert and sympathetic child emerges under such guidance than when he is told to be good or punished for being bad.

So in the church-school groups, the life stories told and read for the children's benefit need to be thought of as *dramatizing the problems of living rather than as illustrating certain abstract qualities*. Such a psychological approach to the problems of human relations naturally leads to more imaginative understanding of other people. It involves identifying oneself with the feelings of others. The old clear-cut distinctions between the good people and the bad people become unsatisfactory. It is found usually that there have been "good" reasons for being "bad" and "bad" reasons for being "good." Such an approach should develop in the younger generation more

HUGH STEPHENS LIBRARY
STEPHENS COLLEGE
COLUMBIA, MISSOURI

ability to feel empathy and to seek for understanding when faced with conflicts.

These more scientific and exploratory ways of dealing with ethical relationships will include learning, on the part of adults, how to help children to look on their own unlovely emotions and to try to understand their meaning. As leaders and parents, we need to learn how and why we should refrain from condemning children's emotions, and from seeking to persuade them to act in spite of how they feel. In emergencies outward restraint is indeed sometimes necessary, but the important learnings of self-control must come from the child's own inner desires.

If but one generation could be skillfully educated in accordance with the new psychological understandings now available of how human nature can be wholesomely changed, and if educators set as their goal the development of such understanding and empathy, I believe the adult world of thirty years hence would find its tensions and hostilities surprisingly reduced, and the ability of orations to negotiate differences tremendously enhanced.

5. Finally, I wish to add very briefly one more important change in our religious education that I see involved if we take up a full partnership with science. This is the *need to universalize our morality* and our feelings of relatedness in order *to include not only all humanity, but also the animal and plant world, and, in fact, all of creation.* The universe has been struggling through a long evolution. We are the fruits of her millions of years of labor. Our flesh is the evolved dust of the stars. Our very life is dependent upon the continuing life and death of other creatures. Without the common green world of grasses we would quickly perish. Our indebtedness is a heritage that links us to all living and nonliving things from the beginning of time. In our pride of human superiority, we have sometimes been disdainful of the values in things of a so-called lower order. We have talked of subduing

89358

the forces of nature to serve our ends. The Living Universe calls us to understand, to appreciate, to co-operate—rather than to conquer.

The Living Universe does not ask us to accept things as they are. She challenges us to join in creating better things. She asks us to help her to improve. Goodness involves respect for material things and animals, and all forms of life. Morality does not concern itself only with relationships between persons. No human fellowship is possible without the use of things.

All the difficult international problems that face mankind today involve the sharing of things—the world's lands, seas, and air; the treasures stored in the earth: oil, coal, copper, uranium, and iron; and all the things that men can make from them. The discovery of and the ability to use the power within the nucleus of the atom has posed for modern men in an age of science the most dramatic and serious ethical question he has ever had to face. An exclusively human ethics is no longer adequate. Our duty to other living creatures and to things is inevitably intertwined with our duty to humanity.

These then are at least five important ways in which education in religion will require change if the knowledge and the methods of science become incorporated into our own and our children's religious education. They are drastic and difficult changes. Indeed, I believe we are facing the possibility and the opportunity to initiate a religious reformation not merely as significant as that of the reformations of the past, but one that could be far deeper and thoroughgoing in its remaking of religion, and far more widespread in its influence; for the very cosmology and psychology of religion would be transformed, and all the religious cultures of the world would eventually be affected.

CHAPTER 4

Mature Religion and Mature Science[*]

by RABBI ROLAND B. GITTELSOHN

Temple Israel, Boston, Massachusetts

I

NO EVALUATION by a clergyman of the relationship between religion and science can be worth its weight in words unless it commences with a clear identification of the perspective from which he speaks. This is true because we live at a time of incredibly swift and profound ideological transition. Such a time is characterized necessarily by semantic confusion. Words that were once precisely meaningful become aggravatingly confused. For some they retain their old meanings, while for others they have already acquired colorations and shadings that are quite new. Thus can words become barriers rather than bridges in the effort to communicate.

This is what has happened in the last two generations to the word *religion*. It is used now to designate men and positions that are seen, upon careful analysis, to share little beyond the label itself. Let me be specific. The Bible-belt Christian fundamentalist of the deep South is called *religious*, as I am. A scientifically oriented agnostic such as Julian Huxley is

* Copyright © 1963 by Saturday Review, Inc.

generally considered to be *non-religious*, as I am not. Yet if I were painstakingly to spell out long lists of specific attitudes toward the universe and human life, I have no doubt that I would end up sharing more with Huxley than with the Southern evangelist. My attitudes toward science must therefore be expected to differ considerably from those of the orthodox Protestant or the Roman Catholic or, for that matter, even of some among my fellow-Jews. This despite the fact that with a certain measure of validity all of us are at this juncture in time considered to be religious. Where, then, do I stand as I propose to ponder science?

II

I am a naturalistic, humanistic theist. Naturalistic, because I believe that God inheres within nature rather than operating upon it from outside itself. Humanistic, because I am convinced that the loftiest human values we have been able to conceive represent the closest our finite minds can come as yet to comprehending the infinite. Theist, because I am persuaded that our spiritual propensities and capacities are reflections of something very close to the crux of Ultimate Reality. Each of the terms thus defined now invites further elaboration.

My identification as a naturalist does not automatically make me a pantheist. I do not equate God with nature or assert that God is nature; rather that God permeates and infuses nature. God is to nature, as it were, what electric current is to a motor: the Creative Energy that transforms what would otherwise either not exist at all or at best be lifeless and inert into a vital process.

I do not believe in what most people mean by miracles. For me, one of the most convincing kinds of evidence that God exists is to be found precisely in the fact that there are no exceptions to the laws of nature. It will be a very long time, if ever, before I shall be able to know all the laws of nature, but I know enough already to be confident that they can be abrogated by neither man nor God. Indeed, if they could be suspended or interrupted by either, I should then have to become an atheist! For then the very Principle and Power of purposive development that I call God would have vanished from the universe.

My humanistic theism means that I cannot see our unique ability as human beings to create and appreciate truth, goodness, and beauty as divorced from the rest of reality. I believe this dimension of man's experience has evolved in response to the nature and structure of the universe no less than has his hand or brain. There must, therefore, be something in the universe itself that is closely akin to this aspect of man's life. Which means to say, there must be God.

Here, then, is the religious position and perspective from which I ponder science. From this point of departure, what do I find?

III

First, an alarming (and, I fear, growing) tendency to resolve the erstwhile conflict between religion and science through by-pass rather than confrontation. There was a time when chiefly religionists were heard to say that religion and science do not conflict because they do not really meet, that they occupy altogether different and unrelated areas of man's concern, that science is preoccupied with facts and religion with values, that what we *believe* as matters of faith cannot be affected one way or another by what we *know* through empirical research. Now—amazingly and regrettably!— a similar chant has been taken up by some among our scientists.

Typical of this view are statements by two eminent psychiatrists. Dr. Harry Solomon, Commissioner of Mental Health for the Commonwealth of Massachusetts, has written the following in private correspondence with the author: "I see no reason why one cannot have deep faith on one hand and be deeply involved in scientific study on the other hand without worrying whether one negates the other." The late Dr. Gregory Zilboorg was even more explicit: "Scientific knowledge is essentially different from religious knowledge, and it is impossible to measure one by the other; ... religious beliefs need no scientific proof, nor are they made less valid by scientific refutations." He achieves the logical climax and consequence of this view by quoting W. T. Stace to the effect that "science is irrelevant to religion." [1]

I must protest with utmost vehemence and vigor this attempt to reconcile religion and science by detour or avoidance. It is not true that religion and science yield two different and unrelated kinds of knowledge. Knowledge is knowledge, whatever its source. There is indeed a difference between knowledge and faith, both of which play significant roles in science as well as religion, but not between one kind of knowledge and another. There is, to be sure, more than one source of knowledge, but not more than one kind. What we know, we know.

I reject no less perfervidly the implied cleaving of man or reality into neat and unrelated compartments, amounting almost to a kind of philosophic schizophrenia. If science and religion have conspired to teach me any one abiding truth, it is that man is one, the universe is one, and man and the universe together are one. This is the central meaning of science and the core of Judaism's watchword: "Hear O Israel, the Lord our God, the Lord is One."

This means that man cannot be divided into a believing creature versus a thinking creature, that his faith and reason, while not identical, are yet indivisible. What he knows must be the basis of what he believes. What he believes must be consonant with what he knows. I have elsewhere expressed myself on this point as follows: "Of course we need faith to carry us beyond the bounds of reason. But that faith must be

[1] *Psychoanalysis and Religion* (New York: Farrar, Straus and Cudahy, 1962), pp. 26, 46, and 105.

built on a foundation of reason, must be consistent with the reasonable and the known, not contradictory to them. If the direction of the knowledge yielded by experience and reason be represented by a solid line, faith must be a dotted line which continues in the same general direction, not one which goes off at a capricious and contradictory angle." [2]

To juxtapose mind and faith, human investigation and divine revelation, as if they were irreconcilable opposites, is for me utterly fallacious. Man's intelligence, his conscience, and his sensitivity are the very best instruments he possesses to ascertain the divine. Revelation is not the miraculous one-way intrusion of the divine into the mundane. It is rather the result of progressive interaction between man and God. Whenever or wherever a human being reaches out to grasp a truth that has never been comprehended before ... or to create or appreciate a higher dimension of beauty ... or to achieve a loftier level of ethical conduct ... there and then God has revealed Himself to man again. Divine revelation is just as apt to take place in a laboratory or studio, on a concert platform or counting-board, as it is in a pulpit.

I like particularly the way Dr. Meier Ben-Horin expresses this concept of revelation, with its creative implications for the relationship between religion and science. Skillfully playing upon the words of the Biblical assertion, "Near is the Lord unto all who call Him, unto all who call Him in truth," he interprets this to mean: "God is called *in truth*. To find a new truth is to come nearer to His nearness." [3]

All of which adds up to my very firm conviction that the only valid ground for a true synthesis of religion and science is to view them as co-ordinated, complementary, and simultaneous approaches to man as a whole and life as a whole.

[2] Roland B. Gittelsohn, *Man's Best Hope* (New York: Random House, 1961), p. 62.
[3] *Judaism*, Summer 1962 issue.

They must not only coexist; they must reinforce and refine each other.

IV

But do they in fact do this? To a greater degree than small minds on either side of the equation have been able to perceive, yes. It is time for both religionists and scientists to realize the extent to which their most significant insights coincide. True, many of the incidental superstitions by which the essential message of religion has in the course of time become encrusted have been discredited. So have some of the earlier dogmatisms of science, or perhaps it would be more accurate to say, of some scientists. But in remarkable respects the newer findings and conclusions of science confirm rather than threaten the earlier intuitions of religion. Perhaps this can best be understood through three stages of exposition.

One: science reveals a universe of ineffably wondrous order. This has always been a prime postulate of high religion. The fact that science speaks more frequently today in the vocabulary of statistical probability than in that of law must not be allowed to obscure the truth involved: that our universe is not a haphazard or capricious puzzle; that despite the many mysteries which will long—perhaps forever—remain, there are reliable, predictable patterns; and in proportion to our success in discovering these patterns we can increasingly understand the universe and manipulate it to our enormous benefit. Every scientific experiment is predicated on the premise that this is so.

Two: science has emerged from the stark mechanism and materialism by which so much of its infancy was marked. It is much more inclined now to interpret reality in terms of energy and process than of matter, even speculating at times on whether they may not be identical. Insofar as human life is concerned, it recognizes the intimate interrelationship and mutual sway of mind and body over each other. Significant numbers of scientists have at least tentatively voiced the hypothesis that primal energy evolved into matter, then the inorganic into the organic, the unconscious into the conscious, the amoral into the moral, the physical into the extra-physical or spiritual—with each successive stage at least potentially present in its predecessor. This is very close indeed to my understanding of religion.

Three: science has provided the strongest bulwark for a point of view that was adumbrated earlier and to which we must now return, namely, that man in all his aspects and proclivities is an integral part of his universe. He is made of the same stuff as the universe. He could perhaps be perceptively defined as the stuff of the universe become conscious of itself. On the level of the physical, science and religion would agree that this is so. What religion would hasten to add is that no less is true of the extra-physical or spiritual in man. It, too, must have its counterpart in the larger cosmos.

Thomas Huxley seemed almost to be groping for this very truth a century ago when he wrote: "... man, physical, intellectual, and moral, is as much a part of nature, as purely a part of the cosmic process, as the humblest weed." [4]

His grandson, Julian, consummated what the elder Huxley had only implied: "The evolutionary point of view ... establishes the reassuring fact that our human ethics have their roots deep in the non-human universe, that our moral principles are not just a whistling in the dark, not just the *ipse dixit* of an isolated humanity, but are by the nature of things related to the rest of reality." [5]

Here we come close to the most exciting confluence of religion and science. To my knowledge, no one has expressed it more eloquently or incisively than the Canadian zoologist, Dr. Norman J. Berrill: "... our knowledge of the universe

[4] T. H. and J. Huxley, *Touchstone for Ethics* (New York: Harper & Brothers, 1947), p. 45.
[5] *Ibid.*, p. 256.

through our senses and our knowledge of the universe through our own inward nature shows that it is orderly, moral and beautiful, that it is akin to intelligence, that love and hope belong in it as fully as light itself, and that the power and will of the human mind is but a symptom of reality; that we, when we are most human, most rational, most aware of love and beauty, reflect and represent the spirit of the universe." [6]

V

This brings us to a question that seems to bother many of my colleagues in the clergy, both Christian and Jewish. Does the foregoing mean that religion is dependent upon science for validation, that we can accept on faith only that which science shows demonstrably to be true? My answer is, of course, in the negative. Here is where our distinction between knowledge and faith comes again into focus. It does not require faith to accept that which has already been proved as fact. Religion will always, must always go beyond science in postulating hypotheses about life, especially about the spiritual dimensions of life—hypotheses and convictions that science may never be able either to prove or disprove.

Science must be depended upon, not necessarily in every instance to validate, but when necessary to veto the assertions of religion when they uphold on faith that which has already been proved impossible in fact. Specifically, science possesses both the right and the duty to deny, with reference to the Biblical account of creation, that this earth with all its precious cargo could possibly have been created in six days or that one pair of fully developed human beings named Adam and Eve ever appeared on our planet at a precise moment of time as the progenitors of the whole human race. Religion, in turn, has

[6] *Man's Emerging Mind* (New York: Dodd, Mead and Co.), p. 286. For a more detailed exposition of the reinforcement that science now brings to the insights of religion, see my *Man's Best Hope*, especially chapters 2 through 8.

both right and duty to proclaim that life developed gradually on the earth—and perhaps elsewhere, too—as an expression of a massive Cosmic Energy or Urge that has been designated through the ages as God. Between religion thus conceived and science thus understood there can be only collaboration, not conflict.

What I am struggling to express here comes close, I suspect, to Erich Fromm's distinction between rational faith and irrational faith. By the latter he means the blind acceptance of any "truth" simply on the authority of some individual or group that has proclaimed it. By the former he means the acceptance of a given doctrine as "true" because my own reason and experience, together with those of any number of authorities, convince me that it is valid.

In this light the obligations and responsibilities of both religion and science become clear. Science must guard against the dogmatic assumption that only that which can be demonstrated in a laboratory can be true. Religion must refrain from arrogantly disputing with science its discoveries of fact. Both must understand that absolute knowledge is possessed by neither, that everything we think we know—whether it be religious doctrine or scientific data—has been filtered through finite and fallible human intelligence. No individual, discipline, or sect has a monopoly on such intelligence. All that any of us has a decent right to claim is that he is doing the very best he can, at this moment in history, and consistent with his own limitations both of knowledge and of faith, to understand life and to live it more decently.

May I be forgiven a brief word of *ex-parte* pleading at this point? Even as science must very properly appeal for religion to keep abreast of man's expanding knowledge, so that it will never claim as true on faith that which has already been discovered to be false in fact, so religion should petition science to remain aware of significant changes within the household of theology. Too often the spokesmen of science act as if nothing had happened to religion since 1800. Instead of setting up straw men in the likeness of medieval faith and exulting over the ease with which they can swiftly be demolished, let science, consistent with its own essential nature, take pains to acquaint itself with the newer voices of religion, voices that have been more than a little responsive to the importunings of science itself.

At this fateful juncture in time, mature religion and mature science can ill afford to continue a quarrel that has long since lost its meaning. It will require the most precious talents of both if either is to survive.

"Science helps us take our bearings in the journey through evolution. Science and religion together enable us to project the probable future. We see ourselves not as the end-result of evolution but as a way-station en route to something incomparably more wonderful. . . .

"Thus, through science and religion together, we arrive at an understanding of meaning in life. We become aware not only of the present as it has evolved from the past, but also of our human responsibility to the future. Neither science nor religion alone can give us this. Only religion modified by the insights of science and science tempered by devotion to spiritual values can save us or make us worth saving." [7]

[7] Gittelsohn, *op. cit.*, p. 188.

CHAPTER 5

Religionswissenschaft

by E. R. GOODENOUGH
Yale University

SOME ESSAYS must begin with a footnote, and the German title of this one certainly demands explanation. I have used the German word because no English term means what I shall be discussing. *Religionswissenschaft* means the scientific study of religion, but not in the modern English sense of the term, for those who "count and measure" have arrogated "science" to themselves, and of course religion cannot be approached on any important level by controlled experiments or differential equations. The German word still means the medieval *scientia*, that is, critical, ordered, analytical study, and it is of scientific study of religion in this sense that I am writing.

Our contemporaries in all directions urge upon us the futility of *Religionswissenschaft*. During the last twenty-five years especially we have been hearing how science, philosophy, and religion move on different levels of knowledge, and that through revelation we go beyond the whole scientific method, because science must draw its conclusions from analyses of material data. The religious man's intellectual problem, on the

63

contrary, it is argued, is essentially to comprehend the depths and implications of revealed truth. To people who thus divide their ways of thinking, any attempt at a science of religion runs into absurdity, is a basic contradiction of terms. For it is to treat the holy, the numinous, the religious, as though it were a matter for profane scrutiny. Nearly a century ago the great Canon Sanday of Oxford, torn between the new analytical temper and his own devout faith in Anglican Christianity, cried out in agony, "We kill in order to dissect." The agony has since then proved too much for many of our most sensitive spirits. Perhaps they will practice science, do so brilliantly, so long as they can keep up the wall of utter contrast between the sacred and the profane, and do their science in such fields as not to impinge on what they call sacred. But the science of religion is meaningless unless we see that it essentially breaks this down, and proposes precisely in the realm of the religious to move from empirical data to hypothesis, and from hypothesis back to data, and to correct hypotheses by data, as nearly as possible in scientific fashion. It will have no meaning unless we do so with the data of all religions, with the data of the religion we were early taught to love quite as fully as with the religions of Asia, Central Africa, or Australia.

Hereby, it seems, we may perhaps see why study of the history of religion, or of *Religionswissenschaft*, has now generally declined, and has never gained any recognized place among the departments of American universities at all. A century ago those who felt most torn in Europe were the men who, like Sanday, applied the new methods of historical criticism to the Bible. American scholars went to Europe during the last half of the nineteenth century, and learned the methods of European criticism, and brought back the German solution of Ritschl and Harnack, that the *Wesen* of Christianity is its social and ethical teaching, a facile solution that Schweitzer very effectively exploded at its roots. Almost simultaneously the Papal Bull of 1912 rejected all such analytical methods for Catholics, and I cannot see how the Pope could have made any other decision. For the analytical study of the sources of Christianity did indeed break down the old distinctions between the sacred and the profane. What had to be God's Word for the Church, for Protestants, really, as well as Catholics, had in the hands of historians become a collection of historical documents from which history was to be gleaned by only the most rigorously detached scrutiny. I recall Kirsopp Lake's saying once to a graduate class, "The genuineness of a saying attributed to Jesus can be judged only by men free if necessary to say without emotion that, so far as they can see, Jesus did teach in the way under discussion, but that on this point they disagreed with Jesus." The historian might reject or accept the saying attributed to Jesus as authentic, but not on personal or ecclesiastical grounds. From the point of view of the historian, Lake was absolutely right: we cannot let our own or our Church's ideas or preferences interfere consciously or unconsciously with our decisions as to what Jesus did or did not teach. But the Pope was right in saying that such an attitude does indeed break down the safeguards of the sacred as the Church has to conceive it if the Church is to continue at all in its traditional way.

Meanwhile in the nineteenth and twentieth centuries men studied the myths and rituals of the world with increasing detachment. The relative merits of Max Müller's school of cosmic origin, Durkheim's social-totemistic origin, Tylor's animism, and Marett's mana, with a variety of other suggestions, could be debated with complete freedom in a secular world whose leaders largely thought in the new channels of a boundlessly optimistic evolutionism. The crudity of man's roots only emphasized the beauty and value of the emergent tree, the civilization of William II of Germany, Edward VII of England, and William Howard Taft of America. For many devout people revelation became progressive revelation, and scholars delighted in tracing the evolution from the crude

Yahweh of the Book of Judges to the Christian God, who, finally, could "love" but not "desire." Frazer became a household word. Anthropologists concerned themselves largely with gathering material on the religions of the world. The new scientific criticism invaded the four leading American centers of religious study, the divinity schools of Harvard, Yale, Union, and Chicago. No one who heard them will ever forget the great lectures on the history of religion given by George Foot Moore.

America's special contribution to the analysis of religion, however, was made by our psychologists. While all the leaders of thinking in the history of religion were Europeans or Englishmen, and Americans were eagerly reading their books, all Europe and England were reading William James, Starbuck, Leuba, and Pratt. These men had a new and startling view of the roots of religion, roots not in a past perhaps a hundred millenniums comfortably removed, but in our own immediate and personal psyches. Religious individualism of America had split the social organization of religion into a hundred controverting fragments, and Americans regarded religion as a private matter in which the state should never interfere except to protect individuals and minorities. Through practically inventing new approaches to the psychology of religion, this American spirit made its idiomatic contribution to the scientific study of religion, a contribution that Europeans with their state churches did not attempt to rival. You will all object, perhaps, that Schleiermacher, Herbert Spencer, and Louis Sabatier had followers when they, each in his own way, proposed a more individual and psychological approach. But Europe and England generally agreed with Durkheim at least in his minimizing such movements, and defining religion as a unified system of beliefs and practices relative to sacred things, which bring their adherents into a single moral community called the Church. Even so great an individualist as Freud all his life saw in religion a block of entrenched beliefs and practices which he had to fight in order to protect the individualistic approach of his own psychology. He thought he was fighting religion, when, as it seems to me, he was founding and practicing one of his own.

Since the series of collapses that followed upon the catastrophe of 1914, the scientific study of religion has fallen off rapidly. Depression took hold of the defeated Germans of 1918, and in this condition their religious leaders, succumbing to the magic of Karl Barth, regarded the scientific approach to anything whatever as the great sin of men, who only made fools of themselves when they supposed that by taking thought they could add to their stature. Christian revelation, the new-old theology said, had taught man the complete sovereignty of God, the pusillanimity of man, and the sacrilege of supposing that man's critical study of anything, religion least of all, could hope to improve man's essential way of life. Two new words for the profane became widely current, namely science and history, and Barth and his followers would fain lead men not only out of the damning preoccupation of their study, but altogether out of the world these words imply, lead men to a world in which they find their existence in a metaphysical reality.

The great financial depression of the late twenties and thirties made such an escape from the world of science and history deeply attractive also to frightened and discouraged men and women of England, France, and America. With the horrors of the Hitlerian war, more and more people, from different points of view, came to accept the new emphasis upon the inherent sinfulness of man and the mockery of his analytical and scientific efforts. Science makes instruments only to destroy us, people cry out in terror, and to them this demonstrates the inherently depraved nature of science, a doctrine, incidentally, they are not above broadcasting by the latest scientific gadgets. The modern age is re-enacting the tragedy of all Greek drama, they say, the tragedy that the gods inevitably bring destruction upon men who in *hubris* try to do the superhuman. One of the leaders of this sort of thinking loves to describe how God rocks in derision on his throne at the spectacle of man's trying by science to help himself, to improve himself in what this preacher calls the world of history. Man's only hope is in a divine act of revelation. The contents of this revelation we can examine, formulate, assimilate, but the critical attitude of science has no relevance to it. I recently listened to a discussion of the bearing of psychology, both experimental and depth psychology, on theology. Clearly most of those in the room considered that the criteria for examining ordinary psychological experiences had no relevance to man's experience of God and revelation. Science was very well in its place, but as a man-made thing it was futile, hopeless, and entirely impious if it invaded the field of religion.

Theological schools and religious leaders now largely preach variations in this message of human futility. In spite of a scattered remnant, it is precisely *Religionswissenschaft* in any meaningful sense that the religious leaders of our generation have rejected. Are we ourselves ready to face the world as a group prepared and eager to modify our operating hypotheses, which in religion means our faiths, if scrutiny of empirical data makes them dubious or suggests better ones?

The remnant of historians of religion with scientific attitude is now largely scattered in a wide variety of fields: linguistics, anthropology, area studies, sociology, and the like. Leaders in these fields have in large part accepted the old definitions of religion, by which such scholars are not only classed as irreligious by most contemporary religious leaders, but are delighted to find themselves thus described, and call themselves irreligious. Scholars in these fields, consequently, have in general turned their attention to other things than what they consider religion. Most anthropologists now have only tangential interest in religious phenomena. Not by chance did anthropologists study religions avidly a century ago, and now study social structure. Religion was the burning issue then. Now social structure, by the rise of Communism, the threats of the dictatorships, and the problems of industrial relations, stands at the forefront of all our minds. We must not fool ourselves: our scholarship reflects our own basic problems, and the modern intelligentsia feel these social problems much more intensely than the problem of the sacred and the profane.

The same change has occurred in psychology, which has largely tried to become scientific by asking only questions that can be answered by counting and measuring. The psyche as a whole lies quite beyond such control, and so at times modern psychology seems almost obsessed with what one might call psychophobia. One cannot set up problems of the sacred and profane in a rat maze and one does not try to do so. Consequently, I know no really important book on the psychology of religion published in the last thirty-five years. Psychologists who work in personality testing have not tried to develop tests that would show sensitivity to the sacred and profane. We have tests of aptitude for almost everything except for reverence of the "sacred."

The great psychologists that have come out of psychoanalysis have divided sharply on this point. Freud, as I said, tried to brush away the whole matter by showing that the illusion of creedal religion was doomed to collapse before such a deeper understanding of man as he was offering. We may well doubt that Freudianism, as it was systematized by his orthodox followers, is any less illusory as a final statement of the nature of man than the statements Freud characterized as illusions; but Freud provokes us to ask whether authoritatively drawn distinctions between the sacred and the profane, what Freud accepted as being religion from the religious experts of his day, really constitute religion, and whether their acceptance basically marks the *homo religiosus*. Jung went further when he put his whole psychology upon a religious basis by proposing that all individuals have their foundation in the collective unconscious. This conception we might well call mana in direct action, or the panpsychism that has haunted Western thinking from Aristotle to Hegel, and which really underlies Buddhism and Hinduism. I am not a Jungian, but we must admit that Jung has done more than any one man of our generation to keep from utter neglect the problems that world-wide similarities in religious experience thrust before us. I must digress a moment to record that among the great experiences of my own life, not generally known, were the hours in 1938 that Jung spent in my own study (not I in his as a patient), when the already huge mass of my material on symbols threatened to overwhelm me, and when, to use his term, I was trying to "integrate" it all by, as always, integrating myself. Like the great therapist he was, he helped me largely by encouraging me to help myself, not by telling me how I should regard the material. There was healing in his wings. But Jung, let us face it, has generally been rejected by our generation, those who call themselves religious and those who call themselves irreligious, and behind rejection of such a brilliant way of thinking must lie a reason. The reason, if in one reason I may summarize the many, is that somehow he has not spoken the word this generation wants to hear. To his ideas, however, we shall keep recurring, not only in this paper, but in all our studies.

This generation wants either an assurance that its true existence is not in the scientific world, or it wants analytical precision. So *Religionswissenschaft* has suffered from the new and specialized sciences, which, in their highly proper craving for precision, have taken science away from religious studies. Linguistic science, for example, has captivated most of the best minds that have gone into Sinology, Indology, and Islamic studies. Or documentary history, and precision in textual editing, now dominate the minds of young men who came into our departments with quite other objectives. The professors have felt that generalizations about the *Religiosität* of the documents might well await accurate texts and genuine *Sprachgefühl*. Who could assail such impeccable and impregnable correctness? Who but those of us still interested in *Religiosität*, since we find ourselves deserted not only by the new theology, but also by those who through their technical skills could help us most? In these departments a remnant of the old interest survives in many people, who still read the religious classics with deep perception of their religious as well as linguistic or literary value. The greatest scientists of our day, however, are by no means denouncing religion. They have little in common, as I know them, with the theologians who demand that scientists keep within their province of carding wool so that the theologians can weave their cloths. The best scientists I know are deeply devout persons who see the numinous through their telescopes or microscopes, and in their test tubes, not as an "other," but as the essential quality of matter, matter as exploding atoms, or galaxies, or as biological processes.

The hope of reviving study of the science of religion lies, I believe, not in courting the traditionalists and theologians, but in coming to recognize that science itself is a religious exercise, a new religion, and that science and religion have fallen apart largely because traditionalists have done what they have always done, failed to recognize a new approach to religion as it has formed itself in their midst, challenging thereby old conceptions and comfortably formulated adjustments. Historians—of religions, that is—must include in their study, and in their sympathy, the new religion of science, or of scientists, along with the religions and thought ways they have hitherto considered. This needs a bit more explaining.

For the term *religion of science* to have any meaning, we must obviously return to ask what we mean by *religion*, since by the old definitions the two are essentially in contrast. I have no illusion that I shall do more than make suggestions for the problem.

As a historian rather than a philosopher, I must say that no definition of religion I have ever heard, or made (and I have made many), has any but suggestive and partial value. The most important words, of course, can never be defined, and deeper understanding of them usually involves discovering the inadequacy of old definitions. Even so precise a term as chemistry can no longer be defined. What, today, is it? Who will now sharply distinguish it from physics or botany? Certainly not the students of chemistry themselves. Nuclear physics can be studied apart from chemistry, or biology, or astronomy, to a point, but only to a point. *A fortiori*, who can set up any but pretty verbal barriers between history, science, and philosophy? Similarly Freudians have come to understand sex better as they have confused the rest of us by seeing its manifestations everywhere, even in the conduct of infants. Man is a physiological animal, a sexual animal, a political animal, an economic animal, a social animal. He is also a religious animal. He is all of these simultaneously, for beneath the distinctive terms is man himself. Those who study man from one point of view rather than another always tend to see their own approach as the one really all-encompassing in human structure. The function and goal of *Religionswissenschaft* is to come better to understand the *homo religiosus*. But all these approaches blend so inextricably that to define the character and compass of any one aspect invades the boundaries of every other. If we do not recognize this, we limit to the point of petty distortion the aspect we try to define. Sociologists and psychologists have no notion of defining their fields in such a way as to exclude the other, or, in fact, of excluding man's religious patterns. Religion, in turn, cannot be forced to define itself in such a way as not to impinge upon, indeed largely to include, at least sociology and psychology. So, if we are not by verbal calisthenics to weaken our understanding of all these fields, we must resort to description that moves from an essential center indefinitely outward, rather than fabricate definitions that work from borders inward.

In brief, then, I see religion arising from the universal phenomenon that we are born and live in an external universe, and with internal depth and emotions, which we neither understand nor control. Man exists largely helpless before the forces of nature and society, and really knows nothing basic about himself, and the meaning and purpose of life, individually or collectively. The conscious mind, and probably even more persistently the unconscious mind, are always confronted by the *tremendum*, both within oneself and without. By modern science man has to a slight degree mitigated the sense of helplessness and confusion he feels before the *tremendum*, but now when men collectively know more than ever in history, we call ourselves the Age of Anxiety, because we are freshly, almost pathologically, sensitive to the ignorance and helplessness that characterize us. Such ignorance has always characterized mankind, characterizes all animal life. But if an animal is hungry, while he looks eagerly for food, so far as we know he has no diffused anxiety about the problem of food supply. Or of death, or sex, or security in general. Without debating whether that be true for mice and rabbits, or for rats that have been psychologically tortured, this generalization will stand better than most, that awareness of our helplessness and ignorance, along with the anxiety they produce, generally characterizes human beings.

Religion steps in for all of us at this point. Man has never been able to accept himself on this level as helpless before the *tremendum*. He must have the illusion, at least, that he can do something to control the apparently uncontrollable, to explain the inexplicable. We may laugh at the savage stories of creation through a cosmic bull, or turtle, or egg, but the understanding most people have of the process of evolution is probably just about as far from reality, and starts from quite as vague a protozoon, or protozoa, as the stories of the savages. It gives us comfort, nevertheless, to believe in evolution. Those least satisfied by the theory of evolution are my friends in biology who know how fragmentary and inadequate the whole theory really is. All great tragedy faces the unintelligibility of life, and terrifies us as it suddenly dangles our helpless ignorance before us. Shakespeare had no answers for Hamlet and Lear. The *Oresteia* loses its dignity when Athena at the end introduces a divine justice that exists in religion, not reality. For Aeschylus had finally to succumb to his craving for divine consolation, and so he projected its reality as Socrates did not. But how few men in history have given their lives rather than deny their own ignorance! For one such man there have been untold millions of Athenian citizens who would murder, and not always mercifully by hemlock, a man who doubted the reality of the myths that they held like curtains to screen themselves from the unintelligibility and uncontrollability of the *tremendum*.

Here seems the essence of religion, the problem of how man can live over against the great unknown, the *tremendum*. Traditional religions have given two basic answers. Most commonly man has screened himself off from the *tremendum* by mythical accounts of the origin and nature of things, by rites that would placate its unpredictable lightnings and whirlwinds, by holy places and seasons, by divinely given codes of laws. In all these ways man has tried to protect himself from what is to him the chaos of the *tremendum*. Man has draped curtains about him, with fine paintings in perspective on them. This perspective could give him the illusion that he lives in the *tremendum* itself while the curtains actually only protect him from its impact. The patterns on other people's curtains are, of course, myths; those on our own are theology. The masses of men must get their myths, their rites, and their codes, their symbols, the designs on their curtains, from the traditions of their social groups. Few can escape them, or make new ones of their own. Since a few can do so, however, our myths of explanation and our rites for controlling nature, or fate, cannot be simply social institutions forced upon all. And those of us who break away are not thereby irreligious, else the Jewish prophets, the Buddha, Socrates, and Jesus were irreligious.

As over against the apotropaic, the second basic formulation is that in which an individual has broken the curtains, or lifted them, to go alone into the Alone, and to face the numinous *tremendum* in itself. Moses on Sinai, the prophets announcing their new visions, Jesus at Gethsemane, the Buddha as he left his earthly kingdom, many young savage candidates to achieve spiritual leadership in the tribe, these represent an utterly different conception of an adjustment to the universal reality from which most men screen themselves. These men left, or still leave, the formulation about them, to court the very *tremendum* itself, and be taken over by it. Buddhist monks practice this approach, and train the more intelligent laymen in it, though it has little appeal to the mass of Buddhists who live almost entirely in their apotropaic exercises.

The history of religions examines this drive of man to adjust himself to the *tremendum*, the masses by screening themselves from it, others by freshly approaching it. About the *tremendum* itself as a whole, we all come out with myths, of course, whether with traditional myths or ones of our own creation, since the *tremendum* as a whole is utterly too much for us. Practical living is impossible without a skeleton of myths that establish values and meaning. The myths of men have given them their courage both to live and love, and to destroy and kill. It is in the name of myths proclaiming a meaning of life that Hitler and Lenin killed, and Gandhi refused to kill. All decisive action, in the last anaysis all action and life, comes from faith, pure faith that the nature of the *tremendum* is thus, and so, and so, and that we have such or such relation to it. If true religion be a matter of formal rev-

elation from the *tremendum*, however, those who assert that
science and its methods have no relation to it cannot be dis-
puted. In that case, study of the history of religion would be
to collect curious information about behavioral aberrations
and strange myths, essentially not religious at all, because not
a part of what we consider revelation. Its members might have
much good information, and practical advice to give diplomats
or businessmen in dealing with peoples of the world, but their
work would have no relation to *Religionswissenschaft*. Perhaps we should assume, on the other hand, in Jungian terms,
that religion is a matter of less formal, but no less real, invasion of humanity by the *tremendum* through the emergence
of universally similar rites and myths. In that case, by accept-
ing the Jungian hypothesis that these materials come to man
through the Collective Unconscious, we can perhaps get increasing insights into the nature of the *tremendum*. But, to be
brutal, this approach may well be only another method for
obscuring from ourselves our ultimate ignorance, and of painting new designs, or a new term, on our curtains. Whether we
think this fair to Jungians or not, most scientists would at once
say that the Jungian approach goes too rapidly from data to
overall conclusions.

Can a really objective approach to the value of the myths
and practices of religions ever be found? Is one myth painted
on the curtain as good as any other? Should we believe anything that makes living and dying comfortable, and destroy
those who would shake our belief and so disturb our comfort? As one Catholic wrote me: "There are too many things
we shall never know. Here it seems to me is the role of the
revealed religions, of which there is only one true one, meaning mine, for the simple reason that Catholicism did it so much
better than any other religion." This is, indeed, the usual pattern of religion, especially in the West, including modern Russia with its Gospel according to Marx. At this point the science
of religion, with the history of religions as one of its chief

tools, can step in. For we shall believe that only our cowardice makes the *tremendum* terrible, and that so long as we admit our ignorance we can step up to the *tremendum* itself in matters of human value as physics does in matters of material value (if we can use the word *material* any more). The method of modern science is, unabashed by general ignorance of reality, to go to the great unknown with little questions that inch their way into bits, consistent bits, of knowledge. I believe that in the science of religion we must learn to do the same.

Personally, I do not see how in the modern world we have a right to speak of, or look for, a science of religion so long as we ourselves live within apotropaic curtains, or live with the stated purpose of having our personalities and critical faculties blurred out in mysticism. For we can no longer use the word *science* in its original sense of the Latin *scientia*, or of Plato's *episteme*. Science now means, as I have said, a method of study in which, by the most exact methods applicable to a given sort of data, we draw up hypotheses from the data, and then verify (or reject) the hypotheses by some fresh return to the data, or by return to fresh data. A cataloguing of data, or a learned collection of information, can no longer pose as scientific knowledge, what the word *Wissenschaft* often meant a century ago. Scientific study takes empirical data and tries to see the principles inherent in them. Science proverbially says it can do nothing with an isolated fact. It can do just as little with inherently miscellaneous facts. For what science seeks always is structural, inherent relationships.

In saying this about science we seem to have begun again describing religion, since religion has been man's passionate attempt to adjust himself to the *tremendum* by understanding its nature and how to use it. It is possible that the rejection of science by religion, and of theology by science, is only the old war of religions on a new front, and that science seems a threat to old formulations of religion precisely because it is a new formulation of man's relation to the *tremendum*, actually a totally new form of religion itself. I believe that that is precisely the case and that the emergence of this type of thinking, which followers of the old religions continue to mark as irreligious, signifies the emergence of a new religion. The new religion takes a new attitude toward the *tremendum:* It no longer hides its head, ostrich-fashion, in myths asserting that the *tremendum* is less perilous than it is; it no longer surrenders to the *tremendum*, and asks to be reabsorbed into it. Instead, refusing either to run away or to surrender, it accepts the *tremendum*, and the individual's helplessness and insignificance before it. It drops no curtain, but faces the overwhelming within and without, while it seeks to find relationships and meaning as far as it can by its own method. The new religion of science, and most of the men and women who practice it, have few illusions. Few of them want to discuss the nature of reality, or work from *a prioris*, except the basic one announced by Einstein, that the only thing unintelligible about the universe is that it should be intelligible. To assert that the universe is universally intelligible would indeed be another painted curtain. Certainly it is not intelligible now. But society finds itself deluged with the apparently limitless flow of dimes from the jackpot of nature that the scientific conception of intelligibility has released upon us. As Theodore Sizer remarked the other day, the new deluge, in the eyes of millions, has been enormously rewarding but depressingly stupefying. In other words, science has released not only gadgets and dimes to engulf us, but has stupefied us with the *tremendum* itself, and that in a way for which we have formed no protective devices. It has often stupefied even the scientists in their private lives, but does not do so in the lives of those truly dedicated to the new point of view, people whom I may call the saints of science. Many of them have a private logion, such as that of the great astronomer Harlow Shapley, who, as he looks in his telescope, or does his celestial mathematics, mutters to himself: "All nature is God, all God is nature." He approaches this nature-God, however, not by traditional forms of worship, but through his observations and calculations, which have become his sacrament. Few human beings have a conception of the immensity of the universe, or of the smallness of man in it, comparable to Shapley's. But the *tremendum* has no terror for him. He looks at it with quiet eyes, astonished, reverent, but unafraid. He carried this attitude over to society and politics when McCarthy created fear and trembling. He regarded Senatorial Committees for Hysteria with the same calm eyes, and spoke up to them as, in his mathematics, he speaks up to the universe. Throughout he keeps his integrity, his dignity, as an ignorant but seeking human being. This is religion pure and undefiled, and we do ourselves, and our subject, small service if we fail to recognize it as such.

Much of this spirit must become ours. For we can hardly call ourselves scientists of religion if we systematically define religion so as to leave out this great approach to the *tremendum* going on all about us, and refuse ourselves to share it. In the mid-twentieth century we will seem ridiculous to our generation if we call ourselves scientists but do not examine our data in the same factual and calm spirit. We cannot announce the nature of the *tremendum*, but must content ourselves with shuttling back and forth between data and hypotheses, happy when one of our hypotheses proves useful, but quite undismayed and willing to discard them when others do not. For our faith, like that of all scientists, will be that the process will eventually advance us to sounder understanding, not that our hypotheses of the moment have ultimate validity.

In such study our audience will be small. We shall have little that will seem valuable to the great mass of men who live within the curtains of a revelation or within the far narrower and uglier curtains of indifferent and insensitive preoccupations, which are the local and private blinders of much of our modern society.

And what, exactly, will be our data?

For *Religionswissenschaft* in general the data will be of many kinds. No field of human activity, really, can be thought irrelevant. We may get most important suggestions from the study of psychology of all sorts, from all sociological studies, including, of course, anthropology and law. Increasingly the new linguistics, whether as a study of the structure of language, the more accurate approaches to etymology, or the whole new philosophy of semantics, will help us. The worlds of creativity in art, literature, and music are worlds of religion. No one person can deal with such diversified data. Many particularly concern themselves with the sacred literatures and ethics, as well as the myths and rituals, of people of the world from earliest times to the present. Insofar as our study of this is scientific, it will involve detailed analyses conducted with full awareness of the best understanding others have achieved from such data up to the point of our own investigation. It is not, if we are analyzing Pahlavi texts from Iran and India, that we will know merely all former suggestions for the meaning of those particular texts, but that we shall know similar analyses elsewhere, so that our work will add at once to the understanding of the particular texts, and also to the general technique of textual analysis. This brings us one step nearer the *tremendum*, since the phenomenology of textual transmission has broad horizons. If analysis of our particular data takes us into strange fields, we go out into them. It is a common experience that one analyzing texts in one language will find cognate texts in another language, so that he must stop and learn the other language. It may be that a scientific study of rabbinical law is going to require knowledge of Greek and Roman law, or, for the Babylonian Talmud, of the laws of Babylonia. In that case the obligation before the scholar is clear. There are limits to this, the limits of human capacity and length of life. We often must publish, using data beyond our expert competence. Such publication must not only state the limits of the author, but be written by an author who will always bear in mind that what he writes is beyond his expert control.

Herein we can never fulfill the ideals of a natural scientist, who can so control his observations that they involve no extraneous variables. But at this point I hear the chuckles from my scientific friends. Of course that is the ideal, they say, but just what experiment of any but routine importance was ever done in any science when all variables were controlled? Scientists try to recognize those variables, and take them into account, they tell me, but the advance of science has largely meant that the next person discovers variables that had not been suspected at all. The *tremendum* again.

We can hope to re-establish a science of religion not insofar as we take over too slavishly the various methods now used in other sciences. Scientists have to invent new methods for appraising each new type of data. Science has only one method, and that is to devise in each case and for each body of data or for each question a method, usually quite *ad hoc*, which will yield the most adequate understanding of that data. But the questions scientists ask of their data are relatively small ones. Science advances only bit by bit, and most scientists regard the questions of philosophy as quite outside their proper realm, indeed as *hubris* when they invade science itself.

Scientists, however, can never lose sight of the fact that the particular problem is always part of a larger problem, for only in that relation lies scientific creativity. We hope to clarify the larger problem by solving the smaller, but in simply solving the smaller we are technicians and antiquarians, not people adding to scientific knowledge at all. The great prophets of science, or the great historians, have been masters of their techniques (though in this they have often had research assistants who could correct them sharply), yet they have been supreme because they have gone beyond the techniques of what I may call the pharisees of science. Creative scientists, like creative painters and musicians, advance into the *tremen-*

dum as they try methods never used, join the hitherto uncon-
nected, break all rules as they seem inadequate, even though
earlier men had found those rules useful. Science, like religion,
has been led and fed by men who have used their micrometers,
but looked beyond them. For the spark of new light always is
an understanding of the data that the data themselves do not
give to those whose eyes focus too narrowly upon them.

In studying the data of man's religious history, we, too,
must look beyond the data. But not too fast. We must look
how and for what? Look by the most detailed study for a
spark of new light on man as a *homo religiosus*. A young geologist remarked to me the other day that the modern scientist
works always confronted by the vastness of unknown nature.
But he does not drop his tools to generalize about it. He works
on his own specific problem. Our specific problems will be
somewhat analogous to those who investigate native herbal
medicaments to see if they can find their value (many had
great value), and so get suggestions of new drugs for our own
use. Somewhat similarly we would ask: What actually lies behind the values men have found in myths, mystic philosophies
and practices, rituals, and symbols? As historians of religion
this will be our specific field of investigation. Before we can do
any valuable generalization, we must do a great deal of careful,
detailed study of local phenomena. We must beware of the oc-
cupational disease of people in our fields, which is to make such
generalizations about religious phenomena as were made by
the great leaders in *Religionswissenschaft* of the last century.
The old method, still by no means abandoned, was to assume
we are proving such generalization if we can give examples
of cases where we think they apply. It is almost impossible not
to fall into this error if we make too large generalizations too
soon. In fields where evidence is hopelessly inadequate, we
must work with hypotheses supported only by a few instances.
But in those cases we work fully aware of the hypothetical nature of our conclusions, as a biologist must do in discussing the

stages of evolution. At the present stage of the science of religion, we would do well to ask small questions until we have established a methodology we can all approve and use.

Such a procedure does not mean that we will ever lose sight of our true objective, total understanding. But we must face the *tremendum qua tremendum*, not reject old curtains only to put up new curtains of hasty generalizations. Most of us will be technicians, turning up carefully verified hypotheses about small and isolated problems. We also will have our reward. Always, however, we shall hope that new Curies and Einsteins will come in our field to use what we have been doing, and go far beyond it into a new dimension. The *tremendum* about us and within us will still have *n* dimensions. *Religionswissenschaft* in the mid-twentieth century can take us not to total understanding (perish the *hubris*), but to somewhat greater comprehension of man in his religious problem. It can do so only as we combine science and religion in our very marrow, combine them into a dedication to learning about religion by the slow, dogged approach of science. I know no other way in which we can hope eventually to understand better the *homo religiosus*, religion itself, and avoid the agony Sanday felt when he killed in order to dissect. For if we still have to kill the old dream that religion is a matter of revelation, through *Religionswissenschaft* we may discover that the scalpel itself has become a sacramental instrument.

That is, we must learn this much, at least, from psychoanalysis, that we cannot understand other people until we understand ourselves. In calling the myths and theologies of religions painted curtains, designs so drawn in perspective that one forgets the flat canvas on which they are painted, I have, of course, only partially described the function and value of traditional religions. To change the figure, the projections of men have often been dream ropes they have thrown up into the *tremendum*, and then have miraculously been able to climb them a little. All human development has taken place as men have dreamed, for example, of social justice, and then spent the millenniums from the beginnings of tribal justice to hopes of the One World in climbing that rope. All who have any understanding of religion know that much of great value has been painted on men's curtains, that mankind has actually climbed on those ropes. We know also that much that was hideously destructive has been taught in the name of religion. The great new hope, I believe, is in *Religionswissenschaft* itself, which proposes minutely to examine the *homo religiosus*, including ourselves as *homines religiosi*, quite aware that over-all and hasty generalizations only curtain us off again from our subject. We should use the curtainless procedures of science, whose essential temper was oddly best expressed by that curtain-bound genius, Cardinal Newman, when, although hating free inquiry of any sort, he wrote:

> "I do not ask to see the distant shore:
> One step enough for me."

Religionswissenschaft writes no popular books, no simplified summaries for sophomores. Perhaps we must make our living doing this, but we must recognize in it no part of our real business, for the soul of the new age sees human existence as the endless road of inquiry. Science offers no royal road to knowledge, but an unblazed trail into the wilderness, where, if we travel with understanding, we travel with awareness of its vastness, but move from tree to tree.

So we shall take to ourselves the advice of the ancient rabbi: "He who grasps much, grasps nothing; he who grasps little, really grasps."

CHAPTER 6

Spiritual Man:
Thoughts on Religion and Science

by DANA McLEAN GREELEY

American Unitarian-Universalist Association

I BELIEVE that religion and science are reconcilable because I believe in One World, and in the monolithic character, or indivisibility, of truth, and because I am persuaded, although it cannot be demonstrated for at least another million years or two, that although we talk about reason on the one hand and intuition on the other, and divide our scholars into scientists and seers, nevertheless man also is one and indivisible, and to say that he knows with the mind on the one hand and with the heart on the other is but a figure of speech. What he knows he knows with all his powers of comprehension. These powers of comprehension fit the universe that has produced them, and can progressively understand it in its entirety—not you and I, perhaps—but these powers of comprehension, when they have become as great in comparison to our present intellects as the Yerkes Observatory, which I visited recently, is in comparison to the magnifying glass that I carried in my pocket as a boy. We were not born to become curious, and then to be deceived; but we were born to achieve wisdom as valid as the mathematics of Whitehead and the music of Beethoven and the love of Saint Francis of Assisi.

At the same time that religion ponders science, we can try to take an objective view of both religion and science. Science is putting increased power into the hands of men every day. Splitting the atom was perhaps as great an invention or achievement as the making of fire, and can bring us untold blessings, or, if it gets out of hand, it can exterminate us from the face of the earth. Religion has been dogmatic and superstitious in the past, or what men have called religion, at least. It has been authoritarian and tyrannical. And it has been cloistered and remote from the world. But it has also challenged men and enlightened them and inspired them; and today, keeping abreast of science, it must be open-minded and free and practical, or there will be no responsible society, and perhaps no society at all, in this last half of the so promising twentieth century. On December 2, 1942, man achieved at the University of Chicago the first self-sustaining chain reaction, and thereby initiated the controlled release of nuclear energy. This was a historic event, as a university publication records. Then, on August 6, 1945, the United States dropped an A-bomb on Hiroshima; and on that day Reuben Gustavson, the vice-president of the University, met on the campus the director of the University Laboratory, which had helped to develop the bomb, and the scientist said to the vice-president, "This is a very sad day for us. Let us hope that we've not placed dynamite in the hands of children." He might have said in different phraseology, "Let us pray for the maturity of the race, and that our ethics will catch up with our physics." Norman Cousins reminded the people of Moscow fairly early in the nuclear arms race that nuclear bombs have been tested that contain the equivalent of twenty million tons of TNT, and to make the power of such a bomb more real for them, he said, "Think of every city that has been bombed in the past; think of Leningrad, Stalingrad, Kiev, Minsk, Warsaw, Berlin,

Frankfurt, Hamburg, Bremen, Munich, Darmstadt, Düsseldorf, Amsterdam, Rotterdam, London, Birmingham, Southampton, Madrid, Shanghai, Nanking, Tokyo, Hiroshima, Nagasaki," and then he added, "Put the destructive power of all those bombings together, and it does not come up to the destructive power of a single bomb that can be carried currently by a single plane or missile, against which there is no defense; no defense except peace." This gives us a small but vivid illustration, regarding just one of man's problems, of the responsibility of religion and ethics in an age of science. If religion remains irrelevant, or abdicates its role, we could be in a far worse fix than when Mount Ararat hospitably reached up its summit through the waters to receive Noah and his family, and two animals and birds of every kind.

But my subject for this paper, in relation to a responsible society, is "Spiritual Man." Who is the contemporary Noah in every one of us who is worthy of being saved? The existentialist advocate would urge us to feel for him and to save him, but in the old-fashioned rationalist manner I want to philosophize about him for a few minutes, and preliminarily even to appraise the value of such philosophizing. Professor Gifford of McGill University says, "From the beginning of civilization it was inevitable that science and philosophy and religion would one day part company. They were held together so long as science and philosophy were by-products of the religious quest." Then he says, "In a mature society they will again be held together; for the knowledge of things, which is science, and the inference from things, which is philosophy, are correlates of the concern about human destiny, which is religion." That is very similar, of course, to Paul Tillich's definition of religion. We have a concern about human destiny and about the nature of the whole cosmos in which we find ourselves. As the green plant turns toward the sun, and as the homing pigeon finds its way high above a hundred miles of broken landscape, and as the salmon crosses an ocean against currents and tides and many hazards, so there is an instinct in us to search for ultimate reality and to discover the whole meaning of life. The world is not flat, and epistemologically we are not blind or helpless any more than Christopher Columbus was. There are endless depths and dimensions for us to explore, but in us life becomes self-conscious and starry-eyed alike, and we were made for that exploring. I am saying something about the contemporary Noah in every one of us that is worthy of being saved when I cite our hunger and thirst for knowledge, or our concern for human destiny. Julian Huxley makes that point with the testimony of anthropologists and archbishops to back him; he insists that the essence of religion springs from man's capacity for awe and reverence, and that the objects of religion, "however much later rationalized by intellect or moralized by ethics, however fossilized by convention or degraded by superstition or fear, are in origin and essence those things, events, and ideas, from which arose the feeling of sacredness." And you and I argue that the whole of life is sacred, and the concept of the creation itself is sacred. That is the very basic presupposition of our discussion of "Spiritual Man." As many appear to be convinced, historic Christianity and Christian theology may be passing away; they were too inextricably wedded to Christian dogma that could not be changed; and when theology begins to follow dogma instead of dogma following theology, so to speak, then it is not for the future. But man's inquisitiveness is not passing away, and his quest for God is not exhausted or outmoded. Science is the search for truth, but theology is the quest for the ultimate meaning of life, and theology is still, and always will be—allow me to say it—the queen of the sciences. There are many schools today that scoff at the idea that we can understand ultimate reality, or know God, or even know that he exists. Theodore Parker, one of the greatest iconoclasts in modern history, regretted that in his century there were no great theologians. "Theology is left," he said, "to men of humble talents, who walk mainly under the cloud of prejudice, and but rarely escape from the trammels of bigotry and superstition." He, the great social reformer, wanted the children of genius and liberty to think about human destiny and to have a concern for ultimate reality. The geologist and the botanist and the biologist and the anthropologist all have noble professions, but it is when they study the universe that has produced the rock and the flower and the animal and man and man's ideals that they become theologians, and that is why, as we have repeated from old, "theology is the queen of the sciences." Dr. Louis Agassiz at Harvard, when he was ready to perform a new experiment, would halt his scientific students and say, "We are about to ask God a question." That was profound reverence. Albert Einstein, in testifying to the intelligibility of the universe, asserted that God meant for him a "superior mind that reveals itself in the world of experience." Channing in America and James Martineau in England, two of the greatest liberals of their lands, have both asserted that to know God is to attain to the highest conception in the universe. I am illustrating man's confidence in his universe, and his hunger for truth.

We have been on this planet a million years or more. Twenty-four centuries ago there was a man in Greece named Democritus who simplified the universe by suggesting that everything was made up of tiny molecules, and they called him a materialist. That was all that was real for him. Two centuries ago there was a man in England named George Berkeley who simplified the universe by extending certain theories of John Locke's and arguing that all we know of the world around us is in our own ideas, a secondary and entirely unsubstantial knowledge, and they called him an idealist. Bacon thought he knew everything, but others, such as Descartes when he knew only that he existed, have fallen almost into solipsism and acknowledged that they knew next to nothing at all. Was Plato wiser, who dwelt mostly with ideas, or Schleiermacher or Sartre, who have dwelt more with feelings and immediate experience? Are the optimists the ones whom we ought to follow, or are the pessimists closer to the truth? I don't think the world is just matter, and neither do you. Nor do I believe that we have only secondary and unverifiable knowledge, and neither do you. Modern philosophical irrationalism or epistemological futilitarianism distresses me as much as atheism in its more negative forms. I believe that nature and the moral law and spiritual reality are all comprehensible, and that our immediate experience and our discovery of God and the Pleiades belong together. And although life must have its tragic elements, there is ground for genuine optimism. "The spirit of man shall reign over all the earth! He is heir of all the ages since the dawn of time." That is not pure fancy; it is insight, and aspiration as well.

Of course, there are various views of man that arise and that linger in history. Emil Brunner, in speaking of the physiochemical view of man, says that he is "subject to the law of gravity, like everything else, that he is a portion of matter composed of hydrogen, carbon, nitrogen, phosphorus, calcium, and other elements. A little thyroid-gland secretion does actually more or less determine the whole of his bodily existence, and affects his psycho-spiritual existence as well." But if one seeks to understand the whole nature of man by studying this aspect only, he is chasing a will-o'-the-wisp. And Brunner thinks that side by side with the materialistic view is the organic-zoological theory. According to this, man is just an animal, albeit the highest and perhaps final offshoot of the mammals, with a peculiarly complicated structure, and a highly differentiated nervous system, which gives him his superiority over other species. But his difference from the animal is only in degree, not in character nor in principle. Brunner talks about the man-in-the-street common-sense view of man, which is unsophisticated, although it may become both practical and poetic. And there is the idealistic view of man—many of the ancients had it, and the German philosophers, Leibnitz,

Kant, Fichte, and Hegel—which affirms essentially that man is spirit, "and therefore immortal, eternal, divine, in the deepest part of his nature. All that is mortal, perverted, limited is non-essential, a kind of foreign addition, perhaps even an illusion." Many expressions of mysticism and psychology alike grow out of this view. Every world religion has its interpretation of man, some of them in the Far East being close to forms of idealism. The Christian view seems a strange one to the scientific mind, one of the most strange. Brunner emphasizes that this is not a theory, but a statement of faith, and that it springs not from a process of analysis or meditation or reflection upon existence, but from its relation to a historical event. "Grace and truth came by Jesus Christ." The Christian doctrine is familiar to us all. Man was created by God in a pure state, as the Greeks thought that Pallas Athene sprang full-blown from the forehead of Zeus. But Eve tempted Adam, and he sinned, and was cursed by God, and from then on was a depraved and lost soul until Christ came to earth to atone for his sin and to redeem him, not universally, but under certain specific conditions.

You and I accept some form of evolutionary philosophy regarding man, and we say that even more wonderful than the story of the Garden of Eden is the upward climb of life, and the mystery or the miracles by which the scum on the pool was supplanted by the fern that waves in the breeze and the butterfly and the eagle and the ape and Aristotle and Shakespeare and Mahatma Gandhi. Science teaches us today that life has advanced from the simplest to the most complex forms. I don't believe that there was ever any fall in a hypothetical Garden of Eden; but if there was a time in the evolution of the race when man's eyes were opened and he first distinguished between good and evil or right and wrong—in other words, when his moral conscience was dawning—that was not a fall, but an ascent. Perhaps he became free from instinct to some extent at that moment, but he won the power of choice and the wisdom of a god, and if Jehovah knew what was happening, He would not have cursed man then, for He is not really jealous, but He would have said at that time more than ever before, reflecting upon His creation, "It is good." As Browning put it, "Man was made to grow," and when he learned to distinguish good from evil, he was growing most significantly.

I don't know how the universe came into being. We read that it could have been a slow process on the one hand, or that there might have been a great explosion of gases on the other hand; but from whence came the gases? It is as hard to conceive of the origin of the universe with nothing beyond it, as of an unlimited universe. Perhaps someday we shall find the answer, but for now we must think of it as a miracle, the very fact of the existence of stars and galaxies and nebulae and planets, and rocks and lava and water and an atmosphere that surrounds the planets.

A second miracle that we cannot yet understand took place about a billion years ago, when over a period of more millions of years perhaps than have elapsed since then, life actually had its origin, and organic substance was added to the inorganic substance of this earth. The scientists know that the sun's rays and the escaping body-heat of the earth and many other factors helped determine the creation of vegetation; but these scientists do not know yet the real secret of the first living cells. As I learn from Harlow Shapley's *Stars and Men*, even "The cell, like the 'indivisible atom,' is now recognized as a highly organized and integrated system built up from extremely small and distinct particles," but whether the ultimate particles of life have been found and identified is very doubtful. And as I say, how they first came into existence, or emerged upon the scene, nobody knows. And yet forests cover the continents, and in places even the desert blossoms like the rose.

And then still a third miracle took place, at least from the layman's point of view. Biological life appeared. Maybe the biologist doesn't recognize any lines of demarcation separating plant life from animal life, but to my untutored observation mobility and even a sort of self-direction became characteristics of life, and there were the beginnings of a nervous system, and the "earth brought forth every living creature after his kind, cattle, and creeping things, and beasts, and the fish of the sea, and the fowl of the air"; and it was so that the toad and gazelle and the skylark could all see the world into which they were born and upon which they fed, and they could hunt their food instead of waiting for it to come to them, and even though they began to eat each other instead of to grow on chlorophyll, we are convinced that they represented a step ahead in the upward march of evolution.

Now I am beginning to speculate, but I would suggest that somehow, as the universe was born in the first place, and as the organic evolved from the inorganic life, and biological life from plant life, so the mind of man has evolved from biological life, and, shall I even say, from the nervous system of the animal. Man has been defined as the animal that laughs, and this has been referred to as constituting his uniqueness. One writer suggests that man's mouth is his distinction, for strangely it is "more than a toothed opening to his stomach, designed to force down food. His weak-jawed, horse-toothed mouth is the great riddle of the plains. He can speak." From Bushman to Florentine, he has a language. But George Wald tells us that the bees communicate with each other; they do it with their wings, but are wings inferior to mouths? And maybe other animals communicate too. Much of their instinct, we reiterate, is keener and more reliable than ours, but without getting into the egocentric position, we can categorically assert that we think more than they do. The mind of man is the fourth level in emergent evolution.

And then came his spiritual sensitiveness and growth. If the terminology will suffice, I will argue that the chimpanzee had a latent mind, and that the Neanderthal Man had a latent soul. The mind and the soul were developing simultaneously in the savage, but his altruism was slow to achieve real stature, and even today, as we started out by acknowledging, our ethics are not up to our science. The cave man had a mind, and above that, said William Herbert Carruth, there developed "A sense of law and beauty." That sense of law and beauty is the key to the spiritual man. Once upon a time the earth was barren, and there was no life here. Now there is life. Yesterday a man in Galilee had a vision of a kingdom that is not of this world, and by the force of his own faith, he encouraged those who were beaten and lame and halt to stand erect and walk, and by the power of his own love, he forgave sinners and taught them self-respect; and when fearful and selfish men conspired against him, he was true to his own principles, and went to the cross to die for peace and good will among men. He called himself, and they called him, the son of man; Emerson said of him: "one man was true to what is in you and me." But we could also suggest that in him there emerged an ethical character that made the reforms of Hammurabi look childish indeed, and a spiritual stature that was prophetic of the potential of man and the future of the race. His followers were fed to the mouths of lions in the Roman Colosseum; and they were not committing suicide, after the manner in which the lemmings make their periodic devastating migrations into the sea in Europe, but they were violating the laws of the survival of the fittest for the sake of a dream and of their moral integrity. That was a new kind of life. And as they died, more and more men became Christians. It was a kind of life that was not evident in molten lava or cold quartz, or in moss or redwoods, or in rats or kangaroos, or even in the minds of Cain or Ramses. I expect the quartz and the redwoods and the rats to endure, and the minds of men to become keener and more capable all the time; but I expect the spirit of love and of dedication to a better world to become more and more dominant in the life of man. He will awaken to his glory. "Before him lies the way of life. He will come into the joy of his divinity."

I don't know for a certainty that everything in my experience is real. I accept the sun and the moon as real, and this desk in my office, and the water that I drink to quench my thirst. But the reports that the scientists render on the nature of matter make me as skeptical at times as Bishop Berkeley, whose skepticism didn't have the advantage of knowing that a stone is more space than atoms, and that atoms are only electrons, and electrons are only charges of energy, and have never been seen. He might have been even more skeptical today than he was then. I accept electricity and energy as real, but in my naïveté I wonder how they are different in iron ore, or lettuce from the garden, or a bolt of lightning, from what they are in music from the organ pipes or the sights and sounds that come from Westminster Abbey in London through my television set. I accept thought as real, the thought that I am getting hungry, or the thought that I love my friends, or the thought that the aurora borealis is more beautiful than the fireworks on the Fourth of July; and I am persuaded that it is not tied to the brain; it can travel from one person to another. Perhaps all these things are varieties of the divine energy, which is all that there is. Perhaps love travels also. Possibly that is another name for the divine energy. God is self-creating energy; and God is love. I wonder whether there is not a spirit of aspiration in the heart of the cosmos itself, and if we had teleological eyes, whether we could not see the future almost as well as we can now see the past. God prays and we pray, and our hearts burn within us for the further fulfillment of life.

I accept many things. But one thing I believe most firmly: that life is no accident; that there is moral and spiritual purpose in star dust and modern democracies; and that a dream is not illusory, and that hope is not in vain. Jesus probably thought the world was coming to an end in a very short time; and in that respect he was wrong. But he was right in his witness to the spiritual character of life, as Jeremiah and Socrates were right before him, and as Luther and Wesley and Channing and

Gandhi and Schweitzer have been right also. D. D. Runes, writing on the nature of man, says that "man is as little the final purpose of divine providence as an elk or a beetle or a salamander." And yet this same writer says that "man is spiritual, essentially spiritual." I do not know whether he is the ultimate end of creation, or will be even in the psychozoic age. Perhaps he is not man as yet. Or perhaps he will be superseded by a being as far above himself as he is above the beetle. But this I do affirm, that he is the highest form of life upon this planet, that he is the creation of the divine will, and that in him the spirit and purpose of the cosmos have reached a level beyond the inorganic, the organic, the biological, and even the intellectual. To survive, and to feed himself, and to procreate are not his genius. Idealism is his genius. He is a dreamer of dreams. Joel said, "It shall come to pass that I shall pour out my spirit upon all flesh; and your sons and daughters shall prophesy, and your old men shall dream dreams, and your young men shall see visions." And man, having reached that stage, has the power to make those dreams come true too. Plato envisaged his republic; John on Patmos saw a new heaven and a new earth, for the first heaven and the first earth had passed away, and there was no more sea; Bacon didn't mind the sea, and he wrote the *New Atlantis*; Thomas More drew the blueprints for his Utopia; and George Ripley and his friends founded Brook Farm as the pattern of their ideal community. These men were all tempted by the world, and at times I am sure they became weary with the world. Their natural animal appetites sometimes distracted them from the higher forms of beauty, and even interrupted their quest for truth. The freedom that we have achieved from instinct, and the will of God, and the fallibility of the human mind, occasioned their vacillation between truth and falsehood. But nevertheless the natural spiritual man that was in them longed for the ideal life of the Republic or of Brook Farm; and so they labored for its fulfillment. "Why are we here?" they are bound to ask, and their answer was that we are here for growth, and to achieve that which is ultimately worthwhile, in ourselves and through our society with each other. The Galilean phrased it for us in a forceful way when he said, "Be ye perfect even as your Father which is in heaven is perfect," which I would interpret in modern parlance to mean, "Let the life process, or the divinity that is within you, reach up for its fulfillment, until the harmony of your own spirit reflects the harmony of the cosmos, and you are what God intended you to be." We are bound to ask why we are here, and even to muse: "Why do we wonder why we are here?" Because we are rational, reflective beings, born of the universe itself, and yet able to detach ourselves from the universe and to equate it as we comprehend it from the small end of our telescope. And because, unlike the animals, in us the purpose of the cosmos has become a conscious purpose, and it commands us as co-creators with God of the world that is to be. Science has not yet found the meaning of life, although it might conceivably do so. But religion has to postulate the meaning of life, or discover it by its own experience. Victor Frankl, who is the successor of Freud and Adler in Vienna, asserts that neither the will-to-pleasure nor the will-to-power is the primary factor in man's life, but that primary factor is "his deep-seated striving and struggling for a higher and ultimate meaning to his existence." We demand this meaning because of our native spiritual hunger, and it is satisfied by the consciousness of spiritual purpose and responsibility. As in the case of a society, so in relation to the universe itself, each of us has a part to play and a task to perform. And Frankl says, "the religious man does not interpret his life only in terms of a task—a morally inescapable personal task—but also in terms of a taskmaster." The Platonists and the transcendentalists alike strove to fulfill the task of realizing a nobler society or the kingdom of God on earth. We cannot separate our spiritual nature or our spiritual vision from our social responsibility. This is the religious meaning of homeostasis. I am sure, as Alfred Emerson says, that there is an end-directedness in living organisms, and man, by understanding this (by using his freedom), can control his own destiny to some extent. But in the fulfillment of that destiny his spiritual growth and his social achievements must be inextricably inter-woven. He cannot pray on his knees on the Sabbath and then prey on his neighbors during the remainder of the week, or offer his gift at the altar of religion without reconciling him-self with his fellow men. His religion is his answer to tyranny and exploitation of men, wherever they exist; and it is by his religion that he knows that righteousness and peace are not options or expediencies in society, but moral necessities.

Professor Carl Zimmerman, the sociologist, has said that five times in Western history the well-fed classes have lost their faith, and simultaneously fallen into a relapse; and that only when they regained their faith have they gone for-ward again. What he means is that they lost their conviction of the meaning and the purpose of life. They lost the con-sciousness of their spiritual nature and destiny. Ralph Burhoe, in reporting on the Institute on Religion in an Age of Science, has stated that perhaps the greatest problem of all "is the tend-ency of the logic of scientific ideas to corrode and dissolve the strength of the Christian beliefs as they have been taught." On this basis we could fall, and very likely are falling, into a relapse in our generation. I would agree that "no aspect of existence—physical, living, or human—is beyond the scope of scientific inquiry." No presumed "revelation" can be inviolate against the examinations of reason. But we need in this age an affirmation of man's spiritual genius and of the power of ideals if we would save civilization, and unify the race as well as split the atom. Many of the old religious beliefs, like many other beliefs, will have to go in the light of advancing science. But new beliefs can take their place that are larger and not smaller than they were. Our God is not the god who walked in the garden in the cool of the evening; and man is not a savage or a slave or a fallen angel, but he is a Hilary or a Tensing, spiritually speaking, striving for the summit of Mount Everest. And God is striving with him.

Let me conclude by asserting that science without religion is amoral; and that religion, without the best knowledge that it can assimilate and use, in the physical and social sciences, is unenlightened or irresponsible. They must bridge the gap, or overcome the barriers that separate them. To change the figure of speech, I have been reminded of Albert Schweitzer's statement, "There is an ocean of warm water, flowing within an ocean of cold water." But I think that I would prefer to say that the love of God and the power of the spirit, or the warmth as well as the holiness of religion, can and should permeate the whole of life.

CHAPTER 7

Aspects of the Human Enterprise

by GEORGE L. MADDOX

Duke University

OF ALL THE ANIMALS, we men are the only ones who wonder where we came from and where we will go. We are the only ones with a history of achievements impressive enough to warrant the presumption of hoping and planning for a future which improves upon the present. We are the only animals who spend significant portions of the present wondering and worrying about our condition. All this is possible, says Ernst Cassirer in his *Essay on Man*, because man is capable of an elaborate use of symbols. This fact

> transforms the whole of human life and introduces a new dimension of reality. Man cannot escape his own achievement. He cannot but adapt to the conditions of his own life. Not living in a merely physical universe, man lives in a symbolic universe. Language, myth, art, and religion are part of that universe.... No longer can man confront reality immediately. He cannot see it, as it were, face to face. Physical reality recedes in proportion as man's symbolic activity ad-

vances.... He has so enveloped himself in linguistic forms, in artistic images, in mythical symbols or religious rites that he cannot see or know anything except by the interposition of this artificial medium.

But the transformation is and can be only partial. The intractable regularities of physical, psychological, and social reality persist to remind men that ultimately they must pay their debts as finite animals. The Promethean hope that somehow the powers of reason will free men from the ultimate contingencies and limitations of their existence is never quite realized. For all their ingenuity, men sooner or later encounter limits. They are able to conceive a stable, secure, and intelligible world for themselves, but their experiences refuse to assure them either of certainty, stability, or security. It is therefore not surprising that men should ritualize their hopes, as Malinowski says in explaining the persistence of magic and religion in the face of advancing knowledge. For what any man knows at any point in his experience is fragmentary, incomplete, and often disturbing. What he knows always advances more slowly than his need to know; and there seems little prospect that his knowledge will ever be sufficient. Life, however, refuses to wait. Decisions cannot wait on certainty. Art, myth, religion, philosophy—all products of human imagination, aspiration, and hope—illustrate the continuing struggle to fuse the ideal and the actual in experience. That the fusion is never quite complete, never quite satisfactory, is reflected in recurrent discussions of the relationship between faith and reason, between religious and scientific perspectives, between the nonrational and rational elements in contemporary life.

This paper inquires into the status of such discussions within a particular segment of contemporary American scientists, the sociologists. The focus of attention will be on whether sociologists as sociologists express interest in such theological issues as the nature and destiny of man or the relevance of personal commitment to what one perceives to be ultimately important about life. Moreover, there is interest in how personal values and professional concerns about the conditions and consequences of various kinds of social interaction are related to one another when the relationship is an admitted concern.

Questions about the frequency and form of conscious interest among sociologists in the convergence of theological and sociological concerns could be, and ideally should be, answered by systematic research. Since there has been no such research, discussion in this paper reflects primarily the experience and observation of an interested participant trained both in the theological tradition of Protestant Christianity and in sociology, in that order, who has worked for the past ten years as a teacher and researcher in academic departments of sociology.

A contemporary sociologist as a sociologist is not likely to be consciously concerned about exploring systematically the relationship between his personal commitment to a theology and his professional commitment to sociology. This is simply not one of the tasks he ordinarily perceives as important in the development of his career or of his discipline. If the issue is brought to his attention at all, he is more likely to be indifferent than hostile. There are a number of reasons why this is so.

Sociologists, like most other members of the scientific community, harbor the suspicion that faith and reason are always potentially at odds and that the demands of each should be kept distinct. The roots of this suspicion run deep in the intellectual and religious traditions of Western civilization, and indications that the suspicion is well founded have appeared with regularity. The ancient myths of Prometheus and Job addressed the issue, and, prophetically, neither provided a very reassuring denouement for the problem posed. Medieval accommodations and coercions managed to keep faith and reason in a working, though precarious, relationship. But conflict was contained, not resolved. During the centuries between then and now, there have been social and intellectual developments which made a simple resolution less rather than more likely. The developments of particular relevance here are (1) the emergence of science as a relatively autonomous social establishment; (2) the ascendancy of an image of man which provides poor support for his self-esteem; and (3) a pervasive secularization of life.

The emergence of science as a relatively autonomous social establishment has occurred within the last four centuries, particularly within the last one. Consider, for example, Copernicus, Lyell, Darwin, Marx, Freud, and Einstein—six men whose careers are important milestones in the history of modern science. The scientists who preceded Copernicus were citizens of communities which did not provide the man of knowledge with sources of income, prestige, and power independent of their relationship to the prevailing religious establishment. Intellectual prowess did not give one license to be indifferent to matters of faith. The man of knowledge was expected to take the initiative in demonstrating that what he knew could be accommodated to what the faithful in the community, which presumably included him, believed. Dialogue between knowers and believers was thus assured. Copernicus was not free from this obligation. But with Lyell the obligation is less apparent; with Darwin still less so. With Marx, Freud, and Einstein, the capacity of a man of knowledge to secure economic resources, prestige, and power independent of his relationship to the prevailing religious establishment is quite apparent. The human enterprise has become specialized; there are now a variety of distinct enterprises.

While it would be incorrect to say that the new man of knowledge is free from community restraints, conformity to any particular theological tradition or an avowed interest in reconciling scientific and theological interests are no longer important aspects of the restraints which communities place on scientists. Thus the biography of a contemporary man of science does not necessarily include a sympathetic exposure to theological concerns just as the man of religion (broadly, the humanities) is not by definition exposed to a sympathetic interpretation of the procedures and aims of science. In fact, it is quite possible, as C. P. Snow has noted in his comments on the "two cultures," for an individual to be almost exclusively preoccupied with the interests of one or the other of these cultures. As a consequence he may lack the conceptual tools for entering into dialogue about possible convergence of interests even if the motivation to do so is assumed. The discovery of new powers of the mind over the past four centuries has been accompanied by a relatively autonomous scientific community within which one, if one chooses, has a new freedom to be indifferent to historic theological concerns. A scientist, particularly a social scientist, may even perceive this indifference, which he prefers to call objectivity, as a virtue.

The notion that a sociologist should be value free in his analysis of human behavior has had and still has many supporters. This posture emphasizes the need for relative detachment, for objectivity, for rising above moral provincialism. It also is potentially a defense against forces in the community which might be mobilized to attack the sociologist who does not share their vested interests and commitments. The utility of disinterest in values for the scientist is demonstrable. But, however useful the value-free notion has been in the pursuit of scientific interests and professional careers, it has not solved the problem of how the scientist lives with himself and others as a man. Nor does it preclude the possibility that the right to reserve moral judgments may become an occasion to make no moral judgments at all. In a word, one's professional commitment to sociology does not preclude personal commitment to values; the one commitment simply does not encourage the other or have as its concomitant a blueprint developing a working relationship between the nonrational and rational elements of the human enterprise.

The development of new powers of the mind over the

past four centuries has also been accompanied by a new indifference to the hopes and aspirations of individual men. Traditionally Western men have had a rather high regard for
themselves. Prometheus has been a traditional hero of the
Western intellectual. And even the Judaic-Christian tradition,
for all its suspicions about the dark places within each individual life, tolerates rather high hopes for at least a remnant of
humankind. Yet the foundations of contemporary man's self-
esteem have been shaken by developments in both the natural
and social sciences, particularly the latter.

The work of natural scientists such as Copernicus and
Lyell broadened man's conception of heaven and earth and, by
implication, emphasized human finiteness. But, in the long run,
their new information did not lead men to think less of themselves. Darwin's inclusion of man in the scheme of natural
history did shake the foundations of human self-esteem mo-
mentarily. Even this notion, however, was accommodated
rather quickly and effectively within the framework of prevailing theology by appropriating an ideology of progress.
Man still fancied himself at the summit of creation. Disenchantment with mankind was not yet the mode.

The ideas of Marx and Freud proved to be less tractable.
Philip Rieff has observed that in the historic images of man
that have served as the character ideals of Western men—*social*
man, *religious* man, *economic* man—a distinction typically has
been made between man's lower and higher needs. That the
lower needs should ultimately be subordinated to the higher
has been an aspiration if not an expectation. Even in the case of
economic man the advocacy of self-interest was tempered by
the assumption that the enlightened egoist in his personal pursuit of creature comforts ultimately contributes to the achievement of the social good. The Marxian conception of man, for
all its materialistic and atheistic overtones, proves no exception; the pursuit of ideals persists.

It is in Freudian thought that the prevailing Western

image of man is most basically challenged. Freud's psychological man, according to Rieff, is profoundly skeptical of a hierarchy of lower and higher values; he is antiheroic, shrewd, uncommitted, and lives by the ideal of insight. He aspires to better living, not the better life. He learns to live with contradictions, emphasizes the near equality of good and bad, and in his tolerance for ambiguity finds the key to the only genuinely stable character.

There are themes in the early tradition of sociology which run counter to this antiheroic image. Belief in the perfectability of men and institutions, the heritage of the Enlightenment, still has its advocates. Moreover, the Social Gospel within the Christian tradition has also had its advocates, particularly among the ministers turned sociologists who appeared with interesting frequency in the early decades of this century in the United States. But by and large the contemporary sociologist is impressed with the extent to which man is a creature of his environment. This, coupled with a somewhat pessimistic and fatalistic assessment of the current state of social affairs, has tended to make David Riesman's familiar *other-directed* man the sociological counterpart of Freud's antiheroic *psychological* man.

The new powers of the mind have made man more comprehensible, perhaps, but at the expense of making him seem quite incidental and irrelevant in the total scheme of things. Contemporary scientists know more about the human being than they have ever known before; yet never in human history has the human being seemed less worth knowing. For many contemporary men, human life has become, in Yeats's phrase, "an immense preparation for something which never happens." A sociological perspective does not preclude the possibility of believing otherwise. Rather, why one should believe otherwise is simply not one of the issues typically addressed in the sociological literature. There are exceptions, some of which will be noted subsequently, but the exceptions are few.

The development of modern science, furthermore, has had as one of its concomitants the pervasive secularization of life. The scientific perspective illustrates one important dimension of this secularization. The scientist as a scientist, for example, is at heart an instrumentalist. Anything is conceivable; any idea is potentially worth a test. There is always more than one way to look at this or that. One learns to speak in terms of probabilities and to understand that certainty persistently eludes the human grasp. In fact, within the scientific community, the search for certainty easily comes to be defined as an illegitimate goal or, at best, a goal to be pursued by the soft-minded individual who has a low tolerance for ambiguity.

As a result of his training in an environment in which this kind of mental set prevails, a sociologist is likely to be more aware than most that the members of different social groups are often committed to different systems of beliefs and practices by means of which they deal with their ultimate problems and concerns. He learns, for example, that the disinterested, the value-free sociologist views infanticide, premarital sexual behavior, and polytheistic religious beliefs within the social context in which they appear. The good life means many different things to the individuals in different groups. A specification of what *really* constitutes the good life is not found in the sociological literature for a simple reason: There is no known scientific basis for determining the ultimate value commitments which define the good life.

In sum, the contemporary sociologist participates in an environment in which he is free to ignore the relationship between theological and scientific concerns and in which he gets little encouragement to pursue the relationship between these concerns. He may have theological concerns and a sense of personal commitment. But the concern about personal commitment to a particular system of beliefs about what is ultimately important is ordinarily neither incited nor nurtured by the scientific interests with which a sociologist is likely to be pre-occupied.

Some sociologists have expressed dissatisfaction with this state of affairs. Social scientists have participated in fellowships of the concerned on college campuses. A few minority reports have even appeared in the professional literature. A brief review of several of these formal dissents will be useful not only to express the nature of the dissatisfaction with the present situation in the profession but also to give some indication of how the concern to relate personal commitment to values and professional social scientific interests is likely to be manifested.

The late Robert Redfield, for example, in one of his last published works expressed his personal discomfort with the notion of cultural relativity that had served so well in his early studies of human behavior in other societies. Specifically, he was disturbed by the implications of being morally neutral with regard to the Nazis' "final solution of the Jew problem," which had so basically challenged one of the foundations of Western civilization, a belief in the inherent dignity of the individual. If one cannot dismiss this behavior as "just the way the Germans go about solving their problems," on what basis does one object? Or, in deciding that one will participate in the economic and social development of underdeveloped countries in ways which a sociologist knows will result in profound changes in their culture and social life, on what grounds does one justify personal involvement in such intervention?

The framework within which Redfield proposed to answer these questions is found in the mainstream of Western civilization. There one finds, he believed, some basically humanitarian values about which there is widespread consensus. He did not share with the reader precisely what these values are or why consensus among large numbers of human beings hallows a particular system of values. He did not indicate, for example, why the inherent dignity of the individual person, a common value preference in the West, is to be preferred to a number of competing alternatives found within other moral precepts prevailing outside the West. Redfield seemed certain of only one thing: To act is to make a moral decision, even if by default. He preferred not to make such decisions by default and struggled with the justification of his own value commitments.

The late C. Wright Mills wrote often and well on what he perceived to be the jeopardy in which the development of large-scale organizations had placed the traditional values of the Enlightenment—Freedom and Reason. He felt that faith in progress, in science, in popular education, and in the political meaning of democracy were being continually undermined by the bureaucratization of our society. Mills did not foresee any simple solutions to the problem he posed. He did choose to hope that freedom and reason would remain cherished values and that they would be used consistently and imaginatively by committed men in the formulation of the problems to be solved. Mills modestly hoped also that some right questions could be asked even if no right answers could be found. If he can be said to have proposed a course of action at all, it lay in the restructuring of society in such a way that the possibility of individual initiative and responsibilty in the governing of men would remain. Mills continued to believe in the perfectability of men and institutions. But what specifically should be done, how it should be done, and who should do it remained problematic for him.

Alvin W. Gouldner also has presented a minority report. In his Presidential Address to the Society for the Study of Social Problems in 1961 he presented a review of the origin and development of the notion that sociologists should be value free. Having noted that the myth of a value-free sociology notion has on occasion been useful for sociologists and for the discipline, Gouldner expressed doubt that a sociologist could be value free or that at the present time he should be.

He does not argue that the sociologist has a superior morality or that his professional skills equip him in some special way to set the goals that the members of society ought to pursue. Rather he argues that if a sociologist as a member of the intellectual community does not participate in the setting of goals and their implementation, who is in any better position or under any greater obligation to shoulder the task? In this address the particular values that a sociologist should have beyond a commitment to entering into dialogue in the classroom and in the community are not specified.

William Kolb, a competent sociologist and in his own words a "committed Christian," is one of the few contemporary sociologists to propose in print a Christian perspective (after the fashion of Reinhold Niebuhr) as the most appropriate commitment for the contemporary sociologist. In the initial volume of the *Journal for the Scientific Study of Religion*, Kolb specifically argues that the image of man in the Judaic-Christian tradition is better suited for the ordering of sociological data than alternative models, which he characterizes as basically deterministic (that is, as placing the human self totally within a web of invariant relations so as to deny freedom of the will). Moreover, he is critical of current functional analysis of religious beliefs and practices in sociology because such analysis stops short of pursuing the crucial question: Which beliefs and practices most closely approximate the Truth about man, his destiny, and the nature of his commitment? Kolb argues that the Judaic-Christian tradition is a closer approximation of that Truth than existing alternatives. In particular he believes that alternative models do not provide adequately for the basis of all responsible moral action, the freedom of the will.

Violence is necessarily done in so brief a review of current dissent among sociologists both to the full range of emerging criticism of a value-free sociology and even to the more systematic elaboration of the perceived relationship between personal and professional commitments in the thought of the four men cited. These men and their criticism of the separation of personal and social commitments do suggest, however, the tenor of current discussions among others within the field of sociology.

The origin of dissatisfaction with a value-free sociology appears to lie in a double sense of failure. Sociology as a discipline has proved to be neither personally nor socially satisfying. On the one hand, the pursuit of a career in sociology has not always provided adequate answers for the existential questions, What is the meaning of my life and what is the nature of my responsibility? On the other hand, what the sociologist has learned about the conditions and consequences of human interaction has not provided the basis for selecting the ultimate ends which men ought to pursue. Detachment from consideration of ultimate ends which a society ought to pursue has become increasingly less easy to justify in a world in which the other fellow's, that other society's value preferences may well become the basis for the ordering of one's own life.

The value preferences which are reflected in the work of these four men are, with the exception of Kolb, essentially those of the Enlightenment. They prefer to believe in the inherent dignity of the individual, in reason, in freedom. They probably speak for the majority of sociologists who have a conscious concern about personal value commitments. Kolb's avowed theism and the emphasis he gives to man's finiteness and dependence are themes of a minority report within a minority report. In no instance does one of the four men cited argue that sociology, or more generally science, does or can provide the basis for determining the ultimate ends that men ought to pursue. They are agreed, however, that they choose to be moral men. That in itself is no mean decision. They are agreed also as to the importance of entering into dialogue in the classroom, in the public forum, and in professional circles.

The impact of such dialogue on students, the public, and other professionals remains to be evaluated.

The fact that they and others like them perceive themselves as involved men as well as detached scientists, as participants in the human enterprise rather than solely the scientific enterprise, leads them to question the historic disinterest in value commitments. But the decision to ask questions about value commitments does not assure them of the right questions, much less the right answers. This has always been so. The fact also remains that conscious concern about the merging of theological and scientific commitments among contemporary sociologists, as among other scientists, is a concern of the minority. But this too is to be expected.

There is little prospect that the present state of affairs will change very much in the foreseeable future. The contemporary sociologist will continue to be preoccupied with attempts to understand those aspects of human behavior which seem amenable to the techniques of inquiry he has or is likely to have at his disposal. All his resources can easily be used in pursuit of those questions which he perceives to be answerable within the framework of commonly accepted canons of scientific proof, leaving little time for theological concerns about the nature and destiny of man or the proper content of a scheme of ultimate values. Moreover, as the product of a society and an educational system which are largely secularized and highly specialized, the chances are quite good that any given contemporary sociologist provides a good illustration of what C. P. Snow is talking about when he discusses the two cultures, the scientific and the humane, which so rarely meet and between which so little dialogue takes place.

Yet the pressure to consider one's personal as well as one's professional commitments is also likely to persist. The pressure will come externally from a society which shows increasing signs of disenchantment with scientists who have hardly proved to be saviors and with science which has hardly proved to be a Second Coming. The pressure will continue to come internally both from men in whose biography there is exposure to philosophy and theology as well as to science and from those who for any reason assume the role of an intellectual within their particular scientific discipline.

Individuals who are committed to the Judaic-Christian traditions and to the specific religious communions that consciously embody these are likely to be dissatisfied with the prevailing humanistic perspective manifested among even the minority of sociologists who are consciously concerned about relating personal and professional commitments. The contemporary sociologist, like his colleagues in other scientific disciplines, is likely to be a devotee of Prometheus if he is going to be a devotee of any image of man.

The important conclusion to be drawn from the current ferment in the field of sociology, limited though it is, is not that the sociologist has failed to conclude this or that about what the nature of his personal commitment ought to be. The important point is that dialogue between the philosopher or theologian and the sociologist is increasingly recognized as both proper and necessary. The beginning is modest, but it is a beginning.

CHAPTER 8

The Challenge to Religion As It Ponders Science

by BENJAMIN E. MAYS

Morehouse College

THE FEAR that science can destroy man's faith in God and render the Christian religion impotent has been and still is without foundation. This writer believes that present or future fear of what science may do to invalidate the fundamentals of the Christian faith is also without foundation. Much of the controversy known as the "warfare" between science and religion was based on the shadows of religion, not on the realities of religion. Even in cases where the findings of science shook the foundation of certain religious beliefs and made untenable the literal interpretation of some Biblical passages, deep beneath the accepted beliefs and the literal interpretations were and are abiding truths that the intelligent mind could not and cannot set aside. For example, one may disbelieve in the literal interpretation of the Jonah story, but one can hardly deny the truth the story is designed to reveal: Man cannot escape the responsibility that God places upon him, nor can he deny that he is obligated to minister to the needs of others, even those of a different race, culture, or nation.

With the hindsight that is often more enlightened than foresight, we realize that the centuries of wrangling between science and religion might have been avoided had there been more sympathy and understanding on both sides. It is fallacious to assert that in the controversy science was always right and that religion was always wrong. Both were equally partial and myopic. The scientist who was inclined to dismiss religion as "mere superstition and mythology" and who claimed too much for science was as blameworthy as the religionist who held tenaciously to his literalism and viewed science as wholly evil. There were mutual ignorance and arrogance on both sides. Time and experience have proved that the conflict was unnecessary. Rabbi Silver asserts:

> The conflict was always between superstition disguised as religion and materialism disguised as science, between pseudo-science and pseudo-religion.
>
> Religion and science are the two hemispheres of human thought. They are different though converging truths. They grow binately. Both science and religion spring from the same seeds of vital human needs.[1]

The stiff opposition to those who advocated the experimental method in science stemmed from the belief that all knowledge and all truths are to be found in the Bible and that to experiment with nature or man to discover more knowledge must surely cast doubt upon the Bible as the source of all knowledge and as the authoritative word of God. So great was the pressure in 1278 that Roger Bacon was put into prison at the age of sixty-six and confined there for twelve years because he advocated the experimental method in science. Al-

---

[1] Abba Hillel Silver, *Religion in a Changing World* (New York: Richard Smith, Inc., 1930), p. 34.

though the experimental method in science triumphed, I wager that the vast majority of the religious people never lost their faith in the Bible and it was then as now a source of comfort for millions of people. It spoke then and it speaks now with authority to people throughout Christendom. The acceptance of experimentation as a basic technique in science did not destroy or weaken the Christian Gospel.

The conflict went on for years between the geocentric and the heliocentric theories of the earth and sun. The earth was considered the center of the universe with the sun and planets revolving around the earth. This theory that the earth was the center—and man, God's chief creature, lived in the center and everything else revolved around man—made man a very important creature and indeed the crown of God's creation. To advocate a theory that would push man from the center of the universe was to degrade him and to deny his centrality in God's creation as recorded in Genesis.

Although the heliocentric theory had been hinted at by Pythagoras in the sixth century before Christ, the war between the religious and the scientific views did not really break out in earnest until the sixteenth century. For thirty years Copernicus was afraid to publish his "proof" that the earth revolved around the sun. He revealed his findings only to a few private friends. Finally Copernicus prepared his noble work, *The Revolution of the Heavenly Bodies*. Still timid and fearful, he entrusted the work to a friend, Osiander, at Nuremberg. Osiander lost courage and wrote an apologetic preface to Copernicus' findings, declaring that the doctrine of the earth's movement was set forth not as fact but as a hypothesis.

When the published book reached Copernicus, he was on his deathbed. The opposition to the heliocentric theory was so great that his friends feared violence upon his corpse; hence, no record of his discovery was engraved on his tombstone. Instead, these words appeared:

> I ask not the grace accorded to Paul; not that given to Peter;
> give me only the favour which Thou didst show to the thief
> on the cross.[2]

It was thirty years before his friends dared inscribe on his
tombstone a record of his discovery.

Galileo fared even worse. When Galileo upheld the Copernican doctrine in 1616, Copernicus' book was seized by the
Curia and his works condemned until corrected to conform
to the Ptolemaic theory. What happened to Galileo is too well
known to recite here. But we can visualize an old man on his
knees at seventy denying the scientific truth in which he believed and to which he had dedicated his life.

Although the Copernican theory has been modified by
modern science, the fear that the heliocentric theory would do
permanent injury to the Christian faith proved to be ground-
less. In man's own eyes he is still the climax of God's creation
and the apex of the evolutionary process. Whether theist or
naturalist, sinner or saint, man generally believes that he is significant and that each person is of intrinsic worth and value.
It is still basic among the devotees of the Christian faith that
God cares for the sons of men.

> I quote approvingly W. T. Stace:
> What bearing can physics or astronomy possibly have upon
> morals? What difference can it make to any ethical theory
> whether the sun goes round the earth or the earth round the
> sun, whether the planetary orbits are circular or elliptical,
> whether the laws of motion and of falling bodies are those
> accepted by Aristotle or those put forward by Galileo? [3]

From the standpoint of theology, neither the experimental method in science nor the heliocentric theory had any-

[2] Quoted from A. D. White, *History of the Warfare Between Science
and Religion* (New York: D. Appleton and Co., 1922), Vol. I, p. 124.
[3] *Religion and the Modern Mind* (Philadelphia: Lippincott Co., 1960),
p. 38.

thing basic to do with man's belief in God as expounded by Jesus in the New Testament and as set forth in the Old Testament by the prophets of the eighth and seventh centuries B.C.

The Darwinian Theory of Evolution and its related doctrines were particularly upsetting to conservative theological beliefs. To advance any theory as to the origin of man and the earth inconsistent with Genesis was, to the literalist, to destroy belief in the whole Bible and to depose God as the creator of man and the universe. It is not surprising, therefore, that Darwin was viciously attacked when he published his *Origin of Species* in 1859 and his *Descent of Man* in 1871. Learned prelates, Catholic and Protestant, from the United States, England, France, Germany, Switzerland, and other countries literally denounced Darwin. Cardinal Manning called Darwin's work a "brutal philosophy" and set forth the view that if his works were true, there is no God and Adam is only an ape. Another religious authority declared that if evolution is true,

> Genesis is a lie, the whole framework of the book of life falls to pieces, and the revelation of God to man, as we Christians know it, is a delusion and a snare.[4]

These and other critics of science were grossly in error in what they thought the findings of science would do to the basic Christian Gospel. They did not know that religion has always stood on its own feet and that if it must live in constant dread of new scientific insight, it is not filling a vital human need and will eventually pass away. Nothing can stop the onward development of science, and I shall endeavor to show that nothing can eradicate the need of vital religion in the life of man. The fear that the doctrine of evolution would destroy the Christian faith and undermine Christian morality was highly exaggerated.

The truth of the matter is that the doctrine of evolution has neither proved nor disproved the existence of God. Evo-

[4] A. D. White, *op. cit.*, Vol. I, p. 71.

lution has neither proved nor disproved the Christian affirmation, "in the beginning God." In an attempt to explain the marvelous things he saw, a sensitive religious soul looked upon the universe and the world and said: "In the beginning God created the heavens and the earth." As I have said in another writing:

> We shall not argue here over the interpretation of the creation story. We shall not split hairs over its historical accuracy. But I believe that in the sweep of the centuries no better answer has been given to tell us how the universe and man came to be than the simple expression "In the beginning God." When we accept all that science has to offer, the riddle of the universe is still unsolved.[5]

As I shall attempt to show later, the more science discovers, and the more man explores outer space, the greater will be the need for a relevant religion if mankind is to survive in the space age or in any age.

Not only has so-called pure science helped religion to mature and stand alone, but medical science has also contributed its share to free religion of superstition and erroneous beliefs. Opposition to medical advance has not and does not come from religious leaders alone but from men of medicine as well.

It is now hard to believe that there was great opposition to inoculation, vaccination, and the use of anesthetics. It was the current belief among some people in England and France in the late eighteenth century and in the early nineteenth century that diseases are sent by God for the punishment of sin. Any attempt to ward off disease, therefore, is to work against God. French theologians at the Sorbonne strongly condemned the practice of inoculation. In 1772 an English clergyman pub-

[5] Benjamin E. Mays, *Seeking to Be a Christian in Race Relations* (New York: The Friendship Press, 1957), p. 1.

lished a sermon entitled "The Dangerous and Sinful Practice of Inoculation."

In this conflict there were clergymen who supported inoculation against disease and men of medicine who opposed it. In 1721 Dr. Zabdiel Boylston, a Boston physician, was hotly criticized by his colleagues for inoculating his own son against smallpox. Some urged the authorities to try Dr. Boylston for murder. It was argued that smallpox was "a judgement on the sins of the people." To try to avert the disease is to provoke God all the more.[6] These superstitions soon passed away and the Christian faith was in no way damaged. Their abolition gave us a more intelligent and understanding view of God.

Looking back into the Egyptian and Greco-Roman worlds, we discover that it was a terrible thing to tamper with the bodies of the dead. During life the body was considered by the early Church, and still is by many Christians, as the Temple of the Holy Spirit. The Apostles' Creed, for example, refers to the Resurrection of the Body, and for some time it was believed that the body should be unmutilated when raised in the Last Judgment. For more than a thousand years surgery was unpopular, and it was seldom performed.[7]

These points are developed here only to show that none of the advances made in scientific discoveries in years gone by have served to invalidate religion. The religious mind has become more mature and the scientist more humble. Science has helped to increase the religious man's respect for knowledge. So now the religious mind welcomes all that science has to offer and feels as secure in its position as does the scientific mind. All mankind is in debt to science. It has brought material comfort, reduced poverty, abolished disease, annihilated distance, while at the same time extending man's life span and increasing his opportunity to enjoy the better things of life. All these things religion recognizes, and the intelligent reli-

6 For full discussion see A. D. White, *op. cit.*, Vol. I, pp. 55 ff.
7 *Ibid.*, pp. 31 ff.

gious mind salutes the scientific mind with respect and appreciation and accepts all that science has to offer to enlighten further the minds of men and improve human welfare.

But even as the religious mind acknowledges its debt to science, so it is not unmindful of the limitations of science nor is it unaware of the dangerous uses to which many of the findings of science have been and may be put. The danger of the latter, however, is not in science but in man.

Let us discuss briefly the limitations of science, and in doing so I am recording only what the scientists themselves readily admit. It is often those of us who are not trained in science who claim for it more than the scientists do themselves. The limitations of science are inherent in the scientific method itself. In its limitations, however, lies its greatest strength. Science has the genius of correcting its own errors.

When we speak of science, we usually mean a method of pursuing the truth or a method of acquiring knowledge. We might say that Copernicus, Kepler, and Galileo were the founders of modern science. They deliberately selected and abstracted from total reality only elements that could be controlled, those elements of reality that could be abstracted, weighed, observed, measured, and described. The scientific method makes it possible for scientists everywhere to test and verify what another scientist has discovered. Following the scientific method, the scientist can predict with accuracy the outcome of an experiment. But no scientist claims that the scientific method can be applied to the whole of reality or the whole of man's experiences. Some may feel that science will someday encompass the totality of human experiences, but no respectable scientist would be so dogmatic as to say that he would exclude as non-real that area of reality which at the moment science must exclude from its area of investigation.

On this point, what Sullivan said several years ago still holds:

Science has become self-conscious and comparatively humble. We are no longer taught that the Scientific Method of approach is the only valid method of acquiring knowledge about reality. Eminent men of science are insisting, with what seems a strange enthusiasm, on the fact that science gives us but a partial knowledge of reality, and we are no longer required to regard as illusory everything that science finds itself able to ignore. . . . We are no longer required to believe that our response to beauty, or the mystic's sense of communion with God, have no objective counterpart. It is perfectly possible that they are, what they have so often been taken to be, clues to the nature of reality. Thus our various experiences are put on a more equal footing, as it were. Our religious aspirations, our perception of beauty, may not be the phenomena they were supposed to be. In this new scientific universe the mystics have a right to exist.[8]

Sullivan says further:

It is evident, even from this brief survey of scientific ideas, that a true scientific theory merely means a successful working hypothesis. It is highly probable that all scientific theories are wrong. Those that we accept are verifiable within our present limits of observation. Truth, then, in science, is a pragmatic affair. A good scientific theory accounts for known facts, and enables us to predict new ones which are then verified by observation.[9]

The limitation of science is well stated by Brunner:

But even among those who do not hold the Christian point of view, and therefore cannot make this distinction between God-knowledge and world-knowledge, there are many who recognize at least one limitation of scientific knowledge. They have come to see that science can never speak with

[8] J. W. N. Sullivan, *The Limitations of Science* (New York: The New American Library of World Literature, Inc., 1949), pp. 138 ff. (Published with arrangement of the Viking Press.)

[9] *Ibid.*, p. 158.

authority about *ends*, but only about means, that it cannot find the *meaning* of anything, but only facts, and that science can therefore do nothing within that region in which human disorder has become most apparent—namely in the sphere of human relationships, the sphere of ethical, social and political problems.[10]

It should be clear then that science deals with a particular class of phenomena and makes no claim to deal with the whole of experience and nature. From this point on, I shall deal with insights and truths that, as of now, cannot be established by science nor proved by science but that are vital and significant to man's existence.

Great insights and truths are revealed and conveyed to man through art, literature, and religion. The paintings of Michelangelo and Raphael, the literary productions of Horace and Shakespeare, the religious truths of Paul and Jesus, the contributions of Fritz Kreisler and Marian Anderson are just as essential to life and just as enduring as the discoveries and findings of science. The religious experiences of Buddha and Jesus, Paul and St. Augustine, Mohammed and St. Francis cannot be captured in a scientific formula. And yet, no one would deny that great truths were revealed to these men and that as a result the world has been as miraculously transformed by their works as it has been by the works of the great scientists. So science gains nothing by trying to invalidate the insights given to man through art, literature, and religion. Similarly, religion has nothing to gain by attempting to discount the indispensable values of science. Science and religion complement and supplement each other just as the eyes and ears complement each other. Science and religion need each other.

Although the defenders of the faith were often wrong in their attitudes toward science, it can hardly be denied that the

[10] Emil Brunner, *Christianity and Civilization* (New York: Charles Scribner's Sons, 1948), pp. 36 ff.

greatest advancements of science have taken place where the Hebraic-Christian faith prepared the climate. Both Christianity and the Jewish religion have an affirmative attitude toward nature, the earth, and man. Man was told to go out and subdue the earth. He was deputized to control it.

Alan Richardson says:

> Whatever may be the nature of the connection between Christian theology and the origins of modern science, it can hardly be without significance that the scientific attitude arose in a civilization which acknowledged one God, who was personal, rational and dependable, and that the most ardent and dedicated pioneers of the new scientific movement were themselves devoted students of the Bible and of Christian theology.[11]

Trueblood also supports this view:

> ... Genuine science is something so delicate and so precious that it cannot thrive except under the best conditions.
> The condition which, so far, has been most conducive to science is that in which the Christian world view is generally accepted.[12]

Likewise, the social sciences have had their influence upon man's religion. Medical science has made man less dependent upon prayer for extending the life span, and psychology and psychiatry have done a good bit to improve man's behavior. These insights have been good for the health of religion, but they have no negative effect upon the moral and ethical truths of the Christian faith.

Just as man cannot live well without science, so he cannot live fully without religion. Every man who accomplishes

[11] *The Bible in the Age of Science* (Philadelphia: The Westminster Press, 1961), p. 27.

[12] D. Elton Trueblood, *The Predicament of Modern Man* (New York: Harper & Brothers, 1944), pp. 41 ff.

anything significant in life must live by faith, dreams, and ideals. The scientist, himself, lives by faith in his method and experiments. Hundreds of scientists have died without discovering what they set out to find. Many men and women have spent their lives seeking a cure for cancer. Not during their lives did success crown their efforts. But their work was not in vain. Today an even larger number of zealous men and women continue the "act of faith" and are convinced that there are answers, resolute in their determination to find them.

Within a period of three thousand years man has fought thirty-three hundred wars. History does not give man much encouragement that wars will be abolished, and science has no formula to guarantee the abolition of war. Yet, it is a dream of peoples everywhere that someday permanent peace will prevail. The League of Nations was an adventure of faith; so is the United Nations. Our diplomats are negotiating all the time, sustained by the conviction that we can find a formula for peace. In our search for peace there isn't much that science can offer. Peace must be built on trust, confidence, faith, regard for the rights of nations, and on justice. These are spiritual elements, and they are real. Man must live in hope for the future even though the outlook be dark. Man cannot live from day to day on the sparse certainties that science can guarantee.

The boy who sets out to plan his future, not knowing what career he will follow, looks to the future with uncertainty. As he sets his goals and moves toward them, he dreams dreams and clings to intangible ideals, taking the gamble that he will succeed in gaining his objectives. He lives daily as a beneficiary of the tangible gifts of science, but the propelling and guiding forces are his ideals, which he cannot reduce to a scientific formula. The youth lives by aspirations, inspirations, faith, and ideals.

Man cannot live by bread or science alone. The family is held together by love, trust, confidence, give-and-take, and by returning good for evil. No family is held together by mere

logic and reasoning nor by abstract justice. Although parents
may wish to deal justly with their children, they know that
again and again love steps in and supersedes justice. There is a
lot of forgiveness in the home. Wife and husband forgive each
other, and parents and children forgive one another. In the
family there is probably no difference between the behavior
of the scientist and the behavior of the man of religion. Both
live on love. Only a small segment of man's life is or can be
fulfilled by the scientific method. The greater part of our lives
is lived in that area that does not and cannot lend itself to the
scientific methodology for investigation.

However much we may admire the stupendous achievements of science and however cheerfully the religious man accepts it as an indispensable ally, we cannot help looking with
dread upon the uses to which the findings of science may be
put. By and large the scientist assumes no responsibility for
the use—be it destructive or constructive—to which his discoveries may be put. Much of the research for developing
more deadly instruments of war is paid for by the government.
The scientists can hardly be blamed if the government uses
their discoveries for "national defense" or world aggression.
Wars will not be fought without making use of the most recent developments in applied science. The more scientifically
advanced a nation becomes, the more other nations stand in
dread of that nation. So a Third World War depends mainly
upon the United States and Russia.

As we recall the horrors of World War II, and remember
to our shame the dropping of the atomic bombs on Nagasaki
and Hiroshima, we shudder as we realize that the developments of nuclear weapons of war are a thousandfold more
deadly than the bombs that were dropped on Japan. As we
spend forty-eight billion dollars a year for national defense,
with the full knowledge that a few bombs can destroy the
whole of the United States and Russia, it is clear that the future of mankind cannot be left in the hands of the government

or the scientist alone. There is nothing inherent in science that aims to improve the character of man and to make mankind better. It is the basic function of religion, and not the function of science, to change the nature of man so that he will not want to destroy his neighbor, to liquidate him in nuclear war, or be so liquidated himself. It is clear that knowledge alone is not adequate to make men live together in harmony and justice. No one will deny that man knows more than ever before, that he has more material comfort than ever before, that disease is being conquered, and that the life span is being extended. But what man can argue with certainty that science and education have made a better man?

The more progress man makes in exploring outer space, the more dangerous existence on this earth becomes. We live now on the precipice of war. As we move into outer space, the more hazardous life on this earth will be. This foreboding presents a challenge to religion. If it is the function of religion to improve the human product, religion has now the greatest responsibility that has ever been given to man. But as long as religious leaders get on the scientific and governmental bandwagon, follow and do not lead, religion will be a puny force in world affairs.

The exploration of outer space and the development that science will make there increase religion's responsibility to make man better. The decisions that must be made relative to control and ownership of outer space are decisions that science cannot make. They will be made by politicians and heads of government. And if religion or sheer common sense cannot influence these decisions, we are headed for catastrophe.

Look at a few of the problems that confront us in outer space. By *outer space* we might as well accept the definition of Donald G. Brennans of M. I. T. when he defines it as "the region above the sensible atmosphere." How far this is, scientists have not agreed. Some claim that

...the atmosphere extends anywhere up to 20,000 miles above the earth's surface. But half of the entire mass of the atmosphere is less than 3½ miles above the earth's surface.[13]

Where does outer space begin? How far above the earth's surface can a nation claim sovereignty? Does a nation own all the space above its territory? There was a Roman law that said: "who owns the land owns it up to the sky" (*cujus est solum, ejus est usque ad coelum*). Who owns the planets and celestial bodies? There must be a fixed boundary line between the earth's atmosphere and outer space. Who will fix the boundary line? Will the nations compete for the control of outer space as they compete to control the earth? Will the nations compete to put nuclear weapons in satellites in orbit about the earth? Will the Third World War be fought in part in outer space?

It is quite conceivable that outer space may become militarized and the nations that control it will have a decided advantage over other nations. If we are now spending forty-eight billion dollars a year for national defense, what will the United States spend if the Cold War enters outer space? It has been estimated that it may cost the United States a hundred billion dollars to land a man on the moon.

The exploration and conquest of outer space could lead to several things: It could enhance the desire of the big powers to build up their prestige. This would be disastrous. On the other hand, outer space could well be used to bring the nations to their senses and lead us to permanent peace. It could enhance learning, further the development of science, lead to the abolition of war, and further the cause of international relations. Which one of these will it be?

It is folly to believe that the scientific development of outer space will alone bring an end to war and cause nations

[13] Lincoln Bloomfield, *Outer Space* (Englewood Cliffs, N.J.: Prentice-Hall, Inc., 1961), p. 154.

and people to love each other better. Just as there is no con-
clusive evidence that a man's character will improve as his
mind increases in knowledge, so there is no evidence that nations will live in peace when life in the universe becomes more
dangerous through militarization of outer space. As these
words are being written, the world congratulates two Russian
astronauts who circled the earth sixty-four and forty-eight
times respectively, traveling at a speed of eighteen thousand
miles an hour and orbiting the globe once in every eighty-
eight minutes. Mankind salutes science and stands aghast. This
is a marvelous feat for science. But there is nothing here that
will improve man's character or his hope for survival. This
presents an urgent challenge to religion.

When I point out the limitations of science, it must be
borne in mind that religion is as old as man and that the Christian religion is approximately two thousand years old. And
yet it has not improved mankind sufficiently for exploitation
to be eliminated, wars to be abolished, human prejudice erad-
icated, and hatred between man and man uprooted. I know,
too, that if science can now destroy the whole of the human
race, it is not easy to know where to find God's justice. Surely
the leaders of Christianity cannot blame scientists and politicians for the state of the world when they themselves have
never consistently exemplified in their lives the Christian virtues they expound. Except in ecclesiastical worship, all too
many Christian leaders have been followers and not leaders.
In everyday affairs, religion is frequently divorced from life.
Christian leaders have no program for disarmament. In world
affairs we follow the leadership of the national government.
In economic life, we follow the leaders of industry. In human
relations we follow the leadership of politicians. In crucial
social matters, Christian leaders, by and large, are conspicuous
by their silence. In such a time as this, religion must have a
"spiritual" sword that cuts through all relativities, idolatries,
and institutions that have been absolutized. Within the con-

text of the Hebraic-Christian faith, "Thou shalt have no other gods before me." Unfortunately religion seeks to lack the "spiritual" sword. This indictment must be made because it is a major function of religion to make man a better creature. If religion falters at this point, why blame science?

Despite this critical appraisal of religious leaders, it is the conviction of this writer that the Christian religion has the word of salvation both for this life and the life to come. It is religion and not science that tells men how to live. It is religion and not education whose chief function it is to nurture the ethical and moral life of mankind. The doctrinal and theological aspects of the Christian religion may be hotly debated, but few men, if any, can doubt the validity of the ethical and moral aspects of Judaism and the Gospel of Christ. Much can also be said of the other great religions of the world, but for our purpose, we will concentrate mainly on the Christian faith. In this faith there are eternal truths that can never be invalidated, either by science or by time.

It is religion and not science that asks the fundamental questions about man. From whence did man come? What is his origin? What is his purpose on the earth? What is his ultimate destiny? The Gospel of Christ indicates how nations, races, classes, and individuals should live and relate themselves to their God, and how they should treat their fellows. The ethical and moral values by which man must live are found not in science but in religion. And these values are independent of time, space, and place. They are not relative to any age or culture; they are everlasting. They are also objective values. Some people have tried to invalidate moral and ethical values by arguing that they are relative and subjective. I reject this point of view.

But before further development of this idea, it should be said here that if logic and science could demonstrate that all arguments ever advanced to prove the existence of God are wrong, they would not thereby prove that God does not exist. Nor can there be any proof that those who claim to find God through experience are wrong in their affirmation of God. No one can prove that the mystic has not encountered God. It cannot be proved that Jesus was a misguided, ignorant man who was mistaken in his views about God. Science may cast doubt on the significance of these experiences, but science cannot prove them false. Likewise, science may make it difficult for some to believe that there is purpose in the universe. But science cannot prove that there is no purpose in the universe. Whether there is or is not purpose, the scientist relies upon dependable order in the universe which he discovers and does not create—an order and uniformity without which he cannot function as a scientist. This may be an accident, but it cannot be proved that order in the universe is an accident.

But let us get back to the Christian ethics and morality, which we hold are just as real and just as objective as discoveries in the natural order. When we argue that moral values are objective and not subjective, we mean what W. T. Stace means when he says:

> A value is subjective if it depends on human desires, feelings, or opinions. It is objective if it does not depend on any such human mental states. And if moral values depend on human psychology, then they do not exist in the universe apart from the existence and the thought of human beings.[14]

Although Stace leans heavily toward the relativity of ethical and moral law, the quotation which follows is significant for our purpose:

> This belief in a single absolute moral law is not the least inconsistent with the fact that in different countries, ages and civilizations, moral ideas vary. The fact that the same thing is thought good in one culture and bad in another does not

[14] *Religion and the Modern Mind* (Philadelphia: Lippincott Co., 1960), p. 114.

show that morals are relative in the sense that the same thing is good in one culture and is bad in another. For one belief or the other may be mistaken, and those who hold it may be ignorant of the true moral law. If stealing is wrong, it is wrong, everywhere and always. If some uncivilized tribe should be found which thinks stealing is a duty, this does not mean that stealing is in fact a duty for them.[15]

Great injury has been done to the Christian faith by those who in the name of social science or in the misapplication of the findings of anthropology argue that all morals are relative and subjective. There are religious truths that experience validates to be eternal and universal. I am well aware that the trend in many circles is against the position advanced here, as the following quotation indicates:

According to the group relativism now popular among social scientists and philosophers, the moral standards of a given society are, within that society, binding upon the individuals who compose it. (Whether there is any logical basis for this contention or not is another question. I should hold that there is not.) But as between societies or cultures, there can be no moral code which is binding. On the view stated by Hobbes, good is what pleases the individual, evil is what displeases him. This is now given up. Group relativism is the view that what pleases (or evokes an attitude of approval, or some other subjective emotional state, in) a society is good *within* that society and for that society, but not outside it. Translated into practice, what this means is that what Germany likes is morally right for Germany, and what Russia likes is morally right for Russia. This is "political relativism," and it is equivalent to the total absence of any morality as between nations, and this is exactly what we see in practice.[16]

But if this position is sound and there can be no agreement on what is universally ethical and moral, there can be

15 *Ibid.*, p. 124.
16 *Ibid.*, p. 133.

little hope for man in an age when we are in a position to destroy the entire human race.

It has always been true and it will always be true that righteousness exalteth a nation but sin is a reproach to any people. To me, it is not an accident that the great civilizations of the past did not endure. These civilizations were built on wars, injustice, and exploitation, and they carried within themselves the germs of decay. It will not be an accident if through nuclear war modern civilizations are likewise destroyed. It is inherent in God's ethical and moral law that he who takes the sword will perish by it, and the soul that sinneth, it shall die. Nothing that science can offer can change these basic moral laws.

It will always be good for the nations if they will allow justice to roll down like waters and righteousness like a mighty stream. The words of the prophet Micah were relevant in his day, are relevant in our time, and will be relevant a million years from now.

> Wherewith shall I come before the Lord, and bow myself before the high God? Shall I come before him with burnt offerings, with calves of a year old? Will the Lord be pleased with thousands of rams, or with ten thousands of rivers of oil? shall I give my firstborn for my transgressions, the fruit of my body for the sin of my soul?
> He hath shewed thee, O man, what is good; and what doth the Lord require of thee, but to do justly, and to love mercy, and to walk humbly with thy God? [17]

Changing times, man's increase in knowledge, the development of new techniques in science, and the new discoveries in outer space will never make these prophetic words obsolete. They are changeless and eternal. Even an atheist or a naturalist can hardly deny that it is good for mankind to do justly and to love mercy.

[17] Micah 6:6–8.

There is nothing relative about the Christian Gospel. When it elaborates the Hebraic doctrine, "Thou shalt not kill," by saying that the man who hates his brother or is angry with him has already committed murder in his heart, it is proclaiming a universal edict and giving the requirements of God and expressing a categorical imperative for man in primitive times, in modern times, and in the years to come. Murder is wrong. People in different ages and in different cultures may have different views about murder. But it is a universally accepted principle that murder is wrong. Customs and the mores do not change this basic fact. We may try to justify it, we may rationalize about it, we may say that murder or war is the lesser of the two evils; it is still wrong. This is the verdict of the Christian Gospel. Findings of science, the use of science for human welfare, and its use for nuclear wars will never be able to discredit or invalidate the Gospel of Christ that murder is sin and that it is against God's moral law.

It was sin before David's time, in his time, and since his time, for a king to put a man at the head of an army, hoping that he would be killed, thus giving the king free access to the man's wife.

At the heart of the Christian Gospel is love. We are told that God gave his son to the world because he loved the world, and because of his love for man Christ died on the Cross. Few people, if any, would argue that hate is better than love. No sane person would declare it as a value for all mankind, proclaim it as a universal principle that hatred is good. No one would want revenge and retaliation to be established as a universal law by which mankind should be governed.

The center of the Christian Gospel is love. Jesus cast aside the old idea that only friends and neighbors are to be loved. He declared that enemies are to be loved because such is the will of God. You have heard that it was said, "you shall love your neighbor and hate your enemy. But I say to you, love your enemies and pray for those who persecute you."

The reason given is "that you may be sons of your Father who is in Heaven; for he makes his sun rise on the evil and on the good, and sends rain on the just and on the unjust." [18]

The efficacy of this teaching is not conditioned by time. If it isn't good practice now to love your enemy, but rather better to seek to destroy him, it was never good practice to love your enemy. It has always been good to love your enemy. The same principle holds whether in a "primitive" society or in a "civilized" society.

This love is dramatically displayed in the story of the good Samaritan. The good Samaritan has been condemned because he did not set up a program to rid the Jericho Road of thieves. Be that as it may, the definition of *neighbor* that his story illustrates commends itself to the centuries and to men everywhere. The time will never come when the practice of the good Samaritan will be out of date.

The Jews and the Samaritans were not in love with each other. Some Jews and some Samaritans looked upon each other with genuine hatred. One day a certain man, apparently a Jew, en route to Jericho, fell into the hands of thieves. They robbed him, beat him, and left him in agony. A priest came along, crossed to the other side, and left him to suffer. So did a Levite, an assistant to the priest. A third man came along, a Samaritan, member of a group despised by the Jews. He stopped and gave aid. He dressed the injured man's wounds, carried him on his beast to an inn, and left money for his expenses. Jesus said the good Samaritan was the neighbor: not the priest, not the Levite.

It is clear from this parable that love for a human being, regard for the other person was the motivating factor that governed the behavior of the good Samaritan.

Neighbor cannot be defined in terms of nationality or race, nor in terms of geography or religion. He who responds with sympathy, love, and understanding to our needs is our

[18] Matthew 5:43–45.

neighbor. Since human needs are physical, social, intellectual, and spiritual, one may in all truth say that whoever administers to any of these needs is a neighbor.

We deal here with an eternal truth. Science can neither mar it nor abolish it. If we, in our exploration of outer space, engage in a devastating war, if through scientific ingenuity we discover that the planets are inhabited and that we can visit other planets as we visit on the earth, it will still be necessary to deal with people on the basis of human need and not on the basis of "planet-ism," nationality, race, or culture. If the human race should be completely destroyed and in the providence of God a new race comes into existence, the new people will find the example of the good Samaritan a good one to live by.

The story of the good Samaritan dramatizes what is so clear throughout the New Testament: that the life of each person is valuable and that God cares for him. We are so valuable and so precious in God's sight that the strands of hair on our heads are numbered, and it is better that a millstone be placed around our necks and we be drowned in the depth of the sea than that we injure one of God's little ones. This doctrine is eternal and it is good at any time and at all times.

"Lord, when did we see you hungry and give you food? Thirsty and give you something to drink? Lonely and made you welcome, naked and clothed you, or when did we see you ill or in prison and go to see you?" The answer was simple and eloquent. "Whatever you did for the humblest of my brothers, you did for me." Who is the humblest of my brothers? The man in need is the humblest; he is the least. Who are the humblest? They are the starved, the diseased, the illiterate, the hospitalized, the imprisoned, the alcoholic, the drug-addicted, the rich man suffering from an incurable disease, the genius on the verge of committing suicide, the man in high office, frustrated, confused, floundering, the man with his back to the wall, not knowing where to turn—all these are the least and they are in need. And they include you and they include me. We are all the humblest. We are all the least. So when we mistreat any man, we mistreat God. Every man who walks the earth is the least. And when we do harm to anyone, we do harm to God. This philosophy of life will stand man in good stead in the midst of "the wrecks of matter and the crush of worlds." Whatever kind of civilization man may build in the future, the Gospel of Christ will be relevant. Although medical science has made man less dependent upon prayer for the extension of life, and psychiatry is now changing man's behavior in ways formerly expected to occur through religious conversion, no branch of science can destroy the eternal values of the Christian faith; nor can man be absolved from individual responsibility by blaming his sins on society.

In this chapter we have emphasized much that is fundamental in the Christian faith, essential for the good life, which it is outside the province of science to give, and rules for conduct that man in no age can ignore, except at his peril. We may worship at the altar of science, but man's salvation and the peace of the nations are to be found in religion. Man cannot live well without science; most assuredly he cannot live the good life without religion.

But the religions of the world need to unite, take the initiative, and call upon the rulers of nations to work out a program of disarmament, cease all nuclear testing, and seek ways and means whereby the billions spent for arms will be spent for human welfare, and the forces of science used to advance knowledge and insure peace. On issues so infinite as these, the three major Christian bodies and the major non-Christian religions are obligated to seize the initiative for achieving world peace and not leave world leadership in this area to politicians. The Roman Catholics under the leadership of the Pope, the Protestants and the Eastern Orthodox under the leadership of the World Council of Churches, and the leaders of the non-Christian religions are called upon to speak to and visit the rulers of the nations to remind them of the folly of the competitive arms race they are waging and urge them to seek in earnest the ways of peace and justice. If ever there was a time when religions needed to take the initiative to get peace established on the earth, this is the time. It is a challenge to the religions of the world to unite in an effort to save mankind from catastrophe and death.

CHAPTER 9

The Recovery of the Whole Man in the Church

by SAMUEL H. MILLER

Dean, Harvard Divinity School

The Human Situation

IN A CURIOUS PASSAGE in one of Gogol's early papers, recently quoted by Wladimir Weidle, we are told of his cosmopolitan passion to see crowded into the same town all kinds of architecture. In his own words: "... A town ought to comprise a great diversity of mass if we want it to give pleasure to our eyes. If only the most contrary tastes could be blended there! If only in one and the same street there might arise a somber gothic edifice, a building decorated in the richest taste of the East, a vast Egyptian construction, a Greek house in its harmonious proportions! If only one could see side by side a milk-white dome, slightly concave, a tall religious spire, an oriental 'mitre,' Italian flat roof, a steep Flemish roof covered with ornaments, a four-faced pyramid, a round column and an angular obelisk!" The image of this conglomerated confusion has remained with me as a kind of revelation of what has actually occurred in the realm of religion. The religious faith of Western civilization no longer constitutes the unifying strength or center of perspective, but has become instead the source of differences in society. Indeed, so widely have the churches diverged from each other that it is only with the greatest difficulty that we can manage to understand each other. Entangled in the web of historic traditions or becoming servants of national prejudices, we are no longer capable of a catholic vision though we still make catholic claims. The church that is to bring order out of the mad eclecticism of Gogol's architectural fantasy is not yet.

And although there are obvious in our world vast and disciplined orders of ecclesiastical longing being manifested in the direction of true ecumenicity, I am not so much interested at the moment in the institutional struggle toward unity, or even in the theological *rapprochement* between the great divisions of Christendom, as I am in the more elemental level that for the moment I shall call the *human situation*. If Gogol's fantasy of architectural diversity is transferred to this realm, the problem becomes much more serious. Modern man finds himself inwardly differentiated, split up, and self-contradictory. He just doesn't go together! His inheritances from Puritan and Cavalier, from Hebrew and Greek, from the Renaissance and the Reformation jostle together like a carnival of ill-assorted oddities. That they become changes of mask or costume for a soul much bewildered by such a loss of integrity is not strange.

This confused conglomeration of inheritances, which obviously must affect any attempt to achieve a religious unity, either inwardly or outwardly, may be seen at a different level again by looking at C. R. Collingwood's study "Speculum Mentis," where the philosopher considers the inner differentiation that the human psyche underwent following the breakup of the medieval world. With the coming of the Renaissance man loses both the external and the internal unity that had been largely his for many centuries. While the outer scene becomes kaleidoscopic with rebellion against church, state, and tradition, the psychic energies of man begin a prolific specialization. Art breaks away from religion, religion from philosophy, philosophy from science, science from tradition. Here occur the great schisms in the soul between reason and faith, between faith and aesthetics, between faith and morals. From this point the soul of man begins to look like Gogol's fantastic congeries of self-appointed autonomous impulses, each a jealous sovereign of its own realm, its own form, and of its own claims. The rank-rebellious individualism of man himself is reflected in the pluralistic energies, each rendered autonomous without regard for an overall unity.

Needless to say, such a state led quickly to where each specialized aspect of man's consciousness, liberated from the harness of the team, sprang into the lead and laid claim to be the premier. Reason was not long in avenging Faith's ancient tyranny; Art broke away from common utility and disdained every authority; Faith shook itself loose from tradition and the state. Each built his own house in his own way and then claimed it was the capitol of the state, the castle of the king.

It is little wonder, then, that when we construct our Church, what ultimately takes shape against the skyline is something far less than catholic. The specialization to which we owe our civilization and its rapid rise to skill and power is inwardly the very origin of our lack of spiritual unity and, in its deeper sense, of our moral integrity. The great Church cannot be built until the inner schisms of man's soul are healed.

Method of Simplification

Now, of course, men have been trying to close these breaches, both within the consciousness of man and also in the social world of history. For the most part they have been attempts at *simplification*. One of the strongest and most persistent tendencies has been that of reason, stemming from the

Renaissance and accumulating power with the ascendancy of science. Another, more recent, simplification has been the Neo-Reformation movement of Karl Barth with its emphasis on Biblical faith as the sovereign norm of man. At the present moment tremendous forces of considerable momentum and extensiveness have been operating to simplify man in terms of social and political materialism. Other forces tend to simplify the situation by divinizing the Church, or by humanizing it.

This simplification by the Church is often by a process of ostracism. Some churches excommunicate sex, others reason; some the Bible, others the world; some science, and others art; some the flesh, and others the mind; some what is written, and others only what is spoken. This fragmenting process, or exfoliation, divides the seamless robe of man's integrity until the pieces are but shreds.

One cannot help but listen respectfully to Jacob Burckhardt's warning of the "terrible simplifiers." Obviously these "terrible simplifiers" were the men who led the political powers that coerced a semblance of unity in the human communities by a show of uniformity. But simplification, terrible or benevolent, has in it great dangers, not the least of which Plato saw in his diagnosis of imbalance as one of the causes of social decay. The "nothing but" men, whether they be "nothing but religion" or "nothing but reason," are already fanatics in the sense of having repressed much that has its rightful share in the full-orbed reality of human life.

What obviously is needed for our time is an understanding large enough, imaginative enough, bold enough, to reach beyond any simple autonomy of a provincial aspect of man's experience, and to penetrate by insight and understanding to that deep ground in which the powers and achievements of his protean nature may be supported and unified, not denied or nullified.

Prophetically enough, Leibnitz the philosopher foresaw something of our condition in a letter he wrote to his friend

Arnauld in 1671. "Today's most crying need is a very profound knowledge of religion. Why? Because a philosophical age is opening where, in the natural and logical course of events, insistence on absolute accuracy in detail is going to spread from the classrooms out into every walk of life. If we cannot satisfy this demand for exact knowledge, the genuine propagation of religion must be abandoned. Very soon the majority of men will be Christians only in externals; enterprising persons with bad spirit will work for the destruction of the faith. Atheism with naturalism will be popular heresies." How Leibnitz hoped this might be averted is interesting. By uniting the sacred professions with secular disciplines he envisaged healing the schism that he feared would work ill for men everywhere. The Cistercians would also be naturalists; the mendicant orders, physicians; the contemplative, mathematicians; the learned orders, historians; missionaries, linguists; theologians, critics; and liturgists, lovers of nature. Suggestive as it is, and as significantly contemporaneous as it is today with many clerical orders taking on scientific disciplines for the larger and more skillful functioning of their ministry, it remains rather ineffective, for two reasons, I suspect. First, it does not indicate how the essentially religious factor would be taken over by scientific disciplines; and secondly, there is not given ample significance to the popular masses, who would be losing their religious orientation at the very time they were gaining a scientific orientation, or at least one they thought was scientific.

The task, then, that we face is a large and very complex one. Nothing less than the reunion of the whole man will yield us a foundation deep enough and broad enough for the building of a *great Church*. When the clerics of Seville arrived at their intention to build a cathedral, their direction to the builders was significant: "Build us," they said, "such a church that future generations will think us mad ever to have attempted such a structure."

Contemporary Man

It will not be unwise of us, then, if we turn to modern man, in whom we have seen the state of spiritual confusion, to consider whether his consent can be gained for what I have called a *great Church*. If he is recalcitrant, or dubious, or resentful, then he will build his own temple in terms of his own concerns and not of ours. E. M. Forster, the novelist, has one of his characters in *Howard's End* say that "We are developing ways which science cannot comprehend and theology dare not contemplate." Here contemporaneous literature overwhelms us with witnesses. What kind of a man, what sort of human being, is being developed before our eyes? There are some frightening visions here, and, like Dante yearning to see Paradise, we must not draw back from the Inferno if we are at last to reach our goal.

In Lewis Mumford's recent Bampton Lectures at Columbia he asked, "Why has our inner life become so impoverished and empty, and why has our outer life become so exorbitant, and its subjective satisfactions even more empty? Why have we become technological gods and moral devils, scientific supermen and aesthetic idiots—idiots, that is, in the Greek sense of being wholly private persons, incapable of communicating with each other or understanding each other?"

There is the mechanized man of Karel Capek and George Orwell; the dehumanized man in a technically fabricated environment of Karl Jaspers; there is the estranged man, separated from past and present and future, from his family, from nature, even from himself, of Albert Camus; there is the superman, of Nietzsche, of Dostoevski, and incidentally of Dachau and Buchenwald, who takes all into his own hands, and kills for the imagined good he can do; there is the man of infinite greed and infinite dissatisfaction and infinite restlessness and infinite guilt, of Thomas Wolfe and John Dos Passos; there is the political man of Koestler and Silone and Orwell.

Can we discern their shape? They have much in common. All of them are without God; for them God is dead. They became gods—they ruled in God's stead, without fear. And yet something went wrong, for instead of being divinized, of finding perfect freedom, life fell apart, became a whirlwind of incommensurate nightmares and boredoms. They are no longer the slaves of height and depth, of sanctity and sin, but now they are caught on the rack of length and breadth. They are stretched in all directions but find peace in none. They no longer believe; they do not need to—there are no margins, no implications, no possibilities, no freedom. Everything is natural and contingent. Having exercised the fictitious, they now become factitious. They accept nothing but facts; facts are their sole food; only it is tasteless, as tasteless as it seems noxious. This is the mechanistic, technological, liberated, non-superstitious man, totally externalized, as John Dewey says.

A recent novel by Ernst Weichert called *The Jeromin Children* illustrates the matter well. Beginning with the passionate renunciation of God and the fiery declaration of atheism, the generations follow one another until at last they reach what might be called a serene and unquestioning secularism. Jumbo, who represents the last stage of the process, can be epitomized as one in whom the question of the meaning of life is no longer raised. Whatever one may call Jumbo, disillusioned or secularized, one cannot fail to recognize the disappearance of certain dimensions of sensibility, which all too obviously leave him less a man than some of his more belief-ful ancestors. They registered, however faultily, some of the reactions that still tokened contact with regions now abandoned.

The question that Jumbo raises for us may not seem as striking or as dramatic as the type of man portrayed by the modern observers I have mentioned or by the rise of the new

barbarian illustrated in the Nazi and Fascist regimes, but for
all that, Jumbo is the very ground and base of operations for
the demonic religions of the new Dionysian state, Karl Heim
puts it succinctly:

> The loss of interest in the religious question is indeed the tacit
> expression of a very radical problem, a problem which is far
> more radical than all those questions of detail which used in
> the days of the older school of apologetics to arouse such
> lively discussions between the Church and her opponents.
> The fundamental question which is now to be debated is not
> concerned with any one single point in the Church's teaching.
> It is concerned with the whole. It is the question whether for
> people of the present time, whose thought is shaped by the
> contemporary conception of the physical universe, any other
> philosophy is still possible than that of secularism.

It is the empty man, the man of no belief, the man of reduced
consciousness who becomes the willing slave of the most irrational beliefs—and becomes dry tinder for the wild fire on any
political orgy.

All of us are in some degree responsible for Jumbo. There
is no simplification possible of the web of historical forces
that have created him. He has been separated from any vital
experience of God for so long; he has been accustomed to a
world bereft of any action that could be ascribed to God; he
has been educated by the brilliant spectacle of science and
industry, and monopolized by their products and power; he
has been the anvil for mighty wars and the ceaseless drip of
radio din—is there any wonder that he is scarcely a fit subject
for the experience of a *great Church?* In fact the Church itself
is responsible in so far as it stubbornly encrusted itself on the
one side with defensive debates to ensure its traditional prejudices and on the other hand betrayed its ancient realities for
the superficial satisfactions of the social man. Science, too, is
responsible, not that she intended by any means to produce,

or even to assist in producing Jumbo, but responsible none the less in the same blind way as the Church, maintaining its autonomy as if Jumbo's whole life could be sustained in healthful balance by her truths alone. Obviously what Jumbo has assumed to be the life of science may be as gross a distortion of true science as his notion of religion is a caricature of real religion. But between a stubborn and senile faith, and an ambitious and presumptive science, man has not only been divided, but he has been reduced in stature. Religion has thus been separated from an everyday relevance, and life in turn has been flattened out, with neither height nor depth to give it substance or weight. Other forces have lent their hands, such as the industrial revolution, the rise of individualism, the ascendancy of the *bourgeoisie* class, but complex as the stream of influence may be, the result is simply a man increasingly less able to make anything of the Church. Yet it is this contemporary man whom we must serve if we are to build the *great Church*. To build a Church for intellectuals, or aesthetes, or even well-certified Christians is not enough. Truth, that is, the fundamental relationship with reality, Marx to the contrary, is not a class possession or a class privilege.

Dimensions of Reality

If the Church, then, is to meet contemporary man and become the articulation of his whole life, there are several questions that must be asked. The first one concerns the dimensions of reality with which the Church must deal. What are the modes of experiences in which the full scope of man's consciousness, mind, heart, spirit, and strength, or in our presently used terms, science, art, faith, and morals can be conceived? This recovery of what the Church is in reference to man might at least give us a direction for our efforts in the rehabilitation of the Church in the economy of modern living. Once we have thus reoriented ourselves, we would still have the task of mediating such a mode of experience to men in whom it had long been atrophied. I am not so sure, however, that that is the primary question. If the Church can be the Church in some such sense as I suggest, there is ample evidence that all through the cracks and crannies of a hysterically supported secularity there can be discerned the movement of what I can only call transcendent principalities and powers, oft hidden but impending evidences of revelation.

Let us look, then, at the dimensions of reality that the *great Church* would seek to articulate. These can be simply listed as the scientific, the aesthetic, the moral, and the religious. The Church cannot avoid even one of them without losing proportion and indicating the repression of a portion of its task. They are not mutually exclusive by any means, but it is easy for an institution, or an epoch, to become neurotically obsessed with one or the other.

The scientific question to ask, as far as religion is concerned, is, What is the nature of reality? The testimony of both traditional religion and of contemporary research is that reality is dynamic, mysteriously and powerfully dynamic. The energies supporting the world are, to say the least, extremely awesome. The nearer we approach them, the nearer we seem to understand the ancient words *creation* and *hell*. It is not without relevance that the new vision of dynamic reality afforded by science seems to point in the direction of many metaphors used by the older theologians, such as "*Allwirksamkeit*," prevenience, and grace. For the scientist intent on the phenomena thrown up by such a dynamic, the implications remain unspoken, hidden in mystery. For the religionist, too, they remain hidden in mystery, but the implications are boldly grasped and with such risk as faith always takes, their "meaning" is referred to God.

There is a corollary to this *rapprochement*; namely, whether reality exceeds the measure of science or not. The religious affirmation at this point emphasizes mystery while science tends to emphasize knowledge. This mystery emphasized by religion, however, is not the mystery that exists in a dark band of the unexplored around the bright circle of our knowledge, a terra incognita waiting for the invasion that would floodlight it. It is the affirmation of a mystery *in* our knowledge, a mystery from which all knowledge comes and by which it is sustained. It is the mystery of being, of being that exceeds knowing. It is thus a fundamental category involved in knowing. It assumes that my knowing does not exhaust the reality of the object known.

Einstein makes it exceedingly plain that science as such does not deign to give a full picture of reality: "Even at the expense of completeness we have to secure purity, clarity, and accurate correspondence between representation and the thing represented. When one realizes how small a part of nature can thus be comprehended and expressed in an exact formulation, while all that is subtle and complex has to be excluded, it is only natural to ask what sort of attraction this work can have." Max Planck similarly says: ". . . The knowable realities of nature cannot be exhaustibly discovered by any branch of science. This means that science is never in the position completely and exhaustibly to explain the problems it has to face. The most penetrative eye cannot see itself any more than a working instrument can work upon itself. The object and subject of an act of knowing can never be identical for we can speak of the act of knowing only when the object to be known is not influenced by the action of the subject who initiates and performs the act of knowing."

It is this pervasive mystery, the mystery of existence as such, which constitutes the ground of our humility, the source of the religious question by which the Church is constituted. For whatever else may be said of the Church, it misses its starting point if it misses the question with which every man begins to live as a man. He is literally flung into a sea of mystery, to cry with Dostoevski, "Does God make anything but riddles?" This is the first awareness of man, whether he is a scientist or a religionist, and it remains for all his harvesting of knowledge the essential experience of being alive as a human being. Science is not total knowledge; it is not omniscience.

It is because of this that both science and religion must be advocates of what I can only call a faithful skepticism. To be faithfully aware of the full orbit of reality and to be skeptically alert to every assumption of total adequacy, or the suppression of experience, or short cuts to truth, or over-simplification of existence—this is our common responsibility. Superstition, whether it be in the religious category or the scientific, is merely the false extension of limited truth to universal pretensions.

The question that arises out of this basic affirmation of the mystery of dynamic reality concerns its formulation. It is the aesthetic question of how this category of experience can be articulated and communicated. It is not a competitive question of whether science is more universal than art. Obviously the descriptive and analytic approach of science to reality in its elementary stages also becomes mathematical and symbolic in its more advanced dealings with reality. The question is whether the essential concreteness, which is the existence itself and its mystery, is retained in the vehicle used for communication. This is done in the symbol or the myth or the ritual. In a sense they are not part of the "natural" framework of events, nor are they abstracted from it. They are concrete, sharing in the mystery of existence, and yet they are significant in their transcendence of individual or historic events. They have meaning, but their meaning is not yet explicit in the rational sense. The meaning exists halfway between that which is implicit in the world itself and any explicit facts separated from it.

As Ernst Cassirer has pointed out, so much of our attention has been given over the last several centuries to scientific reasoning that it has grown increasingly difficult for us to conceive of any other approach to reality. Yet there is no inherent monopoly to truth in discursive reasoning, as the last century of philosophical researches give evidence. And certainly in the broad ideological interpretation of reason itself it is evident we are not dealing with an instrument beyond distortion. Rather what we see now is that scientific reason, like mythical or symbolic thinking, has certain inherent disadvantages. In Clutton-Brock's picturesque phrase, "Science tells a big lie in the interest of many little truths, whereas religion tells many little lies in the interest of a big truth."

Roughly, very roughly indeed, this does indicate the fact that whereas science has proceeded on the basis of precision in measurement and predictable repetition, religion has chosen rather comprehensiveness and singularity. In a sense this is the dimension of wholeness and of the unique, both of which science must disregard, and yet clearly both concern man. For man is incurably metaphysical. He is irresistibly drawn to make an answer to the total mystery, whether he makes it positively or negatively; and he makes it, feeling that it is his own answer, absolutely valid although no other man in the world makes one like it.

The essential corollary of this symbolic mode is that it is highly dubious whether a *great Church* can exist without a symbolic structure. That is to say, it cannot exist alone on a scientific, rationalistic structure of principles and concepts. The reasons for this may be seen in that reality itself is larger than reason, just as human nature cannot be reduced to reason. There are portions of reality known only, as Pascal suggested, by the heart, and on no account did he mean by this metaphor mere emotions. Alfred North Whitehead in his Harvard Tercentenary address in 1936 remarked that "The real problem is to adjust the activities of the learned institution so as to suffuse them with suggestiveness. Human nature loses its most precious quality when it is robbed of its sense of things beyond, unexplored and yet insistent. Learning is sensible, straightforward, and clear if only you keep at bay the suggestiveness of things." To deny this suggestive margin of reality is to countenance what J. Donald Adams in *The New York Times* called the ". . . major fallacy of modern man: that all the answers are contained in intellectual processes."

We can see this matter clearly in the historic situation in which a civilization loses its dynamic cohesion, not because of famines, floods, wars, diseases, but through what Lewis Mumford calls the ". . . accumulated perversion of the symbolic functions." The demolition of the Biblical myth in the sixteenth and seventeenth centuries is a case in point. Another one is the disintegration of Greece in the fourth and fifth centuries, when as Werner Jaeger says:

> . . . as the more binding forces of life—religion, morality and music, which for the Greeks always included poetry—lost their power, so the masses escaped from the formative influence of the spirit. Instead of drawing from the pure spring, they contented themselves with cheap and flashy substitutes. The standards and ideals to which every class in the nation once paid allegiance were still announced, and that too with increased rhetorical embellishment; but less and less real attention was paid to them. People enjoyed hearing about them, and could be enthralled for the moment; but few were moved from the heart by them, and for most people they were useless at the critical moment.

In our time few of us are supported by a dynamic vision held imaginatively as a pattern for belief and action. The "acids of modernity" have eaten away all the bonding of our diversified world, and we have accustomed ourselves to living in bedlam, literally "displaced persons," rootless and endlessly restless.

Here we come upon a factor that distinguished to a large degree the character of the symbol from that of scientific truth. The symbol is never merely an objective sign or representation, or if it is, it ceases to have power in the sense of human meaning. It is objective in that it shares in the thing-nature of the world, but it is ambivalently rooted in the sub-jective structures of man's self. Science, on the other hand, has accumulated its truths by an ascetic discipline of removing as far as possible every vestige of the human factor, not to say of subjectivity. It is the glory of science to say that it has re-spected objectivity, and this is proper for science; but the whole spectrum of light does include the mystery of subjec-tivity as well. Thus it is that the symbol weds both the world and the self in articulations that can never be separated from each other. In our time the symbols of the Church are not necessarily untrue. They have become irrevelant, it is true. But they have lost their power because the subjective struc-tures of reality have atrophied. Our life has been elsewhere. We moved away from them, not they away from us.

Now this leads me to a third question: namely, the moral question. This is essentially the mode of consciousness in which the ego and the world stand opposed, in which the subjective and the objective mingle in conflict and contro-versy. For science, methodically eliminating the element of subjectivity as far as possible from its equations, the ego-world is highly dubious unless it can be rendered into objective terms. But an absolute limit is met in such an effort. The center of subjectiveness, of consciousness, is not objectifiable. Karl Heim calls it non-objective space. Just as the seeing eye can-not see itself, so the ego cannot objectify itself. All that others can do is to presume an ego-center of subjectivity from outer evidences of the body and its action.

Here, then, are two realms, interlocking, sharing in real-ity. Both science and Christianity, let it be said, are agreed on the reality of the outer world, the world of objective space. The inner world, by which that outer world is perceived, strangely enough, is viewed ambiguously by science as if it were unreal, although it is capable of entertaining the vision of reality. For most religionists both realms are part of reality.

It is in this non-objective realm—not as a specific part of man singled out and separated from everything else, but as the dynamic unity and wholeness on which all the parts are dependent for their meaning—that religion affirms three truths: namely, freedom, sanctity, and salvation. None of these are imperceptible from science's point of view, but they are surely not in the direct focus of its attention. The question of *freedom* for science is inevitably linked with deterministic causality. To resist the pattern of cause and consequence is to endure frustration—the very opposite of freedom. To be free in such a structure is to fit it perfectly and to respond efficiently. In objective space anything is free in so far as it fulfills its function.

The strange thing is that when this formula is transferred to human experience, we grow conscious of certain reservations, even of a resistance. There is a sense in which we feel that the human function is not merely to fit into the causal structure, but that there is a margin, an openness, a certain distance that gives us maneuverability to act freely in the face of circumstances. One aspect of this can be felt as perversity (which Dostoevski discerns as related to freedom as he discusses it in *Letters From the Underworld*). This is the basic condition of good and evil, the ground of our anxiety and the possibility of our self-transcendence.

It is easy when discussing the question of freedom to place freedom and determinism in juxtaposition. This I believe to be erroneous. There are many kinds of freedom. That freedom we feel in the non-objective realm of the soul is not opposed to the structures of reality that manifest themselves in nature, but is itself the fulfillment of a larger order than the one we perceive sensually or even logically.

The second factor, which I have named *sanctity*, shares also in a dimension that nature, taken apart from man, does not plainly manifest. Just as freedom and slavery were opposed above, so here sanctity and sin are held in meaningful dialectic. Sanctity in the religious sense is associated with the non-objective world, the realm of the soul, the center of consciousness, and its non-exchangeability. It is sacred in the sense that it is the only point at which the world may be known from the inside. It has no repetitive-value. It is the singular, the *Einmaligkeit*, the knowledgeable center without which the world literally is not known. To sin is to separate oneself from this center of non-objective space; to attach oneself to the world or any part of it merely as part of it; to be irresponsible about one's relationship to the world, to shift, to lie, to deceive as to one's place and position. In a sense this is man's absolute responsibility to be himself.

It follows from this that the ego has a special category of relationships with other selves. Here the moral question arises in its usual restricted sense. Only insofar as all the selves sharing in a society are respected as subjects can a community become normative. Moreover, only as the ego is sustained by a community is it validated and fulfilled. The Church can never be a collection of well-intentioned individualists. It is a cohesive body acquiring and sustaining values and possibilities for each cell. The ego requires the world as much as the world requires the ego.

The third factor in the realm of the soul I boldly term *salvation*. For the world of objectivity this word is nonsense, but for the non-objective world of freedom and sanctity, it is not. The word may be obsolete, but I do not believe it is beyond being salvaged. Salvation is that experience by which consciousness is centered in freedom and sanctity in non-objective space as over against a center determined by the world, apart from human considerations. Just as the category of freedom describes man in relation to the natural world, and the category of sanctity, in relation to humanity, so the category of salvation describes him in relation to the true center of his being. To be saved in this sense is to be free and creative in relation to the world, to respect and be respected by other selves, and beyond these to be a subject grounded in the non-objective dynamic reality of God.

So far we have sought to describe the dimensions of that reality in which man may be reunited in the Church. Dynamic reality and its fundamental mystery, the symbolic function, and the paradox of the ego-world relationships in which freedom, sanctity, and salvation are elicited, comprise our main issues, arising out of science, art, and morality.

The Religious Dimension

The question we ask now is, Is there an essentially religious question that can be asked? Certainly we have already put one foot into the religious realm by our consideration of the soul, its freedom, sanctity, and salvation. Yet I think one may say that it is proper for religion to answer the question of what binds art, science, and morality together in the whole man. And as disappointing as it may seem at first, I should like to give the answer that it is not reason, or sensibility, or integrity. The essential unification of man is by the *spirit*. As disappointing in its vagueness as this answer must seem, I must beg of you to consider it.

There are two ways in which I wish to describe the spirit. The first word I wish to use is *openness*. This is a word, "*das Offene*," which was very popular with Rainer Maria Rilke, the Austrian poet. Throughout his work, strictly disciplined by an intellectual rigor and patience, he sought to render himself hospitable to the full scale of reality. "What he teaches us," says Gabriel Marcel of him, "better than anyone, and what I think such writers as Nietzsche or Kierkegaard have generally either never known or in the end forgotten, is that there exists a receptivity which is really creation itself under another name. The most genuinely receptive being is at the same time the most essentially creative." He renders himself available! His finiteness is not the basis of complaint, but the basis of expecting in every direction visitations of existences and meanings. In one of the *Sonnets to Orpheus* he says:

> Even today, though existence is magical, pouring freshly from hundreds of well-springs,—a playing of purest forces, which none can surprise without humbly adoring. Words still melt into something beyond their embrace.... Music, too, keeps building anew with the insecurest stones her celestial house in unusable space.

This openness appears in the dimensions we have sought to describe as ineluctable mystery, as the readiness of the symbolic both to receive and express that which is not literally describable, or as the infinite possibilities of freedom in the soul's venture with the world.

Moreover this openness may be seen in the interpretation of heart, mind, and strength, of art, science, and morality, in the full unity of the spirit. It is indeed the spirit's strength that it seems nothing of itself, but everything to all things. Perhaps no other word so thoroughly expresses this characteristic as *faith* with all its corollaries of trust, hope, and peace.

The second way of describing the spirit, which adds meaning as well to the first, is that the spirit is the name we give to the dynamic character of reality. Here both science and religion stand together. But both testify to dynamic reality at the ultimate reaches of their experience. It is this power of reality that reinforces the openness and makes intelligible the ancient doctrine of unearned grace. Moreover it is its ubiquity at every level of existence that makes possible the charged power constellations of symbolic and sacramental realities.

The *great Church*, then, unites the divergent energies of man by the spirit, not elicited by magic abracadabra, but implicit in the nature of things, and revealed as far as the openness of man's being allows its entrance and ministry. It is creative, redemptive—or, if you prefer the word, dialectical—and eschatological, which is to say there is a beyond from which power surges. It is both hidden in mystery and revealed in grace. It is still the hope of the world.

Perhaps Gogol's picture of the fantastic jumble of architectural forms is not the best portrayal of our situation, although it has served us for one aspect of it. Karl Heim has told the story of the bombing of Mayence, in which the Church of St. John the Baptist was demolished, leaving only one arch standing, on which the inscription read, "Repent ye, for the Kingdom is at hand." Heim asks whether in our time it is possible to rebuild the Church, beginning with what we have left of our Christian heritage, or whether we must tear down the fragments and build from the ground a new faith, more in keeping with the age. The answer is not a simple categorical yes or no. He will find the structures of reality at their deepest levels not wholly different from what Isaiah and Jesus found.

Several matters, however, are plain. The Church is a religious institution, not a scientific one, nor an artistic one, nor even a moral one. But these are also necessary aspects of reality, and a religion without regard for them will find itself reduced to an esoteric specialty, betraying its own fundamental function in the world—namely, keeping alive a vision of the full orbit of reality.

Such a Church is not built or maintained, it should be said, to keep the planets on their tracks, or to move the sun regularly on its way, or to declare the time of instinct to birds and bees. It is necessary for man, just as a laboratory is necessary for the scientist, or a library for a scholar, or a marketplace for a merchant, in pondering those questions concerning his humanity, when he must deal with the nature and consequences of his own freedom, the highest level at which the dynamic character of reality is manifested. Or when he must recover, by such disciplines as the self-collection in prayer or the ritualistic remembrance of the growing edge of consciousness, the singularity of his being. Or when he confesses his deviations from his own human reality, lest without such occasions he completely lose his way. Whether these gestures be called repentance or philosophical contemplation, they are in essence listening for God's Word, the judgment of reality upon unreality, of the dynamic upon the static.

Here we will seek simplicity to be sure but, as Whitehead urged, we will also distrust it. If we gather up dynamic reality and mystery, the order of law and freedom, the sense of sanctity and sin, the destiny of man saved by a higher law than nature, which comes by a grace—if we gather this total complexity together and utter the word *God* in reverence and in praise, we will not think we have comprehended the structures of reality involved, but we will be humble enough to fling our ragged breath in the direction of that toward which we aspire.

As Walt Whitman once expressed it,

> I swear I will never henceforth have to do
> with the faith that tells the best!
> I will have to do only with the faith that
> leaves the best untold.

CHAPTER 10

Personalistic Religion and Science

by ARTHUR W. MUNK

Albion College

CONTEMPORARY THEOLOGY is deeply infected with subjectivism. Few theologians wrestle with the tough dilemmas that a serious consideration of the relations of religion and science entails. In opposition to this trend, we shall aim at objectivity and synopsis (wholeness). The attempt shall be made to view the problem, that is, especially the problem of the relations of *personalistic* religion and science, in the light of all the basic facts involved.

Relevance and Limitations of Religion

Modern "cultured despisers" of religion usually regard it as largely obsolete—as little more than a fossil which will, on that blessed day when science comes into its own, be relegated to museums. While fastening on its negative aspects, they have forgotten its vast contributions. Strangely enough, there are still many scientists, especially those engaged in the younger sciences such as sociology, who have this attitude. Those in the older sciences are more understanding.

160

High religion, stripped to its essentials, involves at least three positive factors. There is, to begin with, its stress on values, on the qualitative aspects of reality, including, above all else, the value of personality—"human dignity." Not only did the coming of Christianity, with its profound fusion of the best that Palestine and Greece had to offer, awaken our ancestors from a long night of barbarism to an amazing creativity, but it also bestowed upon them this concept of the supreme worth of personality. Moreover, du Noüy speaks of the vast influence of the "wakes" left by the founders of the great religions.[1] In a similar vein William Ernest Hocking not only speaks of high religion as *the mother of the Arts*," but also stresses its "power and freedom to create." [2] It is also interesting to note that the greatest philosopher of history of our times, namely, Arnold J. Toynbee, everywhere bears witness to the creative role of religion.[3]

Closely related to all this is its second significant factor: the mystical. Although mysticism has often been purely subjective, irrational, and actually psychotic, yet, at its best, it seems to indicate that there are deeper levels of reality than the world of ordinary sense experience.[4] Nor is it true that all mystics have been quietists. Some of them, in fact, such as Jesus, St. Paul, Mohammed, St. Francis, and Gandhi have been powerful levers of history.

Finally, in spite of irrational and narrow sectarian tendencies, high religion, like science, aims at objectivity, truth. "You will know the truth and the truth will make you free." [5]

[1] Lecomte du Noüy, *Human Destiny* (New York: Longmans, Green & Co., 1947), p. 255.

[2] *The Meaning of God in Human Experience* (New Haven: Yale University Press, 1912), pp. 14, 485.

[3] *Reconsiderations*, Vol. XII of *Study of History* (New York: Oxford University Press, 1961), pp. 81–102.

[4] William James, *The Varieties of Religious Experience* (New York: Modern Library, 1902), pp. 475–516.

[5] John 8:32.

Like philosophy, it also aims at wholeness, totality. "The earth is the Lord's and the fulness thereof." [6]

In spite of its contributions, religion has its "debit side." [7] There are its subjective and irrational tendencies. While many of our theologians have turned toward the vagaries of subjectivism and obscurantism, on the lower levels, all kinds of fantastic and bizarre cults flourish like green bay trees. Worst of all, dogmatism and authoritarianism are still with us; and, while during other times they produced religious inquisitions, today they furnish the seedbeds for extreme rightist political movements.

Relevance and Limitations of Science

In this chaotic age when irrationalism threatens to hurl us over the precipice and when subjectivism has led to a morbid preoccupation with our own little selves, the scientific stress on objectivity is indispensable. Nothing, in truth, possesses greater therapeutic power than astronomy. Moreover, in a day when the archaist is abroad, and in search for a phantom security tries madly to turn the clock back, the experimental attitude and outlook of the sciences is no less imperative. Unless we are willing to press beyond the frontiers of the known and unless we are willing to be creative commensurate with the demands of the Nuclear Age (on all levels—scientific, social, political, spiritual), we shall follow the dinosaurs into oblivion. It is interesting to note that, in spite of being fully aware of its dangers, Bertrand Russell still maintains that science, with its adventurous spirit, constitutes "one of the glories of man." [8]

[6] Psalm 24:1.
[7] See C. J. Ducasse, *A Philosophical Scrutiny of Religion* (New York: Ronald Press Co., 1953), pp. 168–234; also John L. Fischer, "The Role of Religion as Viewed by the Science of Man," in Harlow Shapley (ed.), *Science Ponders Religion* (New York: Appleton-Century-Crofts, 1960), pp. 226, 230–32.
[8] "Science and Human Life," in James R. Newman (ed.), *What is Science?* (New York: Washington Square Press, 1961), p. 13.

Neither, except during those periods, such as our own, when the philosophers and theologians have not yet succeeded in the process of correlating the new truth with the old, need the advance of science mean skepticism. Ultimately, if we do not give up too soon, there is hope of a larger perspective. After all, no necessary contradiction exists between an experimental science with its eyes fixed on the outer world and an equally courageous, experimental religion which concentrates on the inner world of the spirit. Both, in the final analysis, belong to the same universe and must therefore be related.

Again, science, with its myriads of specialists, furnishes vast bodies of tested knowledge—which the religionist, if he aims at adequacy, must utilize. Although the Hindu mystic may attempt to dismiss scientific knowledge as belonging to the realm of *maya* and the Western positivist may insist that it can tell us nothing about the Ultimate Mystery that possibly lies beyond phenomena, yet, try as we will, we can neither rid ourselves of the fact of nature nor of the suspicion that it has something profound to say to us; for not only does it keep on appearing in its various forms all around us, but, especially when it stirs us with awe and wonder, it seems profoundly suggestive. Perhaps Berkeley was not altogether wrong when he insisted that, basically, nature constitutes something of a sign or "Visual Language," disclosing dimly something about the Mystery which lies back of it.[9] In spite of his phenomenalism, which has helped to shape modern positivism, the great Kant himself goes so far as to suggest that nature may have theological implications.[10] Be that as it may, since science may *illuminate* as well as deepen nature's mysteries, the religionist must have the humility to listen and to ponder what it has to say. The time is ripe for a new and a more adequate

[9] *Alciphron*, Vol. III of *The Works of George Berkeley*, edited by A. A. Luce and T. E. Jessop (New York: Thomas Nelson & Sons, 1950), pp. 159–60.
[10] On Kant's theology, see this writer's article, "Kant's Legacy to Philosophical Theology," *The Philosophical Forum*, 1962.

synthesis of religious insight and scientific knowledge. Failure to rise to the occasion spells chaos.

Finally, there is the vast scientific potential to further and to enrich life through the control and intelligent direction of natural forces. Without science man is helpless in the face of such evils as disease, famine, ignorance, and the threat of over-population: thus, so far as the future is concerned, the constructive aspects of science constitute one of our chief grounds for optimism. Bertrand Russell is at least half right when he insists that it is by "its very nature a liberator." [11]

Yet science, like religion, has its limitations; and these become especially obvious the moment it is regarded as the only approach to life and to the universe.[12] Although far more reliable than the ordinary kind, scientific knowledge is still *human* knowledge and subject to the limitations of the human mind. The history of science shows that again, like religion, it has at all times had its liberals and its conservatives, and that the heterodoxies of today often become the orthodoxies of tomorrow. In Russia Kazan Cathedral has been turned into a "museum" stored with the relics of superstitious faith. To be wholly just, across the street there should also be a museum of science exhibiting the foibles and fables and archaic notions once zealously defended by scientists.[13]

It is interesting to note that today a mature science such as physics clearly recognizes its limitations. Einstein even says

[11] Russell, in Newman (ed.), *op. cit.*, p. 18.

[12] On this section the following have been helpful: J. W. N. Sullivan, *The Limitations of Science* (New York: The New American Library, 1933); L. W. Friedrich (ed.), *The Nature of Physical Knowledge* (Bloomington: Indiana University Press, and Milwaukee: Marquette University Press, 1960); Werner Heisenberg, *The Physicist's Conception of Nature* (New York: Harcourt, Brace & Co., 1958); A. S. Eddington, *The Nature of the Physical World* (New York: The Macmillan Co., 1933); Alfred North Whitehead, *Science and the Modern World* (New York: The Macmillan Co., 1937); and Charles E. Raven, *Science, Religion, and the Future* (New York: The Macmillan Co., 1944).

[13] On the opposition of scientists to Darwin, see Raven, *op. cit.*, pp. 33–50.

that its "very foundations ... have become problematic." [14]
Moreover, since the physicists have come up against certain
great intangibles, chief among which is the fact that matter
itself (that former stronghold of materialism) has been reduced to a mysterious something called *energy*, they are much
more inclined toward a spiritual view of the universe. In
terms of parapsychology, today psychology is also faced with
certain facts that the old classical, mechanistic categories cannot explain.[15]

Nor can there be any doubt that scientific method, with
its stress on analysis and abstraction, involves limitations. In
spite of serious efforts at synthesis, the basic scientific approach
to problems is analytical and piecemeal. Instead of science as
such in terms of one unified discipline, we find, in fact, many
sciences, each with its own special plot. This is still true in
spite of the close relations between such mature sciences as
astronomy, physics, and mathematics, and even though, during
these latter days, disciplines such as biochemistry have been
developed.

The practice of abstraction is closely related to analysis.
Basically it involves the habit of ignoring certain aspects of
reality for the purpose of concentrating on others. There is, of
course, nothing wrong with this as long as the scientist knows
what he is doing. The mischief begins when he tries to substitute these particular aspects for the living whole. Collingwood
has shown, in a masterly way, the various stages through
which this process proceeds till nothing is left but mathematical symbols.[16] This also calls to mind Eddington's famous
illustration of the reduction of the real flesh and blood ele-

[14] See the chapter, "Physics and Reality," in Einstein's *Out of My Later
Years* (New York: Philosophical Library, 1950), p. 59.
[15] For an excellent account of parapsychology, see J. B. Rhine, *New
World of the Mind* (New York: William Sloane Associates, 1953).
[16] See the chapter by Frank J. Collinwood, "Is 'Physical Knowledge'
Limited by Its Quantitative Approach to Reality?" in Friedrich (ed.), *op.
cit.*, pp. 25–46.

phant sliding down a hill to nothing but "pointer readings."[17]
Worse still, some of our modern Pythagoreans attempt to reduce the very universe itself, with all its majesty and splendor,
to mathematical equations; and mathematics, as Whitehead has
pointed out, constitutes "the most complete abstractions" at-
tainable by man.[18] This effort at ultimate abstraction is, in fact,
to fall into what Borden P. Bowne has called "the fallacy of
the universal"—the attempt to substitute empty concepts and
mere symbols for real entities.[19]

Symbols, after all, are merely signs which point to a reality or realities beyond themselves; and, apart from this objective reference, they are empty and meaningless. Moreover,
although mathematics supplies us with one of the keys to the
universe, at the same time, since the universe is dynamic while
mathematical concepts are static, it most certainly cannot supply us with the one and only key. Nor can the modern Pythag-
orean prove his case by trying to rob change of all metaphysical significance in his deference to permanence; for the
truth of the matter is that we always and everywhere find
change and permanence linked together, and one is meaningless without the other. There is also more than a grain of
truth in Bowne's insistence that "only the definite and only
the active can be viewed as ontologically real."[20]

The worst feature of the scientific emphasis on analysis
and abstraction is that it inevitably leads to reductionism. Witness the efforts of certain classical economists to reduce man to
that monstrosity known as "the economic man"; and, likewise,
the attempt of certain biologists, psychologists, and even philosophers,[21] in their desire to be "objective," to reduce man to

17 Eddington, *op. cit.*, pp. 251–53.
18 Whitehead, *op. cit.*, p. 51.
19 *Metaphysics*, rev. ed. (New York: American Book Co., 1898), pp.
14–15.
20 Bowne, *op. cit.*, p. 17.
21 Chief among these are the logical positivists; see Gustav Bergmann,
The Metaphysics of Logical Positivism (New York: Longmans, Green & Co.,
1954), pp. 171–74.

a behavioristic process. Often they do not realize that this means thoroughgoing determinism with the implication that, if all men (which includes all scientists) are absolutely determined, then science itself, since it is also the result of conditioning, loses all objectivity. In a day when many scientists have given up the deterministic dogma, some still cling to it with a surprising tenacity. The trouble with thoroughgoing determinism is not only—as we have shown—that it is self-contradictory, but also, in undermining man's sense of moral responsibility, it transforms him into a kind of amoral reaction system devoid of human dignity and capable of any deed no matter how monstrous.[22]

Mention must also be made of the fact that some scientists, as scientific specialists in certain restricted fields, assume the role of metaphysicians. It cannot be denied, of course, that metaphysical adequacy demands a knowledge of the essentials of science. Nor can there be any objection to scientists becoming philosophers or vice versa. In each instance, however, a real attempt must be made to master the field. Moreover, in this day, when physics, in the words of Bridgman, finds itself "verging toward 'philosophy,'"[23] instead of falling into the temptation of trying to view the universe from the narrow perspective of his particular field, the physicist must aim at the broadest possible standpoint. The great danger is that the scientist may attempt to view reality merely from the quantitative standpoint and make the mad effort to force the universe to fit the Procrustean bed of abstractions furnished by one particular science. No one less than Werner Heisenberg has given the timely warning that, instead of being able to develop a total *"world-view,"* natural science, since it is

[22] On the moral implications of determinism, see Sidney Hook, "Necessity, Indeterminism, and Sentimentalism," in Sidney Hook (ed.), *Determinism and Freedom* (New York: Collier Books, 1961), p. 191.

[23] See Percy Bridgman, "Determinism in Modern Science," in Hook (ed.), *op. cit.*, pp. 59–60.

based on a limited perspective, *"can have only a correspondingly limited validity."* [24]

Finally, today science is no longer regarded by the thoughtful as a virtual messiah. Karl Jaspers brings three charges against science and technology: by their corrosive effect on what remains of the "great traditions," they leave men morally and spiritually naked; they dehumanize and depersonalize men by transforming them into virtual robots; and, worst of all, they may destroy mankind. [25] Similarly, many scientists, among them Einstein (while he was yet alive), Bertrand Russell, and Linus Pauling, have warned us that, if science gets out of hand, the end result may be nothing less than the annihilation of the human race. [26]

Three things have become evident from this discussion: that science is not only relevant but even indispensable; that it has serious limitations; and that, since it stresses the metrical or quantitative aspects of reality at the expense of the qualitative, it is not only metaphysically inadequate but actually a threat to man and all his values. To these a fourth must be added, namely, that, since our highest values spring from man's moral and spiritual capacities as they have flowered in the great religions, a serious attempt must be made to fuse the positive aspects of religion and science. In what follows an effort will be made to set the stage for such a fusion.

Impersonalistic versus *Personalistic* Religion

In religion as well as in philosophy, the great debate is between impersonalism and personalism. There are three im-

---

[24] *Op. cit.*, p. 152.

[25] *Future of Mankind*, trans. by E. B. Ashton (Chicago: University of Chicago Press, 1961), pp. 73–74, 318 ff., 337; see also this writer's review of this book in *The Christian Century*, December 27, 1961, pp. 1559–60.

[26] See Einstein's "Military Intrusion in Science," and "The Menace of Mass Destruction," in *op. cit.*, pp. 212–14, 204–06; Russell, in Newman (ed.), *op. cit.*, p. 9; and Pauling, *No More War!* (New York: Dodd, Mead & Co., 1958).

personalistic types of religion with their impersonalistic conceptions of God. The first is the deistic, which stems from
Aristotle: it is that of an indifferent Deity who, as First Cause,
keeps the world process going but has no concern for it. Perhaps the best modern example is Sir James Jeans' concept of
God as a kind of Cosmic Mathematician.[27] This is abstraction-
ism with a vengeance.

The second type of impersonalism is pantheism. God is
viewed as the timeless Absolute of which finite beings and
things are mere passing aspects—like the changing, appearing,
and disappearing clouds as seen against the vast background of
the unchanging heavens. Although India is the home of classical pantheism, it is also found in the West, especially in the
Greek Eleatics, in Plotinus, and in Spinoza. Moreover, so far
as contemporary scientists are concerned, Einstein's conception of God, which was strongly influenced by Spinoza, comes
closest to pantheism.[28]

The third form of impersonalism may be designated naturalistic and humanistic. On the one hand, there are the naturalistic theists, such as Henry Nelson Wieman, who conceive
God in terms of an integrating, value-producing process operating both in nature and in human life, and, on the other,
outright humanists, such as Max Otto and E. Eustace Haydon,
for whom God is little more than a symbol indicative of
man's highest values. Metaphysically speaking, the difference
between the two groups is not great; for both are naturalists.

Instead of conceiving Ultimate Reality in terms of an impersonal process or principle or simply as the All, personalists
or theists think of God as the Supreme Person. This means
neither a crude flesh and blood and thunder deity (the "Mr.

[27] *The Mysterious Universe* (New York: The Macmillan Co., 1934),
pp. 186–87.
[28] See his "Science and Religion," in *op. cit.*, pp. 21–30; also Virgil G.
Hinshaw's comment, in Paul Arthur Schilpp (ed.), *Albert Einstein: Philosopher Scientist* (Evanston, Ill.: Library of Living Philosophers, Inc.), Vol.
II, pp. 659–60.

Jehovah" of popular theology) nor a vast ghostly Shape haunting the universe. On the contrary, God is conceived as self-Conscious Cosmic Mind and Will. He is like the highest aspects of human personality when raised to the *Cosmic* level; and, although He is invisible and unpicturable like our own thoughts and volitions, He is even more real; for, as the human self reveals itself through the body, so, likewise, but on a far vaster scale, God reveals Himself through the entire universe—including the natural processes and laws which science discovers. Personalists also regard God as the Ultimate Source of all the qualitative aspects of reality.

The great debate between personalists today, a debate of which most scientists are not even aware,[29] is that going on between those who still cling to the old classical concept of an omnipotent God and those who think that He is in some sense limited in power.[30] Although this idea of the limited or struggling God is as old as Plato's *Timaeus,* in our day, especially in the light of the theory of evolution and the nuclear revolution, it has attracted many minds. Among these are such names as Alfred North Whitehead, W. P. Montague, Edgar S. Brightman, and Peter Bertocci.

At this juncture, however, something must be said about the significance of theism and personalism as a whole. Not only are the four great prophetic religions, Christianity, Judaism, Islam, and Zoroastrianism, profoundly theistic, but, in spite of strong impersonal elements, there are also theistic tendencies in both Buddhism and Hinduism. Among the great philosophical theists we find Socrates, Plato, Epictetus, Mo-

---

[29] Although the relations of science and religion are discussed at length in Shapley (ed.), *op. cit.,* yet, surprisingly enough, this concept of God is not even mentioned.

[30] For an interesting discussion and defense of this concept, see Edgar Sheffield Brightman, *The Problem of God* (New York: Abingdon Press, 1930). For a similar view, see also this writer's *History and God* (New York: Ronald Press Co., 1952).

tzu, St. Augustine, St. Thomas Aquinas, Ramanuja (India's second-greatest thinker), Descartes, Leibniz, Locke, Berkeley, Kant, Hegel (in spite of certain pantheistic factors), Bergson and Mill (in their later years), James, Royce, the Neo-Thomists, some of the modern existentialists, and the modern philosophical personalists from Lotze and Bowne to Brightman, Flewelling, Werkmeister, and Bertocci.[31] Similarly, among the scientists, we find Copernicus, Galileo, Newton, Kepler, Faraday, Maxwell, Ampère, Pasteur, Eddington, du Noüy, and many others.[32] Moreover, today many scientists, especially physicists, are showing a marked interest in philosophy and religion. This seems to be true even in Russia.[33]

The best way to examine any religious system is to subject its basic world view or world hypothesis to the coherence test. This raises the crucial question: which world hypothesis (the impersonalistic or the personalistic) offers the most adequate explanation of the basic facts with which the universe confronts us? Although the personalistic systems have difficulty in explaining the *dysteleological* facts (disorder, disvalue, the seeming indifference of the universe, and the thousands of ills that plague mankind hourly), the impersonalistic have greater difficulty in explaining the *teleological*, especially in terms of "the wider teleological argument" [34]—which we can only epitomize here.

No personalist or theist is so naive as to contend that the

[31] On theism in general, see James Collins, *God in Modern Philosophy* (Chicago: Henry Regnery Co., 1959); and on personalism, see Edgar Sheffield Brightman, "Personalism (Including Personal Idealism)," in Vergilius Ferm (ed.), *A History of Philosophical Systems* (New York: Philosophical Library, 1950), pp. 340–52.

[32] For an interesting analysis, see Gerald Holton, "Notes on the Religious Orientation of Scientists," in Shapley (ed.), *op. cit.*, pp. 52–64.

[33] See the article, "Will Reds Develop New 'Religion'?" by Harrison E. Salisbury of New York Times Service, in *The Detroit Free Press*, Feb. 13, 1962, p. 1.

[34] For an excellent presentation, see Peter Anthony Bertocci, *Introduction to the Philosophy of Religion* (New York: Prentice-Hall, 1951), pp. 329–88.

new physics proves his thesis. He does insist, however, that, in reducing matter to an intangible energy, it has not only blown the old materialism with its hard atoms sky-high, but it has also prepared the way for a resurgence of idealism and personalism. No physicist knows what energy is ultimately. Since it is basically action, and, since we know energy at first hand in terms of our own acts of will, it may well be that, ultimately, energy, especially structured energy as we find it in the organization of the atom, is really a manifestation of Cosmic Will. Again, while mechanists have tried to crowd mind out of the universe by simply ignoring its creativity, today, in its emphasis on the importance of the observer, relativity has brought it back. Nor, as Frank fondly imagines, is the observer merely "introduced as a figure of speech" which can be eliminated without loss,[35] for, as Heisenberg reminds us, not only is it impossible to "speak of the behaviour of the particle independently of the process of observation," but science itself "always presupposes the existence of man" with all of his capacities.[36] Thus, after trying vainly to reduce man to a mere process or a cipher, science has been forced by the facts to testify to his significance as center of meaning and creativity. This enhances the personalistic theory that man is our best clue to the nature of Reality.

To this must be added the ponderous, massive facts of order, structure, unity, organization, and intelligibility that we find in nature—without which science would be impossible and reason could not operate. Nature did not have to manifest any of these characteristics. Although these facts do not demonstrate the existence of Cosmic Mind and Will, yet, somewhat after the manner in which such facts as vestigial remains, embryology, fossils, etc., suggest evolution, they suggest a

[35] Philipp Frank, *Philosophy of Science* (Englewood Cliffs, N.J.: Prentice-Hall, 1956), p. 230.
[36] See *op. cit.*, pp. 14–16.

Cosmic Mind and Will operating quietly and almost imperceptibly behind the scenes.

Evolution suggests two great questions that science alone cannot answer: Why should it have occurred at all? And what light does it shed on the nature of the underlying creative principle? Some have tried to explain it wholly in terms of natural selection operating on chance variations.[37] These scientists have not read Darwin correctly; for he insists not only that natural selection cannot account "for the incipient stages of useful structures," but also that, as a biologist, he has "nothing to do" either "with the origin of the mental powers" or the origin "of life itself." [38] Natural selection, in fact, exercises a purely negative rather than a creative function. There are three aspects of the evolutionary process that neither natural selection alone nor in conjunction with chance variations can explain adequately: novelties, especially in terms of "the arrival" of "fit" individuals and their "arrival in so many forms; [39] the strange upward push of evolution from level to level—as though in obedience to a plan—in a universe that, according to the Second Law of Thermodynamics, is running down;[40] and the development of a fit environment. These three aspects involve the correlation of so many factors that mere chance seems wholly inadequate. The concept of emergence, since it is a descriptive rather than an explanatory term, will not help matters. It describes what appears and in what order it appears, but it does not tell us *why* it appears.

To crown it all, there is the miracle of man himself with all his creativity, especially his reflective self-consciousness. If, from a purely quantitative standpoint, man is a dwarf, from

[37] See, for example, Hudson Hoagland, "Some Reflections on Science and Religion," in Shapley (ed.), *op. cit.*, p. 23.

[38] See his *Origin of Species,* in Charles W. Eliot (ed.), *The Harvard Classics* (New York: P. F. Collier & Son, 1909), Vol. II, pp. 243–44, 251.

[39] Bowne, *op. cit.*, p. 280.

[40] On this point, see the excellent discussion by du Noüy, *op. cit.*, pp. 224–25.

the standpoint of his highest capacities, he is a giant. In short, it is reasonable to suppose that the universe is more like its highest products than like its lowest; for, while an effect need not resemble its cause, yet the cause must be adequate to produce and to explain the effect.

Finally, there is the realm of higher values. Nature did not have to be intelligible, challenging man to the quest for truth; nor did the mind have to be so constituted as to be capable of discovering truth. Similarly, the world might have been colorless; it did not have to be beautiful; nor did man have to possess the capacity for appreciation. Here again are two correlations which seem to demand a *teleological* explanation. Moreover, in terms of the moral and spiritual ideal, man seems to feel the grip of Something transcendent which will not let him go in spite of his many failures. The higher religions also bear witness to the fact that there has been religious as well as biological and social and scientific evolution; and, if there have been great scientific geniuses, there have also been great moral and spiritual geniuses, out of whose herculean labors has risen man's vision of a better world.

Suffice it to say then that, in view of the many converging lines of evidence, the personalistic or theistic theory of reality, like the theory of evolution in biology, seems to be the most adequate. Although in neither case is complete demonstration possible, yet, in the light of certain massive lines of evidence all pointing in the same direction, both are superior to their nearest rivals.

The impersonalist will of course immediately point to the vast array of dysteleological facts. This writer is quite willing to admit that the old classical theism, with its concept of an omnipotent God, is archaic. Evolution, with its revelation of the cost of progress as species after species went down blind alleys to perish, the production of monstrosities such as *Tyrannosaurus*, and the general "randomness" of which George

Gaylord Simpson makes so much,[41] has given it its *coup de grâce*.

Since everywhere experience discloses certain basic types of facts, namely, order versus disorder, good versus evil, beauty versus ugliness, we must expand our world hypothesis to include all of these facts; and many personalists have done precisely this thing, in terms of the God who struggles with the wild forces of chaos. Just what these wild, chaotic forces are, ultimately, no one knows;[42] but both in the destructive force which is released when the nucleus of the atom is cracked and in the wild, elemental forces of the subconscious that underlie our own self-consciousness, we may get a glimpse of this limiting power. Be this as it may, since the concept of a powerful but struggling God serves to explain both the teleological and the dysteleological facts, and since many thinkers have remained theists and others have found their way back to theism and personalism by this route when all other routes seemed closed, it deserves much more serious attention, especially on the part of scientists, than it has received.

Is Personalism Incompatible with Science?

Although religion has been largely personalistic, science has been predominantly impersonalistic and even mechanistic. Many scientists have been hostile to the very idea of a personal God. Einstein even went so far as to insist that the idea of the "personal God" has caused most of this conflict.[43] Scientists object to personalistic religion for a number of reasons.

First of all, they bring the charge of anthropomorphism.

[41] In *The Meaning of Evolution*, rev. ed. (New York: New American Library, 1949), p. 38.

[42] In some elemental sense, they are probably psychic, the manifestation of something like Schopenhauer's blind Will.

[43] See his "Science and Religion," in *op. cit.*, p. 27. Likewise in the volume by Shapley, while some of the contributors are theists, most of them are very critical of personalism.

Usually they have in mind either the wise and kind "Mr. Jehovah" to whom Warder Clyde Allee was introduced by his Quaker parents,[44] or the fierce, erratic Supernatural Magician whose chief business was to throw sinners into hell, but who, when his favorites were in trouble, could sometimes be cajoled into interfering with the natural order. Some also contend that not only is there little or no evidence for the existence of a personal God, but, since personalism uses self-conscious mind and will as its clue, it is subjective, while science is decidedly empirical and objective. From a pragmatic standpoint, they may likewise insist that it was only after science dropped teleological concepts and began thinking in mechanical and mathematical terms that it succeeded in understanding and mastering nature. Finally, many scientists believe that God's empire is shrinking and that he is on his way out.

In answer to these charges, the personalist will point to the massive nature of the empirical evidence for God's existence, and he will insist that the time is ripe for scientists to rethink their theology. He will also insist that they distinguish between the crude anthropomorphism of popular theology and the profound personalism of modern theistic philosophers; for, while the former imputes man's total nature, including his weaknesses, to God, the latter contend that, since man seems to be creation's highest product, it is reasonable to suppose that the Ultimate Cause is something like the highest in man. All of our thinking, in fact, is in a certain sense subjective and anthropomorphic. Instead of merely reflecting nature like a mirror, we grasp nature indirectly through the mind's ability to interpret sense data by means of ideas. The great danger is that if we do not try to understand Ultimate Reality in terms of its highest product, we employ a kind of second-rate anthropomorphism. This is what the scientist does when he takes the term *machine*—a human concept derived from a human invention—and tries to apply it to the universe as a whole.

[44] See his interesting article in Newman (ed.), *op. cit.*, p. 244.

Because the mind is in a certain sense subjective and intangible is no sign that it is not real. Not only does all knowledge, including scientific knowledge, come in terms of the subjective processes of thought, thus presupposing their reality, but every attempt to deny the inner self also presupposes it. Besides, so far as intangibles are concerned, if the mind is intangible, so is the mysterious energy to which matter is reducible. Moreover, *coherence* rather than tangibility constitutes the test of truth. The fact must also be stressed that while the mechanistic approach has opened many doors and must continue to be used as long as it is fruitful, it has already become evident that it has obvious limitations when applied to Reality as a whole. In other words, it must not be pressed too far.

Elsewhere this writer has dealt at length with the objection that science is displacing God.[45] Here a few general observations must suffice. It cannot be denied that the conception of God as wrathful Tyrant and Supernatural Magician is being displaced with each new scientific discovery. It is far otherwise, however, with the conception of God as self-conscious Mind and Will struggling with the forces of chaos and constantly expressing Himself, not only through all the various levels of law and order in the universe, but also through all its qualitative aspects—and supremely through the highest creative capacities of man himself, including the latter's scientific triumphs. Not only does this conception not conflict with the claims of science, but also, since God is conceived as involved in all of life and as active on all levels, rather than as shrinking, His realm is really expanding. It also means that man can come to the aid of God as well as God to the aid of man, in the common task of building a new world.

Perhaps it is well to close this section with a résumé of the personalistic implications of science itself. It has already

[45] *Perplexing Problems of Religion* (St. Louis: Bethany Press, 1954), pp. 73–77.

become clear that all scientific knowledge is personal in the sense that it comes through mind and is tested by mind. We never know nature apart from mind: it is always nature plus mind and nature by means of mind. Again, all scientific conquests of nature really represent conquests of mind. Reflective self-consciousness is, in truth, the greatest miracle in the universe.

Finally, there are the implications of the new astronomy, the new physics, and the new psychology. Not only does each new conquest of space represent a triumph of mind, but the fact that astronomers are becoming increasingly certain that reflective mind is not restricted to one small planet serves to increase the probabilities in favor of the personalistic hypothesis.[46] It has likewise become clear that the new physics makes it much easier to conceive the universe in idealistic and personalistic terms. The same also applies to the new psychology, that is, parapsychology.[47]

Personalism and the Future of Man

This concluding paragraph was written the morning after this writer had listened to a lecture by a missile expert. Instead of posing as a tough scientist working hand in hand with the military, he kept saying: "I do not know what all this will lead to." He feared that the time is not far distant when some nation might actually put a stream of satellites around the earth, each armed with hydrogen bomb warheads and subject to the whim of some man who, simply by pushing a button, might bring the final calamity.

As many others have observed, today the big question is not so much, What does the future hold for man? but rather,

[46] See Donald H. Menzel, "Other Worlds Than Ours," in *The Atlantic*, November, 1955, p. 25.

[47] On parapsychology, besides Rhine, *op. cit.*, see the statement by Edwin C. Kemble of Harvard, in Shapley, *op. cit.*, p. 249.

Does man have a future? Although personalistic religion with its stress on human dignity undoubtedly furnishes the best basis for a world society, especially since it places the concept of human dignity in a cosmic perspective, which impersonalism cannot do, yet the fact remains that, if man is to have a future and a worthy future, there must be a common effort such as the world has never seen before. This means that all men of good will, regardless of their particular creed, must join hands in the great unfinished task of making a new world. The hour is late.[48]

[48] For an exploration of the peace problem, see this writer's *A Way of Survival* (New York: Bookman Associates, 1954).

CHAPTER 11

Changing Cultural Climate

by LYMAN RUTLEDGE

Unitarian-Universalist Fellowship

I

THE ISLANDS where these conferences are held may serve to illustrate the main contention of this paper. There are nine in the archipelago known as the Isles of Shoals—nine at high tide when Seavey is separated from White and Malaga from Smuttynose, but only seven at low tide when the smaller islands are seen to be connected with their near neighbors, bringing vividly before us the fact that all islands and continents are connected under the surface. The definition of an island therefore does not represent separate entities, but only separate manifestations of the same entity.

As we look from our island abode into the deep waters surrounding, we are reminded that animal life began in the ocean, not on the land. We would never have become *homo*, much less *sapiens*, if the same elemental forces that lifted the islands and surrounded them with the waters of separation had not also developed a cycle of interaction between plant and animal life. By this process an atmosphere was brewed containing a formula of carbon, hydrogen, oxygen, and nitrogen

180

conducive to the growth of animal forms far beyond the stage
of fish or reptile.

In much the same way mankind has unwittingly created
a cultural atmosphere conducive to the continued development of his higher nature into forms as yet beyond his vision.
We surmise that man has not yet attained his physical maturity, but we are certain that he has only begun to develop his
cultural life. Indeed we have not yet come awake to the profound influence of cultural climate. It is only beginning to
dawn upon us that as our animal nature responds to a so-
called physical environment, so our personalities respond to
a non-physical or cultural environment. We are only glimps-
ing the fact that our cultural climate is literally reshaping the
earth. It is now within our power either to extinguish all
higher forms of animal life, or to promote their development.
This power is being exercised through the cultural climate
that emerges from our day-by-day living.

II

When Captain John Smith visited these islands in 1614,
he wrote, "What sport doth yield a more pleasing content,
and less hurt or charge than angling with a hooke; and crossing the sweet ayre from Ile to Ile, over the silent streams of a
calm sea, wherein the most curious may find pleasure, profit
and content?" [1] From that day to this the climate of the Isles
of Shoals has been praised for its health-restoring effect, and
its exceptional charm. John Smith was caught up for the moment in the sheer joy of living. His whole nature responded to
the crisp, resilient air and the refreshing breeze that cools but
does not chill.

In later centuries, notably the nineteenth, physicians in
mainland cities prescribed a few weeks at the Shoals, and often
spent vacations here. In 1845 a Mr. Williams of England, a

---

[1] *Travels and Works*, p. 213.

man of means but in failing health, was sent here by his New York physician, and made this his summer home for many years. He it was who suggested to Mr. Thomas B. Laighton, then keeper of White Island Light, that he build a health-resort hotel on Appledore; and thus began a new tradition that gave the islands a cultural atmosphere in keeping with its physical climate. Here for many years Dr. Joseph Warren and Dr. S. Weir Mitchell of Philadelphia, Dr. Henry I. Bowditch and Dr. H. R. Stedman of Boston, Dr. Richter, and others came with patients.

The secret they well knew was that the rugged terrain, the tonic atmosphere, and the aesthetic charm of sky and sea called forth the inner resources of the patient. The favorable environment induced him to heal himself.

Cultural climate has a similar effect on mental and emotional states. The best in art, literature, music, society is tonic to the soul. The obligations of citizenship are a challenge. The best in human nature responds and rises to a keener sense of personal well-being than physical environment alone can induce.

Today as we enjoy what we are pleased to call a salubrious climate, we are little aware of the high wind currents and upper jet streams that have become the stock in trade of weather forecasters. The discovery of jet streams came late in the science of meteorology. The significance of upper jets in cultural climate will come still later. The parallel between the two is striking.

Cultural jet streams drift over human history, giving direction to the winds of destiny, shepherding clouds of controversy, mothering spring breeze and winter hurricane. Little men are buffeted hither and yon like dust in a fitful swirl, whisked down beaten paths into broad highways, and suddenly dropped, like autumn leaves, into unexpected graves. Even as no micro-organism on a grain of dust has the least premonition of its relationship to upper currents, so we of the human family are unaware that we are being swept up by on-rushing trends in our cultural atmosphere.

III

Three main currents command our attention: "The Will to Live," "Religious Expression," and "Scientific Approach."

The will to live is the one characteristic common to all living organisms. Albert Schweitzer, observing the play of wild beasts in the African jungle, suddenly felt a flash of insight—the answer to a question that had troubled him for many years. He says:

> Lost in thought I sat on the deck of the barge, struggling to find the elementary and universal conception of the ethical which I had not discovered in any philosophy. Sheet after sheet I covered with disconnected sentences, merely to keep myself concentrated on the problem. Late on the third day, at the very moment when, at sunset, we were making our way through a herd of hippopotamuses, there flashed upon my mind, unforeseen and unsought, the phrase, "Reverence for Life." The iron door had yielded. . . . Now I knew that the ethical acceptance of the world and of life, together with the ideals of civilization contained in this concept, has a foundation in thought. . . .
>
> The most immediate fact of man's consciousness is the assertion: "I am life which wills to live, in the midst of life which wills to live." [2]

Lower orders of life, from micro-organisms to elephants, are animated by this elemental urge, but man alone is aware of it, and his awareness goes far beyond his instinct for self-preservation. It reaches out toward the fulfillment of his highest potentialities. He feels within his nature the keen desire for knowledge, the hope for better living, the mounting am-

---

[2] Albert Schweitzer, *Out of My Life and Thought* (New York: Henry Holt & Co., 1949), pp. 156–57.

bition to express his higher nature in some lasting or permanent form. Hence he cannot accept any philosophy, doctrine, dogma, or interpretation of the universe that denies him this larger exercise of his faculties.

Not content with the limits of his own experience he looks into the heart of being and sees that the "will to live" has its counterpart in all forms of material substance. The rock holds its shape, the atom maintains its integrity, the stars hold to their courses.

Moreover, each one of these is forever expressing more than its own individual existence; it has emergent characteristics that enter into human awareness, as when sodium and chlorine are united in the savoriness of salt, or when carbon, hydrogen, and oxygen emerge into the sweetness of sugar. What do these elements know about their own savoriness or sweetness? These qualities are known only to the living tongue that tastes. Even so man gives to the humble elements a fulfillment that they cannot know themselves, and he, like them, contributes to a realm of being beyond his own awareness. Are not wisdom, insight, and the whole galaxy of "human virtues" emergent qualities that gladden the heart of the world?

Some may wonder whether this is not leading to a dangerous form of mysticism. I certainly hope not, for to me it is a logical and inevitable interpretation of demonstrable "facts."

Religion is the dynamic that we feel in our "will to live," and from which arise our finest qualities, whatever they may be, as faithfully as the diamond lends its brilliance to the joy of humankind.

IV

The main currents of religious feeling are expressed through religious institutions, which in turn preserve the traditions, rituals, and teachings associated with deeper experience. All these taken together we shall designate as the

Church, and those who preside over them, the priesthood, meaning thereby to include all world religions, denominations, and sects of whatever name or origin. Our present concern is with the cultural atmosphere that presides over all religious expression. We shall not belabor the question as to the actual climate created by religious institutions—the Church and its priesthood—but shall try to present the ideal toward which they all aspire.

The general atmosphere of the Church is charged with faith and hope based on the assurance of divine infallibility and absolute authority. "To doubt would be disloyalty, to falter would be sin." These expressions arise from man's inmost feeling of confidence in the universe as a whole, in the "moving power which presides," and in his own intuition. "Whatsoever a man doeth, seemeth right in his own eyes." That which is recognized in the Church as "Divine Revelation," "the infallible word of God," "the beatific vision," is the fruit of intuitive knowledge. The intuition itself is of divine origin, and conscience is said to be "the life of God in the soul of man." There can be no higher authority, hence no greater assurance. Within this climate has grown up a remarkable assemblage of virtues. To name them is to describe the spiritual climate that all good churchmen and priests are striving to create.

Entering the doors of the Church (Temple, Synagogue, Mosque, or Meetinghouse) the communicant feels the presence of a Benevolent Ruler of Human Destiny, "whose power creates and whose wisdom guides." Emanating from this divine source is an atmosphere of assurance—"For underneath are the everlasting arms"—and compassion—"He remembereth not our transgressions," but "Healeth our diseases."

Here is a climate of faith, hope, and aspiration. The windows of this sanctuary open out upon a friendly universe. Man sees there no hostility to man, no vengeful wrath or needless torture, but the ever-present challenge to "overcome evil with good," and in all things do his best. In this atmosphere the soul feels at home and happy, for here is the spirit of universal brotherhood—of good will toward all men, with kindliness, charity, and mutual understanding tempering daily life. Here the virtues of loyalty, integrity, and humility come to blossom, and the fountains of Divine Love are forever flowing.

In this climate our better natures respond with emotions of joy and peace, of awe and holiness, of wonder, adoration, and praise.

In the presence of the Most High we are made to feel our own unworthiness and corresponding desire to be forgiven for our weakness, while we renew our efforts to lead better lives. For the religious sentiment is life feeling after its own fulfillment, pushing toward its higher destiny.

V

Since religion as a dynamic force comprehends the whole of life, it includes science in its onward sweep, and we find ourselves asking what contribution science is making to our cultural climate, specifically to religious expression. It is difficult to find language suitable to this theme, since most of us do not think of laboratories as shrines, scientists as high priests, nor their work as spiritual. Nevertheless men of science are fulfilling the requirements of religion in many ways that they would be reluctant to acknowledge.

First and most valuable to human society is the personality of the scientist himself. To make this less personal I have cast the thought in the idiom of the King James version:

> Behold the man of science—
> He seeketh out the dark corners of the earth.
> He mounteth with wings into heaven,
> Nor doth he ignore the dust beneath his feet.
> He will not slumber nor sleep
> Until he hath reached his goal.

He is withal a man of faith,
For if he had no faith he would not seek.
Yea, his faith is firmer than rock,
Stronger than tempered steel,
Purer than fountains of life,
And will not be broken or moved.

Honor and justice are his robes.
He knoweth not the envy of wealth,
Nor doth he reach for power,
Nor lift his hand against his fellow man.

If there be virtue in humility,
Behold, the scientist surpasseth all,
For when he findeth one small grain of truth—
A jewel for the crown of Wisdom—

He giveth it freely unto all mankind,
And praiseth his colleagues for their skill.
In quietness and modesty doth he toil,
And boasteth not of his accomplishment.

He is a friend to all the sons of man.
Yea, though he be of alien race,
Of foreign blood, of high or low degree,
He placeth laurels on the honored brow.

Behold, I have given him the pen,
Saith the Most High,
That he may write the Sacred Word
Which I have spoken.
For I have laid before all men
The Book of Life—
Even the Earth and all the stars,
And every living thing.
These are my Words
Wherein my being is expressed;
My Wisdom spelleth out the stars;
My Power is written in the dust;

My Love is spoken in the heart.
And thou, the scientist, art my scribe,
To read the Open Book,
To translate my spoken word
Into human language for thy fellow men.
Though in modesty thou namest not my name,
I welcome thee into my heart of hearts.

The second contribution from science is to theology—the intellectual phase of religious experience. For science has from the beginning produced the material from which the theologian has built his mighty works. The scientist does not arrogate to himself the privilege of constructing religious doctrines, dogmas, or theological opinions. He confines himself to the careful observation, analysis, and description of the world as he finds it. But from this description the theologian creates the image of the divine. From age to age the description changes —as from a flat earth, borne on the backs of elephants or turtles, to the round earth circling through space. Slowly the theologian changes his view and feeling, as from the image of God in human form to God as a spirit in whom we live and move and have our being. As the scientist delves deeper into the nature of the material universe, spreading the heavens into an infinitude of light, opening the atom to release an almighty power, so the theologian (in his heart if not in his words) expands and enriches his theology.

The theologian, however, in our Western world, has failed to perceive the advantage of the scientific attitude, namely that of humility in the presence of truth. The scientist ventures his own opinion tentatively, formulates his "laws of nature," subject to change, discards old theories when new knowledge proves them inadequate, claims no unique or superior revelation, claims no absolute authority, and submits all his findings to public criticism. The theologians have felt from early ages that they must speak with divine authority, and their interpretations must be accepted as divine revelation, therefore as absolute truth which "changeth not nor is changed." This is the chief point of conflict between science and religion. It may be dispelled by a simple change of attitude. The theologian, if he had the faith of a scientist, would confess that his theology is a human opinion, not a divine revelation, and is therefore held tentatively, subject to change as greater truth is brought to light.

The third contribution of science is in the area of physical well-being. All great religions have much to say about the healing power of their various rituals and special beliefs. But of all means thus far advanced to heal disease or improve the physical stamina of the race, the scientific approach is most effective. Hippocrates first began the careful observation of symptoms, and taught his pupils to note accurately the effect of each drug, medicine, or specific treatment. Following his instruction, the medical profession has healed more diseases than all the shrines, rituals, and so-called miracles of the ages have done. If then the religionists were sincere in their desire to fulfill their own teaching in regard to physical well-being, they would ask science to apply its healing power. Does this not apply equally to mental health? Is it not our obligation, as well as our supreme opportunity, to ask science to evaluate our efforts to restore health and sanity to our communicants?

Science contributes not only to our intellectual, mental, and physical life, but also to our emotions. Here we observe no direct application of the scientific process, but merely the influence of intellect over emotional states. Our thinking may excite, depress, enrich, or impoverish our feelings. Note the play of emotion as one discovers that the diamond he has bought at a high price is only paste. Nothing has changed except knowledge.

> "My heart leaps up when I behold
> A rainbow in the sky,"

for my nature responds to harmony of color in the broken arc, but now the magic of the intellect nurtured by the wisdom of science opens before my mind's eye a vision of rainbow colors filling all the heavens. My emotions respond to the ineffable thought—the heavens become a blaze of glory, a revelation of supernal beauty.

So the whole world is a fragment of a rainbow, and as the scientist reveals to the eager mind more and more of its true nature, our feeling of awe and wonder steadily deepens. We can no longer speak of Nature as casual, or secular, or "merely natural." Science has taught us to see it as a pattern of motion whose inner beauty outshines the sun. The mystery of its origin may never be solved. Its ultimate destiny may never be surmised, but its present life is the miracle of miracles, stirring our deepest emotions.

What then may be said for our response to our own individual experience? "Teach me myself, myself to know." I am done with all the childish concepts of man. We see him now as a living unit in a living universe, sharing its grandeur, feeling its beauty, aware of its movement, for we are in fact the universe speaking. Each person is a focal point in universal experience. Nor can he by any or all means separate himself from his total environment. It is his function as a living organism to feel the surge of universal life, and express the joy of eternal being. If he is unhappy or disillusioned, it is because he has failed to understand the nature of life, and of the universe to which he belongs. Science can help him to understand.

VI

Religion and science alike develop their rituals from the universal will to live. The devout worshiper of whatever denomination or sect is doing what he is taught to believe will bring him more and better life, or will enhance the life of others. His passion is to save his own soul and redeem the world. If he "splits shingles for the glory of God," it is because he thinks God is served by honest toil. If in solitude he retreats from the company of men and seeks communion with the Most High it is because he believes his own life will be exalted by this act.

Science follows a very different ritual. The formal service of the Church gives place to the informal search for factual information. The shrine gives place to the laboratory and the counting of beads to the analysis of statistics. The scientist in his methodical experiments and interpretations is doing what he believes will enrich his own mind and serve mankind on the highest level. The difference is not in motivation but in method.

The age-long conflict between religion and science stems from the dual nature of human personality. Intellect and emotion should normally function harmoniously together, but when in conflict they develop a schizophrenic turmoil wherein each asserts its authority over the other. Emotions and intellect are woven together in the fabric of experience. To separate the two or throw them into conflict is fatal. Each without the other is less than human.

For better understanding we may note here that intellect sees, whereas emotions only feel. Thought is one step removed from emotion, and both are a step removed from action. Insight is a function of the cerebrum, sensation of the cerebellum, and action of both. Professor A. A. Roback devoted a large volume to the study of the veto power of the cerebrum. His argument was that the mind inhibits action while weighing alternatives, then releases emotional energy in action toward the chosen goal. He went so far as to say that the ability to say No is the one chief distinction of man, setting him above all other primates.

Thought has no energy of its own, and emotions have no vision. The mind may see clearly what course to follow, yet remain inactive.

Since the intellect has no energy or emotion of its own, it is spoken of as heartless. We are quite familiar with the cool reason and cold logic in contrast to warm feelings and hot passion. When emotions insist on having their own way in the face of "better judgment," the intellect is coerced into a series of handsprings called "rationalizing." Thus the emotions whip the intellect into saying it believes what no rational mind can believe, and this is the origin of the conflict between science and religion. It is really a fight for supremacy between emotion and intellect. Shakespeare often touched upon this inner conflict, and outdid the psychologist in his description of it.

"How all occasions do inform against me," exclaims Hamlet in despair.

> "Sure, he that made us with such large discourse,
> Looking before and after, gave us not
> That capability and god-like reason
> To fust in us unusd. Now, whether it be
> Bestial oblivion, or some craven scruple
> Of thinking too precisely on the event,
>   ... I do not know
> Why yet I live to say 'this thing's to do,'
> Sith I have cause and will, and strength, and means,
> To do it....
>   Rightly to be great
> Is not to stir without great argument,
> But greatly to find quarrel in a straw
> When honor's at the stake." [3]

> "Thus conscience doth make cowards of us all;
> And thus the native hue of resolution

[3] William Shakespeare, *Hamlet*, Act IV, Scene 4.

Is sicklied o'er with the pale cast of thought,
And enterprises of great pith and moment
With this regard their currents turn awry,
And lose the name of action." [4]

Emotions, on the other hand, have energy but poor vision. "Love is blind." People act on "blind impulse."

"I am the very slave of circumstances and impulse..." said Byron, "borne away with every breath!" [5]

The ideal, everywhere acknowledged, is the well-integrated personality, wherein emotions are disciplined by thought, and energy guided by reason. Literature is replete with admonitions: "Look before you leap," "Be sure you are right, then go ahead." Charles F. Dole once defined the purpose of religious education as "Encouraging the young to think clearly, feel deeply, and act nobly."

We conclude that emotion without reason may be a dangerous impulse, that reason without emotion may be a devastating futility. Religion helps to preserve the normal temperature of good health, the intellect warmed by emotion, passion cooled by meditation.

VII

It would seem, after six thousand years of living experience, that man would have resolved this inner conflict and created a cultural climate more in keeping with the ideals so eloquently expressed by both science and religion. Yet we have failed in all these centuries to eradicate crime, poverty, and disease. We have lived to witness the most horrendous massacres known to man—the most devastating wars, and the most menacing threats of annihilation. Why does war still

[4] *Ibid.*, Act III, Scene 1.
[5] Lord Byron, *Sardanapalus,* Act IV, Scene 1.

scourge the nations, and why is peace so unattainable? Why did Professor Lawrence Kubie of Yale say in a commencement address that ours is a "Culture of Doom"? Why did Professor William McDougall, while at Harvard, say that he could see the American people "dancing gaily down the broad highway to destruction"? Why have so many of our most thoughtful citizens told us that ours is a "sick society"? We wonder what has happened—or failed to happen? In the words of the Apostle Paul, "Who shall deliver us from the body of this death?"

VIII

Our Institute on Religion in an Age of Science grew out of such questions as these. In 1950 a few individuals felt that one great barrier was a "communication failure." It was observed that leaders in Church and State, Industry, Arts, and Sciences were developing jargons, or special vocabularies, of their own. Debates and long discussions grew out of careless use of words. The point at issue was often lost in the fog of unfamiliar expressions. Our great need was for better understanding among representatives of various faiths. With this in mind a conference was arranged to bring religious leaders together for a week on Star Island. Each was to present some aspect of his own denominational background, and all were to consider that the united or co-ordinated effort of all might do to help solve the world's great problems. The conference was assembled under the name of "The Coming Great Church." It soon became evident that the name itself was afflicted with the very disease it hoped to cure. It gave the impression that someone was trying to form a new Church to supersede all others. The intent was to see whether the Church as an institution—existing Churches, not a new Church—might not become more effective if the acknowledged leaders were to learn each other's vocabularies, i.e., their points of view.

Such a result, it was hoped, might grow out of the personal acquaintance and free discussions at the Islands. The results were in a high degree convincing. Men and women of many faiths attended, and carried home a new inspiration. The conference grew steadily for three summers and then resolved itself into a permanent organization under the present name, "The Institute on Religion in an Age of Science." Here again there was some misunderstanding of the name, for some still thought the purpose was to foster a new religion. It had to be explained—all too frequently—that no such venture was contemplated, but the original policy and method was being continued in a broader field. The question constantly in the foreground was what religion and science could do jointly for the betterment of mankind. No one has yet undertaken to predict the ultimate outcome, but since their inception the meetings have yielded some valuable publications. The chapel addresses by Dr. Edwin P. Booth have been published in two small volumes, *The Greater Church* (1951) and *Religion in an Age of Science—A Tract for the Times* (1954). More recently eighteen typical addresses by noted scientists have been published in the volume entitled *Science Ponders Religion*, edited by Professor Harlow Shapley (1960). Now comes this companion volume, *Religion Ponders Science*. These unfortunately cannot reflect some of the most important aspects of the conferences, namely the steady integration of thought and feeling, the stimulating effect of long discussions, and the subtle influence of the Island environment.

The timeliness of these conferences is attested by the growing number of similar gatherings and organizations that have emerged in various parts of the country, notably the Society for the Scientific Study of Religion on the Atlantic seaboard and in California. These are not committed to the discovery or launching of a "new religion" but to a better understanding of life and its potentialities.

IX

During the last half century, men of deeper insight have begun to chart cultural jet streams on a comprehensive scale. Like weather prophets, they study conditions that whip us into war, poison us with cultural fall-out, lull us into lethal slumber, or nurse us back to health. H. G. Wells produced an *Outline of History*. Oswald Spengler in *The Decline of the West* wrought out a mathematical study of human events, attempting to show the rhythmic rise and fall of cultural tides. Vernon Louis Parrington wrote *Main Currents in American Thought;* Will Durant, *The Story of Civilization;* and Arnold Toynbee, *A Study of History*. Toynbee in his chapter on "Standardization through Disintegration" introduces our theme. He reminds us that Penelope wove a new pattern each day, and each night unpicked the day's work, but though she seemed forever bound to the task of doing and undoing, her toil was not in vain, because she had a "song in her soul, 'With him I will be reunited.' " Toynbee then says:

> If, as it turns out, even Penelope has not drawn her threads in vain, what of the mightier weaver whose work is our study, and whose song finds human expression in the verse of Goethe?

> "In currents of life, in tempests of motion,
> In fervour of act, in the fire, in the storm,
> > Hither and thither,
> > Over and under,
> > Wend I and wander;
> > Birth and the grave,
> > Limitless ocean,
> > Where the restless wave
> > Undulates ever,
> > Under and over
> > Their seething strife

> Heaving and weaving
> The changes of life.
> At the whirring loom of Time unawed
> I work the living mantle of God."

Toynbee continues:

The work of the Spirit of Earth, as he weaves and draws his threads on the Loom of Time, is the temporal history of man as this manifests itself in the geneses and growths and breakdowns and disintegrations of human societies; and in all this welter of life and tempest of action we can hear the beat of elemental rhythm.[6]

X

Cultural climate changes with changing emphasis, and here is the key to possible control.

Seen in the perspective outlined in the foregoing pages, the Church is dedicated to man's life in its wholeness, and includes science as a means to a larger end. If the Church as an institution were true to its larger obligation—were to change emphasis from fixed dogma to advancing knowledge—it would develop many localized functions, and a vast army of specialized administrators. These would include scientists from all disciplines, philosophers of all schools, historians, research workers, and experimenters.

There would be creative artists in various fields—music, sculpture, drama, painting—to express man's aesthetic feeling.

The Church would create an atmosphere of honest, devoted seeking after truth, of constant happy expression of man's highest thought and deepest feeling. It would lead him to the arena of noblest action, and open to him the doors of new and greater opportunity. It would inspire him with the

[6] Arnold Toynbee, *A Study of History* (Abridged edition; New York: Oxford Univ. Press, 1947), p. 556.

thought that he does not need to wait for death to usher him into the presence of the Almighty, for he is already standing in that presence, and need only bow in humble recognition. Thus religion and science together would create a cultural climate wherein the Law and the Prophets would be fulfilled and all mankind would have life, and have it more abundantly.

Chapter 12

A Philosopher of Religion Ponders Science

---

by PAUL ARTHUR SCHILPP

Northwestern University

THE AVERAGE RELIGIONIST does not *ponder* science; he enjoys its results in applied science by using them. *To ponder* means "to think deeply about, to weigh." The ordinary religionist, as such, is not that much interested in science—except insofar as he may be afraid of what science might do to his religion.

The Nature of Ethical Religion

Before we can ponder science—or anything else, for that matter—from some specific standpoint, the nature and position of that standpoint must be clarified. Which means that, if we are to ponder science from the standpoint of religion, we had better make clear what we mean by religion. This all the more so because religion has meant an almost infinite variety of things to different people.

For the purposes of this discussion I shall define *ethical religion* as follows:

"Commitment to the highest, noblest, sublimest, and best that I can think, imagine or understand; and a Way of Life commensurate with the greatness of that to which I have committed myself."

In other words, for this writer neither dogma nor creed nor orthodoxy nor ritual nor institution nor sacred writings nor transcendence are the *core* or *essence* of ethical religion. Its core or essence are *Commitment* and a *Way of Life!* And, although I have used superlatives in my definition of ethical religion, none of the terms are meant to be taken as ultimates, still less as absolutes. Like human life itself, the terms are meant to be open-ended.

What a person values most highly and is ready to give himself to without reservation constitutes that person's *real* —that is to say, actually practiced rather than given lip-service —religion. In the case of most Americans, for example, their *real* religion is not the God they claim to worship on Sunday or on Friday evening, but America, the nation-state. It is this nation-state to which they give their supreme loyalty and devotion; just as materialism (theistic materialism in order to distinguish it from the atheistic "dialectical" materialism of the Communists) is most Americans' real philosophy.

The orthodox religionist seems, almost at all times, to have been afraid of the truths discovered by science. Remember Galileo's fate at the hands of the orthodox religion of his day! Or churchmen's attitude towards Charles Darwin and the evolutionary hypothesis. Even now, when we have entered the Space Age, there are plenty of religionists who still prefer to think of our Earth, this tiny planet of one of the lesser suns in one of the smaller galaxies, as the hub of the universe and of God as the particular God of this Earth, primarily—if not, indeed, exclusively—concerned with the fate of each individual on this planet; and of the coming, death, and (so-called) resurrection of Christ as almighty God's means of salvation and redemption for "sinful" man on this planet. A provincial point of view this, in our Space Age, to put it mildly!

There are those who, not merely in the name of religion but of general human value-judgment, have been arguing for an at least temporary moratorium on science—because of the threat to human existence as the result of the achievement of nuclear fission. Such a suggestion renders service neither to science nor to religion. If "truth shall make us free," then even only relatively free men cannot give up its pursuit without irreparable damage to our very freedom. I have almost unbounded respect and admiration for the late Mahatma Gandhi. In his attempt, however, to hold India back from industrialization he was not merely sadly mistaken, but was at least in part responsible for the all too slow progress India was able to make at the time. Knowledge used for evil ends is no good reason for impugning the knowledge; it is the wrong *use* of the knowledge that is at fault. Nuclear fission, for example, will be able, even in the very near future, to bring untold blessings to mankind in all kinds of areas, such as power, health and medicine, etc. It does not have to be used for the destruction of the human race. If it should finally be so used, this will not be the result of the newly found knowledge, but the fault of the immoral and unethical behavior of men, of governments, and of nations.

And it is true that science as such will not be able to stop governments and nations from such immoral conduct. Here is a function *par excellence* of ethical religion.

For a religion whose supreme values (whether thought of as humanistic mundane or as transcendental) are truth, goodness, and beauty (rather than nationalism or material prosperity), its view of science is relatively simple, if not, indeed, self-evident.

The Nature of Empirical Natural Science

Empirical science, I take it, is the serious and systematic search for describable and (at least within limits) verifiable truths (not *Truth!*) in specific and specifiable areas. For our purposes it is unnecessary to name those areas, except to say that they are all areas capable of yielding to descriptive and, for the most part, quantitative analysis and measurement—where qualitative aspects, even when present, are by definition ruled out of consideration.

With those qualifications, science is essentially a search for such truths. The scientist always wants to know how things behave and what makes them tick as they do. If from such analysis of phenomena he is able to arrive at generalized conclusions that stand up under probing tests of empirical and verifiable observation, he is very happy indeed. In fact, the more generalized (and the more generally applicable) he finds them, the better. For this is the procedure by which we have gotten the statements of what we now refer to as natural laws (or the laws of nature). Einstein's search, on which he was engaged to the day of his death, was for a unified field-theory, a mathematical formula that would, in one formulation, have accounted for all the facts, data, and events of the physical universe and its operations. Whether or not such a single, all-inclusive mathematical formulation, descriptive of the entire physical universe, is or is not possible, this writer is not qualified to judge. What is important for our consideration is the fact that the scientist's commitment is to a search for truth, a search that is endless and relentless, whether it leads to a monistic or pluralistic universe.

Such search—dedication, commitment—itself bears out religion (at least one aspect of ethical religion): commitment to truth, no matter where it might lead, irrespective of consequences, *and* however finite, limited, and relative any actually discovered truth may be. For over against too many orthodox religionists who seem to make claims of having gotten hold of infinite, absolute, and no longer limited Truth, our scientists—despite the tremendous success of their achievements—have long since recognized and admitted the fact that even scientific truth (in any area or realm) is at best always only finite, limited, and relative. This recognition is a fact deserving of more than passing notice. For it not merely keeps the scientist forever on his toes, checking and rechecking and revising his results, not merely constantly on the lookout for something new and previously unnoticed, but also intellectually humble. He is always aware of his limitations—if he is a real scientist, that is to say. He knows not merely that he himself will never utter the last word on any problem or subject, but that that last word will never be spoken by any scientist at any time. For the scientist there is no "faith once and for all delivered" to him; no, not even his faith in an orderly universe—without which faith it may nevertheless be admitted science itself would become unthinkable, even though he may be as unaware of this faith as of the air he breathes. But this faith—though, in the nature of the case, never ultimately provable, for to prove it would require that the scientist stand outside of space and beyond time (a vantage point he obviously never can occupy)—is, after all, based on a world of evidential data. These data, though they do not entitle the scientist to claim certainty or finality for his faith, do as a matter of fact give him enough to go on and to continue his work with not merely the hope but—in the light of his past experience—with the confident knowledge of continued success.

Science versus *"Scientism"*

A distinction must, however, be made and kept in mind between science and "scientism." Science is one thing, but "scientism" is another. Being scientific—in the areas in which (empirical) science is applicable—is fine; but being "scientistic" is not! To make of science an absolute is no less dogmatic than is religious dogmatism. Fortunately, relatively few scientists (and no really great ones) are guilty at this point. Scientism is, for the most part, left to non-scientists, such as certain brands of philosophers, psychologists, etc.

Despite its tremendous achievements, science, after all, is not everything: it is not art, it is not philosophy, it is not religion, it is not economics, or political science, or history, etc., etc. The true, careful scientist never gets these areas confused. And, although he may sincerely (and, I might add, rightfully) wish that scholars even in those areas might be more scientific in many of their judgments and conclusions, he is quite aware of the fact that different branches of human interest and knowledge have need of and require different procedures.

Science and Values

Returning to a discussion of science proper, the problem of supreme interest to the philosopher of religion is that of the place and function of value-considerations, if any, in science. Even though it may be true that science, *as such*, is *not concerned with* value, it does not follow from this that science is wholly objective, as has sometimes been falsely claimed. An entirely objective science would have to eliminate the subjective altogether, which is another way of saying it would have to eliminate the scientist, who, like everyone else, is of course a subject. C. Judson Herrick, one of the world's great biologists, writing in his most recent book, says: "... we can see the surrounding world only through human eyes, and our apparatus of perception is at best an imperfect instrument." [1] To which we must add that all the extensions of our human

[1] *The Evolution of Human Nature* (Austin: University of Texas Press, 1956), p. 1.

perceptive organs scientists have devised, invented, and created are themselves only human inventions, and all the results gotten from the use of those extensions still have to be read and interpreted by finite human minds with all their—both subjective and objective—limitations. What is more, when we are told (by the uncritical) that emotions and human motivation are carefully kept out of the scientist's work, we need to be reminded what *makes* a scientist. *Interest* makes a scientist; and interest, which motivates him to become a scientist in the first place, is an emotive reaction. So that emotive and intellectual value-judgments *are* involved in science after all. Without such value-judgments there would be no science, because no scientists.

These remarks must not be interpreted to say more than they say. They are intended merely to point to the self-evident fact that the subjective cannot be eliminated from science, because science would not exist without scientists. And every scientist obviously is a subject. They point further to the fact that, if you eliminate the emotive motivating power of interest, there could be no science. They do *not*, most emphatically not, mean to imply that scientific results are *merely* subjective. Nothing could be further from the truth. For scientific results are never accepted as such if they are not and until they have been verified by numerous other, scientifically educated, subjects. The subjectivity of the scientist cannot be eliminated any more than can his emotive motivation of interest. But relative objectivity is gained by virtue of the fact that all scientific hypotheses, theories, conclusions, and results not merely are constantly open to public (scientific) inspection, but are in fact never accepted as results till they have thus been publicly tested and verified.

Despite the essentially descriptive character of empirical (natural)[2] science, we have now already seen at least three

[2] The phrase "social science" would seem to be a misnomer. There are social studies, but, probably, no social "sciences," no matter how descriptive

kinds of value and valuation involved in empirical science, namely (1) the scientist's original *interest* in becoming a scientist (rather than something else) in the first place. (2) The *importance* assigned to the basic—though rarely mentioned, if, indeed, even thought of or recognized as an act of faith—hypothesis of an orderly universe, without which (even if unspoken) hypothesis the scientist would be stopped dead in his tracks, inasmuch as it is the necessary underlying hypothesis without which he not merely could never arrive at any (scientific) conclusions, but there would actually be no point in making (let alone recording) even his first single observation, for no observation could possibly tell him anything concerning any other and/or future observation. And (3) the value the scientist assigns to scientific *truths*, even though he knows that even the best attested and most widely accepted scientific truths are always subject to correction and improved statement.

But there is, apparently, a still other (4) value-aspect in the attitude and behavior of—at least some, if not indeed many —scientists: the attitude of what may be called *awe*, *wonder*, or even *reverence*. As India's great Philosopher-President puts it, "Man is intended not only to understand and construct but also to wonder and admire." [3] I sometimes have the feeling that some of our scientists actually seem to be more reverent in the presence of mere physical and biological phenomena than many of our "Reverends" seem to be in the (so-called) presence of their God. The glib way many religionists have of talking not merely *about* their God but even *to* him—even

---

some of these social studies aim sometimes to be. For men, social relations and societies simply are not subject to the kind of controlled experimentation and prediction that are precisely two of the major determinative aspects of the scientific method as this method is used and applied in the natural sciences.

[3] Sarvepalli Radhakrishnan, *Recovery of Faith* (New York: Harper & Brothers, 1955), p. 62.

to the extent of finding it necessary to inform him of all the things that, in the light of the claimed "omniscience" of God he obviously must know already—does not convince me of any very reverent attitude on the worshiper's part. Contrast this with Nobel Laureate (in physics) Max Born, who writes: "God's actions are as mysterious in classical Brownian motion as in radio-activity and quantum radiation, or in life at large." [4] Or with Einstein's famous remark to the effect that "The most incomprehensible fact of the universe is that it is comprehensible." And again: "Certain it is that a conviction, *akin to religious feeling*, of the rationality or intelligibility of the world lies behind all scientific work of a high order." [5] And once more:

> The fairest thing we can experience is the mysterious. It is the fundamental *emotion* [sic!] which stands at the cradle of true art and true science. He who knows it not and can no longer wonder, no longer feel amazement, is as good as dead, a snuffed-out candle. It was the experience of mystery—even if mixed with fear—that engendered religion. A knowledge of the existence of something we cannot penetrate, our perceptions of the profoundest reason and the most radiant beauty, which our minds seem to reach only in their most elementary forms;—it is this knowledge and this emotion that constitute the truly religious attitude; in this sense, and in this sense only, I am a deeply religious man.... Enough for me are the mystery of the eternity of life and the inkling of the marvellous structure of reality, together with the single-hearted endeavour to comprehend a portion, be it ever so tiny, of the Reason that manifests itself in nature. [6]

[4] In his essay "Einstein's Statistical Theories," in Paul Arthur Schilpp (ed.), *Albert Einstein: Philosopher-Scientist* (Evanston, Ill.: Library of Living Philosophers, Inc., 1949), p. 176.

[5] Albert Einstein in reply to questions of a Japanese scholar, reprinted in Einstein's *Ideas and Opinions* (New York: Crown Publishers, 1954), p. 262.

[6] Albert Einstein, *The World As I See It* (New York: Covici Friede, 1934), p. 242.

If such statements do not reveal an attitude of reverence, I fail to see what the word could mean. Each of them is the expression of a value-judgment. Is there any good reason why the scientist—not *qua* scientist but *qua* person who is a scientist—should not approach his work with reverence and come away from its results in a spirit of wonder and awe? Einstein at least found the pantheistic God of Spinoza much more awe-inspiring than the celestial errand-boy concept of God that characterizes so much orthodox theistic religion.

I am about to suggest still another (5) use of value-judgment, which, although by no means original,[7] marks a rather sharp departure from generally accepted scientific custom, procedure, and even motivation. I refer to what may rightfully be called the *social responsibility* of the scientist.

The time was—and that not so long ago either—when even the suggestion of such a thing would have caused extreme consternation on the part of almost every reputable scientist. "Truth for truth's sake" was the motto; and the scientist rather proudly boasted of the fact that he was not only in no way responsible for any possible use or applications of his discoveries, but that for him to have even the slightest interest in such "ulterior considerations" amounted practically to a betrayal of his scientific commitment.

The change from that position had begun even before the first atomic flash over the desert of New Mexico on July 16, 1945. For it has by now become common knowledge that many of America's leading scientists, who had worked on the so-called "Manhattan Project," which led to the detonation of the first atomic bomb, had very serious qualms about their participation in the project. "Science for science's own sake" (or truth for truth's) was good enough under ordinary cir-

[7] It has, as a matter of fact, been made by most of the recent presidents of the American Association for the Advancement of Science in their annual presidential addresses, to cite merely one group of leading scientists. It is only fair, however, to say that other scientists have also expressed themselves in similar vein.

cumstances, they seemed to say. But these were far from ordinary circumstances. *If* this "ultimate" weapon actually worked—and many of the scientists actually were *afraid* that it would work—its use in the hands of irresponsible persons or nations actually could mean the end of the human race on this planet. And although the scientists who had created the bombs could obviously not be held responsible for either irresponsible politicians, military personnel, or nations, they did feel that, as creators of these infernal weapons, they could not be held guiltless.

Ever since circa 1942, then, and largely in view of the possibility of the misuse of the destructive power of nuclear energy, scientists have, rather suddenly, begun to become conscious of their social responsibility—not merely in terms of the fact that they are also, of course, citizens, but precisely as persons who, in their capacity as scientists, have a particular kind of privileged knowledge.

And, if one who himself is *not* a scientist and therefore speaks from the outside may be permitted to say so, it was high time that scientists should at long last thus become conscious of their responsibility precisely *as* scientists vis-à-vis the fate of the entire human race.

There still are, of course, even atomic scientists who will do anything in their own field for money, for advancement, for reputation. (But is this not true in any other field as well?) And there certainly are also those who in the name of a so-called (but probably misguided) patriotism will not shrink back from anything, but are ready to put their scientific "know-how" unreservedly into the hands of their country and, more particularly, into those of the military establishment of their country. One would have to disregard or overlook ordinary human nature not to recognize that such persons can always be found in any society and therefore also among scientists. After all, scientists, too, are only human.

But the American Association of Atomic Scientists and their monthly *Bulletin,* inaugurated shortly after Hiroshima, also prove how very large is the proportion of atomic scientists who, in addition to being the intrepid pursuers of scientific truth, also have a social conscience and recognize their responsibility to human society precisely *qua* atomic scientists.

In season and out, for eighteen years now, they have been trying to arouse, not merely the American people, but the peoples of the world to the relative closeness of the Zero hour so far as the further existence of the human race on this planet is concerned.

Lest I be accused of letting my wish be father to the thought, I can do no better, at this point, than to reproduce a few paragraphs from a very remarkable book, written by the widow of the late Nobel Laureate in physics, Dr. Enrico Fermi, who himself was the Associate Director of the Los Alamos (N.M.) Laboratory of the Manhattan District from August, 1944, to December 31, 1945, the period during which the atom bomb was finally created and perfected, tried out at Alamogordo (N.M.), and dropped on both Hiroshima and Nagasaki. Surely no one could come closer to speaking from the inside than Mrs. Fermi. Here is what she has to say on this subject:

> I was not prepared for the change that the explosion at Hiroshima brought about in our husbands at Los Alamos. I had never heard them mention the atomic bomb, and now they talked of nothing else. So far they had focused all their attention on their research, and now the entire world was their concern. To me they had seemed to be working with their usual zeal and dedication, and now they assumed for themselves the responsibility for Hiroshima and Nagasaki, for the evils that atomic power might cause anywhere, at any time.
>
> Through the years that followed the opening of hostili-

ties in Europe, the scientists in the United States had joined the war effort with remarkable readiness. . . .

Scientists have always lived in a certain protective isolation from the rest of the world, within the walls of their proverbial ivory tower. They were not concerned with the practical use of their achievements. Inside the ivory tower, contributions to science were an end in themselves.

Enrico [Fermi] is fond of stressing this point. It used to be one of his favorite topics in popular lectures. . . .

Our husbands were not different from other generations of scientists. Helped by the physical separation of Los Alamos from the world, they worked in a certain isolation. They knew they were striving to make something that would likely shorten the duration of the war. It was their duty to concentrate all their powers upon this single aim.

Perhaps they were not emotionally prepared for the absence of a time interval between scientific completion and the actual use of their discovery. I don't believe they had visualized a destruction whose equivalent in tons of TNT they had calculated with utmost accuracy. . . .

A man of such a fertile imagination as Leo Szilard could not fail to foresee the difficulties that atomic power would bring in international relations. In March, 1945, he wrote an extensive memorandum in which he advocated international control of atomic energy and gave suggestions for a study of the modalities to be followed in its application. President Roosevelt, to whom the memorandum was addressed, died before he could see it. Szilard presented it to James F. Byrnes [Secretary of State] on May 28. . . .

A committee on "Social and Political Implications of Atomic Energy" was appointed by the director of the Met. Lab [at the University of Chicago]. The committee included seven men, and Professor James Franck was chosen among them to be the chairman. On June 11, 1945, they submitted a report to Secretary of War Henry L. Stimson. In this report the seven scientists not only advocated international control but took a firm stand on the use of an atomic bomb: if we Americans should explode such a destructive bomb on Japan, we would place ourselves in a poor position to propose ban of atomic weapons and international control, once the war was ended. The committee recommended a technical demonstration of the new weapon in front of representatives of the UN. Recommendations along these lines were reiterated by a group of 64 scientists connected with the Metallurgical Project, in a direct petition to President Truman. . . .

In Los Alamos the paging system announced the news [of the bomb dropped on Hiroshima] in the Tech Area, and the men were stunned. A blow is no less painful for being expected.

As the papers published descriptions of destruction in Hiroshima in greater and greater detail, the men in Los Alamos asked themselves whether they could truly delegate all moral responsibility to the government and to the Army. . . .

Among the scientists in Los Alamos the sense of guilt may have been felt more or less deeply, more or less consciously. It was there, undeniably. . . .

In October, 1945, scientists who thought along these lines formed the Association of Los Alamos Scientists (which in the following January merged with other similar groups into the Federation of American Scientists). Their central policy, stated in a newsletter, was to "urge and in every way sponsor the initiation of international discussion leading to a world authority in which would be vested the control of nuclear energy."

Prompted by a crusading spirit, members of the Association of Los Alamos Scientists sought opportunities to bring their views to the public, to promote public understanding and free exchange of ideas between themselves and laymen. They drafted statements, they wrote articles, they gave speeches.[8]

The straightforwardness of Mrs. Fermi's most revealing story leaves nothing to be desired; it is eloquent in its very

[8] Laura Fermi, *Atoms in the Family* (Chicago: The University of Chicago Press, 1954), pp. 241–46. All passages here used by the express permission of the publishers.

simplicity. And, although she frankly admits that there were rather far-reaching differences among nuclear scientists on matters of method and procedure, there appears to have been practical unanimity among them on the necessity of creating a world of law and order, of "international control, of world government, of everlasting peace." [9] None of these are natural science concepts!

Our so-called *social* scientists are not only not nearly so unified in their commitment to these one-world concepts, but seem all too ready to discount such unanimity among the natural scientists as an invasion on their part into areas in which they cannot claim competency.

But it seems to me that the natural scientists have a practically irrefutable answer: We may be neither political scientists nor economists nor historians, but more than anyone else we do know the destructive power of the weapons now available and therefore have not merely the right but the duty to warn mankind and all governments before it is forever too late!

Thus the world's scientists—more than ten thousand of them, as chemistry Nobel Laureate Linus Pauling has been able to show by actual signatures—have entered the arena of world politics; and this not just as ordinary citizens, but precisely in their capacity as empirical natural scientists. Whereas most of the world's religions have been divisive, it is once again being demonstrated that science is unitive. And what humanity desperately needs today is not endlessly splintering division, but unity. Have the scientists, per chance, stolen the thunder that religionists should not merely be preaching but practicing?

Listen:

Science has brought forth this danger, but the real problem is in the minds and hearts of men. We will not change the

[9] *Ibid.*, p. 243.

hearts of other men by mechanisms, but by changing *our* hearts and speaking bravely.

We must be generous in giving to the world the knowledge we have of the forces of nature, after establishing safeguards against abuse.

We must be not merely willing but actively eager to submit ourselves to binding authority necessary for world security.

We must realize we cannot simultaneously plan for war and peace.

When we are clear in heart and mind—only then shall we find courage to surmount the fear which haunts the world.[10]

Are these the words, the admonition, the preaching, if you will, of clergyman, theologian, philosopher—or—scientist? How many guesses would you like? The greatest of all natural scientists of this (if not of any) century, Albert Einstein, wrote these words in 1946! That was over seventeen years ago. Has the world, have governments, have so-called religionists listened? Look at today's world, and you have your answer.

Perhaps we should turn the problem of creating One World over to the world's scientists. So far certainly they have given far more evidence of being able to work and get along with each other than any other group I am able to think of. The so-called Pugwash Conferences are only the best-known demonstration of this observation. Governments certainly, so far from getting humanity together, seem to succeed only in keeping the international pot boiling at ever increasing temperatures. What is more, their unswerving dedication to the myth of national sovereignty makes their behavior almost inevitable. Educators, on the other hand, ought to be able to do better. Unfortunately, however, I find that too many educators find it necessary to bolster up the national consciousness, which is not too surprising when we remember that educators

[10] Printed in *The New York Times Magazine*, June 23, 1946, sct. 6, p. 7.

in public-school systems have little chance of lasting in their positions unless they support the *status quo* and indoctrinate their pupils and students with the required "patriotism." There are, of course, notable exceptions, and we may be grateful that their number is increasing. But they still constitute a minority.

And religionists? Most of them proclaim day in and day out the Brotherhood of Man under the acknowledged Fatherhood of God—and then go out and splinter up into innumerable sects in so-called Protestantism, into Roman Catholic, Eastern Orthodox, and Protestant "Christians," so called! And all of these combined have a way of referring to religionists in all other religions as heathens and pagans—as if you had to leave the so-called Christian Occident to find paganism! Oh, how these religionists do *not* love each other! Is there anyone sanguine enough to expect even so much as a *united Christendom* from the Vatican Council? No, I fear religion—at any rate institutional religion—is not the agency to which we can expectantly look for the uniting of all mankind. And yet, without such a world-union the chances of mankind's survival are very slim indeed.

Consequently I come back to science once more. Science, which knows no racial, national, religious, or any other boundaries, might yet be the means of mankind's salvation. I for one am quite free to confess that I much prefer to be saved by science than to be blown to smithereens by the politicians, generals, educators, and clergy of the world. And I suspect that I am not the only one who feels this way about it.

Towards the Unity of Religion

Of course, if religious leaders (as well as followers) could find their way to such spiritual insight and ethical commitment as is found in the writings of India's new Philosopher-President, Dr. Sarvepalli Radhakrishnan, the story might be different. Here is the way he puts it:

There are no fundamental differences among the people of the world. They have all the deep human feelings, the craving for justice above all class interests, horror of bloodshed and violence. They are working for a religion which teaches the possibility and the necessity of man's union with himself, with nature, with his fellowmen, and with the Eternal Spirit of which the visible universe is but a manifestation and upholds the emergence of a complete consciousness as the destiny of man. Our historical religions will have to transform themselves into the universal faith or they will fade away.[11]

Were one to judge by present appearances and directions, these historical religions will indeed "fade away" before they will be willing to "transform themselves." It need not be so; but . . . After all, even conservative and "orthodox" Christians have never denied that Jesus died for man's sake, *not* for God's sake, nor for Americans nor British nor Italians nor what have you. It was a child—*any* child, not a Jewish nor Roman nor Egyptian nor any other particular nationality, but *any* child —that Jesus put into their midst and said: "of such is the kingdom of God." Why does it seem so difficult for most "religious" people to transfer their loyalty and devotion, their dedication and commitment to all mankind, then? I do not know the answer to this question; I can only observe what actually seems to be the case.

Reasons for Gratitude to Science

These facts make the universality of science and the universalism of scientists all the more impressive. Let me summarize, then, why, as a philosopher of religion, I am grateful to science.

[11] S. Radhakrishnan, "The Religion of the Spirit and the World's Need: Fragments of a Confession," in Paul A. Schilpp (ed.) *The Philosophy of Sarvepalli Radhakrishnan* (New York: Tudor Publishing Co., 1952), p. 81.

I am grateful to science:

(1) for its commitment to truth and for its untrammeled pursuit of it;

(2) for its having pushed out the horizons of verifiable human knowledge to a degree unimagined even a century ago;

(3) for its honest recognition and admission of the fact that the best any science can do is to give us probability and a high degree of approximation; i.e., that absolute certainty—except in mathematics, which is a hypothetically deductive system (i.e., a man-invented game)—is forever beyond the reach of finite man;

(4) for its demonstration of the fact that certainty is not necessary for human progress—all scientific achievements (both theoretical and applied) have been made without certainty or finality;

(5) for its opening of a door to vast realms at the same time that it closed another: having closed the door on absolutes, certainty, and finality, it opened the door to practically limitless possibilities (at least we do not know where the limits are);

(6) for its creation and development of the scientific method: that invaluable tool that has accomplished more for man's life on this planet than any other tool ever invented or used by man;

(7) for its attitude of open-mindedness;

(8) for the essential unity of science across all barriers of race, nationality, religion, etc.;

(9) for all the things, from necessities to luxuries, which it has made possible through its offspring, applied science.

These, as is readily seen, are invaluable contributions. Even to the religious needs and aspirations of man they are of no mean significance. For a religion that is not dedicated to truth (to say nothing of being afraid of it!) certainly is not worth having. And even from the relativism of science religion could and should learn a valuable lesson. The import of universalism I have already commented upon.

Conflict Between Science and Religion?

In conclusion, one thing should be clear: if, when, and where science and religion are, or should ever be, in conflict, the wise man will listen to science and re-examine his religion at that point. Not because science is infallible—we have seen that it is not and does not claim to be—but because scientific results and conclusions, though still relative, are always based on demonstrable and socially verifiable evidence, something religion does not and cannot claim.

It is my contention, however, that there not only is no need but not even any justification for any conflict between science and religion. Science is concerned with the observation and description of ascertainable facts and with whatever generalized conclusions it may be able to derive therefrom. Religion is—or, at any rate, should be—concerned with man's highest and noblest commitments. How any significant conflict could arise between these respective aims is difficult for me to conceive. And this all the more so in view of the fact that the search for and commitment to truth is itself one of man's highest and noblest commitments, although by no means the only one. When the religionist is true to his own highest commitments, he will find that he is never far away from those of his scientific colleague and friend.

CHAPTER 13

Science and Religious Faith in Mutual Support*

by JAMES HOUSTON SHRADER**

Eastern Nazarene College

ANCIENT MAN, in his struggle to keep alive, felt that there was something in the nature of things that could be importuned to help in the struggle against the forces of nature. This mysterious power seemed to respond when properly approached (as "experts" prescribed). One path thereto lay through earthbound material practices; the other, through a supra-material spiritual system of ritual. The first followed the line of magic; the second, the line of religion. Each was personified in the magician and the priest respectively. Since magic involved

* Condensed from *The Christian Scholar*, Volume XLIV/3, Fall, 1961.

** Dr. James Houston Shrader, active in the Star Island conferences on Religion in an Age of Science, is the founder and editor of *Religious Inquiry*. He is chairman emeritus of the Division of Science and Mathematics and Professor of Chemistry at Eastern Nazarene College, Wollaston, Massachusetts. This article is a condensation and rearrangement of talks given before the Conference on Science and Religion at Claremont, California, May, 1959, the Intercollegiate Chemistry Society at Harvard University in December, 1959, and the Covenant Congregational Church, Waltham, Massachusetts, in March, 1960. His ideas are more fully developed in a forthcoming book.

control of the physical aspect of things, it developed later into science. Since religion involved beliefs and other mysterious relationships with supernatural powers, it developed a philosophy (theology) and numerous other metaphysical expressions in the different races of men. Antagonism between the two disciplines eventuated into what we now call "the warfare between science and religion." Really, the antagonism is between science and theology, *not* religion. Religion is fact; theology is philosophy.

Man's Needs

Fundamentally man's basic urge is to survive, to keep alive. This expresses itself in the immediate, direct, and instant hunger of the body for food and water. These needs come first of all man's desires. These are the most basic because if not met, man dies—and then there is no further problem for him.

But when these desires are met, even during their gratification, others begin to assert themselves. Among these are the requirements for shelter, for clothing, for sleep, and so on. All these have been called animal needs.

When these have been more or less satisfied, man seeks safety and security, which are close to the level of his basic urge to survive. Rising above this need appears the feeling for belongingness. Man craves to love and be loved. The importance of this is recognized in the fact that medical authorities and social workers have found that when infants are deprived of affection, they fail to develop normally and often wither away and die. It is a *must* in psychotherapy.

Having all these, man is not satisfied. He seeks approval and commendation from himself and from society. A related craving beckons him on to self-realization, as the psychologists call it. This bespeaks the urge "to make something of ourselves." Man wants to excel in some sport or to win in games, in other words, to triumph in competitive struggle. All this bespeaks his urge to express himself.

Beyond these lies another need, namely, the basic urge to understand and to know the reason for the existence and behavior of things all about us. The thirst for knowledge, the sense of the aesthetic, the social urge to share, all these are experiences universal to mankind. They have existed in man since primordial times. The Greeks valued all this in the ideas of truth, beauty, and goodness.

While man was learning to keep alive and to control his environment to a degree, he began to inquire into the nature of his surroundings. He trembled at the noise of thunder; he was impressed with the occurrence of disease and death as mysteries; he marveled at earthquakes, lunar and solar eclipses, floods, tornadoes. He was attracted by the sublimity and grandeur of nature. Even paleolithic man's burial remains attest this concern. Throughout the whole history of the human race man has struggled to keep alive, to associate and to communicate with his fellows, and to seek encounter with the forces or powers that he intuitively felt gave meaning to his being and existence. These latter interests lie in that area of man's psyche, or mind, that is called the "spirit." From this platform, so to speak, man reaches "up" to what he feels is the transcendent reality.

This upreach of spirit expresses the religious motif. It is the oldest, the most widely prevalent, the most stable, the most inspirationally creative, the most culturally expressive of *homo sapiens*. Every art of civilization had its beginnings in religion.[1] It is the oldest of man's institutions and its followers number more than those of any non-religious culture-group.

[1] A. L. Kroeber, *Configurations of Culture Growth* (Berkeley: University of California Press, 1944), pp. 803–04; 844.
Pitirim A. Sorokin, *Society, Culture and Personality* (New York: Harper & Brothers, 1947), p. 225.

Hierarchy of Needs

There seems to be a regular hierarchy of needs, a sort of graded sequence.[2] When the "lower," or animal, needs are met, the "higher" ones begin to assert themselves. This advance, so to speak, is indicated by the decreasing emphasis on animal needs and an increasing emphasis on the purely abstract ones as man develops his culture and experience. The former may be grouped roughly about the physical requirements of the body; the latter, in the area of the spirit (the latest and most highly developed characteristic of mind) for "controlled expression" in language and art, in theory, myth, and religion.[3] The further development of this area constitutes man's expression of "soul," [4] the highest level of goal-seeking. Such a differentiation between body and spirit is not considered to be real in any basic sense: both are highly integrated parts of one living organism.

Wholeness. The analogy between the hierarchical sequence of man's needs and a continuous light spectrum is illustrated in Diagram I. At the red end I have placed the basic animal needs for food and water. Then sequentially I have placed the rising levels of needs, until 'way over at the violet end of the spectrum I have placed the highest psychological needs, namely, those of the realization of the virtues of goodness, truth, and beauty. In the ultraviolet, beyond the sensory area, I have placed religious expression as transcendent of the physical and sensory. These areas of needs all merge into one

2 Abraham H. Maslow, *Motivation and Personality* (New York: Harper & Brothers, 1954), p. 97; chap. 5.

M. F. Ashley Montagu, *The Direction of Human Development* (New York: Harper & Brothers, 1955), pp. 150 f.

3 Adolph Portmann, "Biology and the Phenomenon of the Spirit," *Spirit and Nature* (New York: Pantheon Books, 1954), pp. 467–68.

4 Edmund W. Sinnott, *The Biology of the Spirit* (New York: The Viking Press, 1955), pp. 155–60.

——, *Matter, Mind and Man: The Biology of Human Nature* (New York: Harper & Brothers, 1957), p. 112.

another imperceptibly with no lines of demarcation between them.

These spiritual areas have needs that are just as demanding as are those of the other areas of man's being, as, for example, his need for vitamins. These spiritual needs express man's aspirations for fulfilling himself in areas beyond those

(1)	(2)	(3)	(4)	(5)	(6)	(7)	(8)
Red		*Orange*	*Yellow*	*Green*	*Blue*	*Violet*	*Ultra-violet*

————————————————— Light Spectrum —————————————————

◄————————————————— The Whole Person —————————————————►

Animal needs	Safety & security	Self actual- ization	Belong- ingness	Approval	Knowl- edge	Aesthet- ics	Religion

Area served uniquely by science — decreasingly

━━━━ ━ ━ ━━ ━━ ━ ━ ━ ━ ━ ━ ━ ━

Area served uniquely by religion

━━━ ━ ━━ ━━ ━ ━ ━ ━ ━ ━ ━ ━ ━ ━ ━ ━ ━ ━

Natural sciences	*Psychology*	*Social sciences*	*Humanities*	*Religion*
astronomy biology chemistry physics		anthropology economics • political science • sociology	education • historiography literature • philosophy •	aesthetics mysticism religion

• These subjects were not included in my perceptual base

DIAGRAM I

of only physical well-being; they express his total experience.

Here we see *why* and *where* religion fits into the human experience of *wholeness*. The *why* is the organism's expression of its correspondence with suprasensory areas of reality—that realm of being which ties man into his total environment: to earth as the ground of his physical life, to society as his community milieu, and to the cosmos as the ground of his uniqueness in the creation (nature). The *why* is the motivation to assuage this hunger.

The *where* is the highest level of psychic development—

the ultrasensory. It is this element that makes man different from all other living organisms. This is possible because only man is able psychically to apprehend this realm by virtue of his sensitivity to the cosmic (divine) signals.

Values. The means of gratifying our needs are the grounds for our values. We price that which we want and so we pay to get it. As gratification urges become satiated, our cultural growth creates new needs that we strive for. The requirements of the organism are the biological ground for its basic values. All living human beings have them. We see them in a modified degree in the order of animals below that of man. These traits are built into the nature of things. They all indicate the way "the winds of the universe are blowing," as Dewey expressed it. These basic needs are fundamental for the health of the organism. Since our purposive endeavor is to live, then gratification of these needs cannot be wrong. (Of course, when abused, they may destroy us, as, for example, when too much water drowns us.) The test of value is organismic health in a coherent setting that harmonizes with the best we know. These needs indicate the direction that nature indicates for the person to travel. In this manner the virtues of love, altruism, good will, beneficence, sociality, and co-operation can be traced back in an unbroken line through the brotherhood of man, the gregariousness of animals, and the associative reactivity of inorganic entities, all expressing the same basic urge at their respective levels of consciousness and/or reactive sensitivity. The study of all such phenomena is the subject matter and objectives of the discipline of science.

Science and Methodology

Science, as I use the word here, expresses the point of view that insists on a rational explanation of the experience of apprehending phenomena by experiments and observations, leading to the formulation of explanatory theories that can be publicly validated. Its emphasis is facts and their public verification of overall hypotheses, theories, and doctrines.

The word *religion* in this paper means a group-shared system of thought and action that orients the person in his ultimate concern physically, socially, and spiritually to Cosmic Reality,[5] the philosophic name for *God*. It is comprised within the currently popular phrase "ultimate concern" but gives a sharper focus to one particular facet, so to speak, of man's interest.

Knowledge is grounded on man's personal experience. Common-sense knowledge is what the man in the street understands to be the nature of things. This outlook gives him a kind of practical know-how that usually gets him by, so to speak. The kind of experience that leads to such conclusions is the procedure of science.

Methodology of Science. In brief, the method of science comprises three main steps: First, the scientist gathers all the relevant facts that he can as apparently related to the question before him. Second, he devises a theory that seems to him to be a plausible explanation of these facts. This idea is at first called a hypothesis. It is always a guess, albeit an enlightened guess, that he believes will best describe all similar events. It might just as well be called a belief or a doctrine. All these words mean about the same thing with only relatively slightly different connotations. Third, if predictions from the hypothesis work out to give results as postulated, he considers that the hypothesis may be correct.

But such compliance does not mean that the theory is absolutely true. Maybe some other one might likewise fit the phenomenon. Such has happened many times in the history of science. In fact, science can never absolutely *prove* irrevocably anything to be true. There is always the possibility that later knowledge may give a better basis for another answer. A re-

[5] James H. Shrader, "What is Religion?" *Religious Inquiry*, No. 20 (April, 1958), pp. 1-4.

cent example is Einstein's relativity theory that supersedes Newton's theory of gravitation.

When a hypothesis has been confirmed several times, it assumes the "higher" level of being a theory, and when this is well substantiated over a long time, it is called a law.

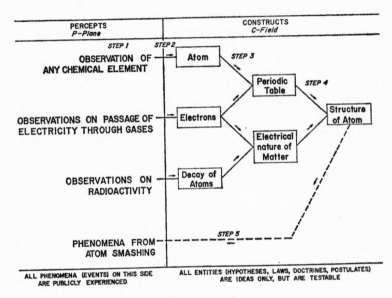

DIAGRAM II

Operationally, this procedure as followed in the instant paper, is illustrated in Diagram II, as based on the epistemology of Margenau.[6] The heavy vertical line represents the plane of nature, and all the objects of sense and phenomena of experience lie in this area of perception. Each such "given" event is called a "percept" in this nomenclature.

Experience moves from these sensory, spontaneous, given data to rational reflection that seeks to relate them to wholes

[6] Henry Margenau, *The Nature of Physical Reality* (New York: McGraw-Hill Book Co., 1950), chaps. 4, 5, 6.

or inter-connected patterns of knowledge and insight into the structure and functioning of nature. Each such hypothesis is called a "construct."

The guiding relations between percepts and constructs, the leap from fact to hypothesis, are called "rules of correspondence." These are in fact metaphysical principles, correlating explanations with immediate experience. In the diagrams those rules of correspondence that connect percepts with constructs are represented by double lines; those that connect constructs with one another are called formal ones and are single lines. In other words, a formal connection sets a construct in a purely logical relation with another construct; an epistemic (double line) connection links the construct with *data* (facts of experience).

By this procedure we move in an orderly manner from the multifarious events of everyday life—a great haze of all kinds of *experiences*—to an insight into nature that shows it to be an orderly, consistent, harmonious pattern that is so reliable, so to speak, and cognizable that man can predict what nature will do under certain circumstances that he himself can impose. In other words, he can invent a science that enables him to control certain aspects of nature because he understands nature.

Constructs are explanations that purport to relate diverse phenomena into a coherent whole. They remain as speculations unless and until they are verified in experience as being true. If A, then B. Verification involves behavior by the observer as if the construct (A) were true (B). So he plans experiments (experiences), assembles equipment, and then proceeds to create conditions whereby the idea can be observed in its application as predictable events. He exercises faith that the test will reveal the correctness of the construct. Verification involves the step of personal commitment.

This procedure is illustrated in Diagram II.

Starting with any material (element) such as iron or gold, we subdivide it until we have the smallest part that our art can apply; there still remains a sizable particle. We *believe* that this can be subdivided into an atom—too small to be seen as such but postulated to be an entity. This is the *atomic theory*. On this hypothesis we arrange the atoms in a conceptual scheme called the Periodic Table; this advances our knowledge by reason of the insight it gives of the relations between the elements and therefore a broader perspective from which to advance our knowledge. This leads to a further hypothesis as to the structure of the atom. Starting with the percept of a piece of copper (step #1), we postulate the hypothesis of the atom (step #2). From this hypothesis (a construct), we postulate further that all atoms have a definite relation to all other atoms (step #3), and then by step #4, we postulate the structure. All this was inductive reasoning.

Now, if the hypothesis of the structure is correct, then we can deduce that the atom can be broken down into electrical (charged) particles (step #5): radioactivity (atom-smashing by neutron bombardment), which is publicly known by anybody who is interested in looking for it. We started with experienced facts, set up hypotheses to explain these facts, and then validated the hypotheses by deductively arriving back again at a different set of facts. The sequence is facts to hypotheses (constructs) and then back to facts.

Application of Scientific Methodology to Religion

In just the same way that the scientist starts with data from the phenomena that he experiences all around him and then builds hypotheses on them to explain their behavior, so I have done in seeking to understand what religion "is all about." Since we cannot deal adequately with only an isolated area of man but must consider him as a whole—body, mind, spirit, and soul, as defined by Sinnott [7]—I have surveyed wide and varied fields of man's behavior and interests that are embraced in the disciplines of physical science, biology, psychology, anthropology, sociology, historiography, aesthetics, mysticism, and religion. These supply public information as expressive of man's reactions to these multifarious fields of experience. By this behavior and expressions, we interpret his characteristics—similarly to the way that we determine the structure of matter and its properties by observing how it behaves under various stimuli (reagents or reactors). On the other hand, the reaction of a known body (the reactant) to its reactors gives some idea of the corresponding nature of properties of the reactors themselves. Their interaction works in both directions—each reveals what the other is like.

Applying this method to the subject of religion, I abstracted out of all available, observable phenomena that which is sensory and also that which is expressively subjective (publicly known). This gave me a list of phenomena in each of the fields investigated, a compilation of phenomena over the whole spectrum of man's behavior—the whole man (see Diagram III). I postulated that these data are explainable as parts of a larger patterned structure. These parts are constructs, all linked into a network of supporting ideas. As we progress to the right with ever broader conceptualizations, we come finally to the extreme right, to Reality. This I have designated by the symbol "X."

Out of nine diagrams representing the above fields, comprising over one hundred constructs, I have selected, for the sake of simplicity, one concept from the respective P-plane and the constructs that arise from it. The constructs from one percept integrate with those from other percepts, making a single, harmonious, integrated network of constructs—all based on nine planes of atomized phenomena.

It illustrates how we can proceed inductively from public

[7] Edmund W. Sinnott, *loc. cit.*

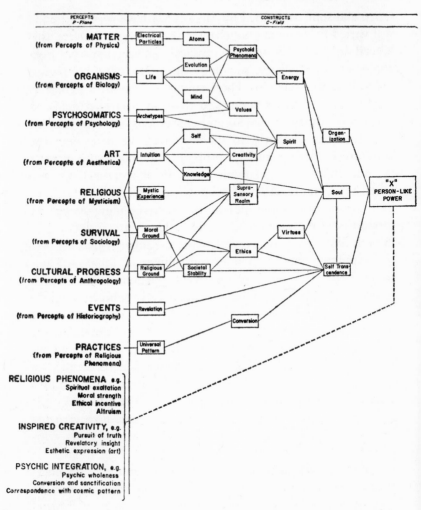

DIAGRAM III

Illustrative Composite Diagram of Constructs from Percepts
in the Nine Disciplines

knowledge of religious phenomena (that exists to some extent in every field of human activity) to doctrines (beliefs) that are supported at the start on verifiable evidence, publicly observed (facts of everyday experience). Then by deduction, I show by testable theorems (not shown here, for lack of space) to ascertain whether or not the construct (doctrine) is valid. For example, starting from the percept of organisms, I set up the construct (hypothesis) of life. From the latter I set up another, "higher" construct of mind. On this I set up a broader one of values, and then spirit, soul, and finally, by "the leap of faith," an irrational but not unreasonable step on to "X."

Consonant with the scientific methodology I then test the truth of this construct by operational theorems. For example, since I postulate that "X" (as Cosmic Reality or *God*) possesses the characteristics of personality, then the use of appropriate practices (analogously to the use of formulas and instruments in physical science) should be expected to entail a type of response such as that between two persons, namely, spiritual and other psychic rapport. Failure to experience such a response does not discredit the idea any more than the attempt to utilize radio signals without a receiving set negates the idea of radio waves. In religion the "receiving set" is a person who has committed himself to God in ultimate concern, thereby providing the sensitive psychic conditions necessary for receipt of spiritual power.

The simplest idea that would explain all the observed phenomena that living human beings encounter is to postulate the being of a conscious Cosmic reality. This instant approach is unique on two counts: it utilizes current scientific methodology and it is based on a wider spectrum, so to speak, of human artifacts than any other base with which I am acquainted. I give as much importance to man's consciousness, for example, as to inorganic nature and cosmic organization. Much subjective experience is publicly known: everybody knows what is meant by someone when he says that he has a toothache.

We all know when a person is in love. Education certainly is subjective, and yet we can test it, even quantitatively. The whole art of medical practice is based on the interpretation of subjective states. Here also lie the fields of jurisprudence, political science, social relations, and much of psychology and mysticism.

Again referring to "X" as having all the characteristics of the highest development of man (and presumably much more besides), we can best visualize it as a transcendent living person.

It is no merely cold, distant, First Cause, nor a "Divine Engineer" as such, nor an impersonal Pure Being. It is a conception of a Cosmic Spring from which stream influences ("forces") that man can visualize (or symbolize) best as the idea of a benign father, again, as "Our Heavenly Father." It means that whatever God may be in the totality of his Being, He at least possesses all the traits that a living human being has, and personality is one. They must be alike to a degree in order to communicate.

The Christian Religion

The foregoing is the way that the Christian religion started. When John the Baptist was in prison, he sent his disciples to inquire of Jesus as to whether he was the one, after all, for whom the Jews had all been looking. Jesus did not say straight out that of course he was the one, as John himself had previously asserted. Jesus said something entirely different, and highly significant. He said, "Go and tell John what you hear and see: the blind receive their sight, and the lame walk, the lepers are cleansed, and the deaf hear, the dead are raised up, and the poor have good news preached to them' (Matt. 11:4,5). In other words he told John to look around and ponder on what all this meant. Inference was held by Jesus to be more convincing than authoritative assertion.

In like vein, the Apostle John in the first epistle recounts "That which . . . we have heard, which we have seen with our eyes, which we have looked upon and touched" (I John 1:1).

These events and others emphasize the importance of living experiences to validate religious truth. In fact, it was upon such down-to-earth facts that Jesus exhorted his followers to accept his teachings. He taught that "through their fruits ye shall know them." The Christian religion originally was a fact-based, doctrinal system whereby God the Father was seen only through Jesus, as St. John affirms. The evidence for belief in God was indirect. This makes it a construct. So, belief in God is a doctrine (hypothesis) that man subscribes to as he encounters the record of the life and spiritual insights of Jesus. First came the observed facts of Jesus' life and ministry, and then came the doctrinal statements later. The writer of the Book of Hebrews asserts: "For whoever would draw near to God must believe that he exists and that he rewards those who seek him" (Heb. 11:6). Again the sequence: facts from experience, belief in God as based on these facts, and then expectancy of answered prayer, all summed up as facts, doctrine, facts.

Here we see the formula of the methodology of science: first the observed facts, then on them the formulated hypotheses that make these phenomena or events meaningful, and finally their validation through verification of prediction (rewards). The two disciplines follow a similar procedure.

Service of Science to Religion. Science serves the religious realm in a number of ways. In the first place, science makes increasingly possible our power to overcome the inertia of nature and to utilize it more and more so that we are enabled to devote time and effort to meeting our needs in the higher realms of consciousness as described above.

In the second place, science provides a mass of validated information for the construction of a cosmology that helps us to understand man's relation to the universe, and his responsibility to comply with nature's laws of health, and with interplanetary societal responsibilities.

The success attendant upon the study of nature shows that man's mind is dependable for understanding nature. This is confirmed by his ability to predict what nature will do. It even shows that his reasoning (mathematics) can forecast what he has never experienced, for example, the planets Neptune and Pluto, and the famous formula $E = mc^2$.

Furthermore, it furnishes a dependable methodology for arriving at a hypothesis, or conceptualization, of religion that harmonizes with all other experience, thus making religion the most natural thing in the world. No longer would it have to rely on a man-made, complicated structure or system of doctrines (often contradictory) but would provide a basis for a simple, Jesus-like approach to God.

It does something more. Its methodology for erecting constructs on a basis of facts gives us an interlocking structure of concepts (doctrines) that are so mutually supporting that if any one or even several should later be found to be incorrect, this new information should not necessarily invalidate nor even shake the strength and dependability of the whole structure. Its doctrinal structure would constitute a vast network of inter-related hypotheses (beliefs) that are connected by cross-references to other constructs in the system, analogous to struts on a bridge. This is illustrated in Diagram III. Here it is seen that the removal of any of several constructs (and even some percepts) does not entail the collapse of the structure.

Finally, religion so conceived is more strongly based and convincing than when it rests entirely on authoritarian pronouncements of alleged private revelation, especially when these have vested interests, professional positions to maintain, or ecclesiastical status to defend. Here is a basis that can be used to appeal to anyone who respects science but not religion. As for example, skeptical intelligentsia, agnostics, irreligionists, or communists.

Service of Religion to Science. In the sixth century B.C., Pythagoras linked science and religion in a mystical interpretation of a rational order in the universe. Geometry arose by the priests of Egypt for measuring the land that had been inundated by the Nile. Astronomy arose in Babylon to set the times for sacred festivals. The temples stored the knowledge of the times, and were centers of the healing arts. In England for centuries medicine and nursing were the work of monks and nuns; St. Bartholomew is the oldest hospital. Practically all of England's older schools, as well as the greater part of Oxford and Cambridge, are religious foundations.

Starting from the fountainhead of Christian theology as molded by Greek philosophy, men's minds became trained to recognize a cosmic sense of order—the conception of the personal energy of Jehovah and the rationality of a Greek philosopher. The scholastics became gropingly aware of the organization of the universe, something not evident to unreflective men. This religious classicism developed the techniques of philosophical discourse. This made science possible. Science in its spectacular modern form arose in a Christian setting. As Whitehead expressed it, this long training inculcated in man's mind the idea that there is a secret order of things that can be unveiled: the rationality of God. The clearest common expression of this feeling is *natural law*.[8]

Experimental science emerged as an effective new intellectual discipline by the fostering of the Reformation.[9] The Greek preference for metaphysics had been further developed by Christian theology. The new emphasis on Jewish elements

[8] A. M. Whitehead, *Science and the Modern World* (New York: The Macmillan Co., 1925), chap. 1.

[9] Arnold S. Nash, *The University and the Modern World* (New York: The Macmillan Co., 1943), chap. 2.

in Christian tradition brought an increased interest in nature, without which experimental science was impossible.

It was the rise of the great universities out of the cathedral system in Europe that conserved the learning of the ancients. Science in its spectacular modern form arose in a Christian setting, was organized by Christian men of science (such as Galileo, Newton, and, earlier, Roger Bacon), and was promoted in Christian institutions of learning. Einstein is quoted as stating: "Certain it is that a conviction akin to religious feeling, of the rationality or intelligibility of the world lies behind all scientific work of a high order." [10]

Wherever Christianity has penetrated, the cause of education has flourished. These are the great centers where science has been encouraged to open up new avenues of knowledge that the world at large recognizes in technology. Science and technology have captured the world's imagination and have provided an intellectual discipline that has won the world's respect and general acceptance.

The rise of science has introduced and fostered a universally sharpened moral sense. Without the strong ethical idealism of intellectual honesty, conscientious devotion to acknowledging credit for the work of others, tolerance for the opinions of others, freedom of thought and speech for oneself and for others, personal honor, independence of thinking, originality and creativity in the pursuit of truth regardless of and independent of personal advantage or disadvantage taking priority over all other demands,[11] science today would not be possible.

[10] Oliver L. Reiser, *The Integration of Human Knowledge* (Boston: Peter Sargent, 1958), p. 311.

[11] J. Bronowski, *Science and Human Values* (New York: Julian Messner, Inc., 1956), pp. 77 f.

Conclusion

In summary, we see that science serves religion: (1) by facilitating man's control over nature in order to be free to pursue the quest for the higher values; (2) by providing a dependable methodology for conceptualizing religious truth that is harmonious with all of nature in one great cosmological whole; (3) by giving an interlocking network of mutually supporting doctrines; and (4) by furnishing a methodology that has received world-wide acceptance.

On the other hand, religion serves science: (1) by fostering science, particularly astronomy, medicine, and mathematics in connection with religious festivals and social service; (2) by training man's thinking into channels of rationality and philosophical rigor; (3) by breaking the power of Greek ideas of contempt for nature and restoring interest in the study of nature; (4) by developing the great universities and centers of learning around the cathedrals, thereby preserving the ancient insights and fostering exploration into the new; (5) by introducing education at high and low levels wherever organized Christianity has penetrated; and (6) by fostering a high moral sense and ethical practice that is universally recognized.

The methodology of both disciplines follows, or may follow, similar patterns of sequential facts, constructs, and then facts again—"check and double-check." In ordinary language we call these the data of experience, the explanations of these data, and the prediction of new data by seeking to apply previous experience. Religious thinking as well as scientific both collaboratively rise from earth-bound dimensions to cosmic ones, as Tennyson has so well expressed:

> "One God, one law, one element
> and one far-off event
> To which the whole creation moves."

CHAPTER 14

Religion and Emergent Evolution

by ALFRED P. STIERNOTTE

St. Lawrence University

THERE SEEM to be two major tendencies in religion at the present time: Neo-Orthodoxy and Neo-Naturalism. This is not the place to discuss Neo-Orthodoxy except to say that its doctrine of extreme transcendence and its neglect of divine immanence, its interpretations of divine activity in terms of supernatural interventions, its provincial exclusiveness in affirming revelation for the Christian religion and denying it for others—these characteristics of Neo-Orthodoxy suggest that it is a modern tendency which makes extremely difficult a *rapprochement* between science and religion. When Canon Charles E. Raven lectured at Yale University in 1958 I inquired whether he thought Neo-Orthodoxy had assisted in a new understanding of the relation of science to religion. He bluntly replied, "Neo-Orthodoxy has been a disaster!"

Neo-Naturalism is based on the doctrine of divine immanence, and it would seem that the strengthening of religious liberalism lies precisely in a new vindication of divine immanence, as is attested by Bernard Eugene Meland:

I regard the doctrine of immanence as a crucial premise to be retained because upon its retention, to whatever degree, however altered or reconstructed, rests what I would call the sanity of the theological enterprise. . . . Now immanence simply presupposes that there are structures within the reach and recognition of man which disclose God's working in some form and to some degree.[1]

These structures have been recognized and classified with such a high degree of verification that they form part of the widest generalization of science, that of emergent evolution. A continuity of process is implied, and when taken with utmost seriousness it does away utterly with dualistic theologies and supernatural interventions. Canon Raven frankly states that

> he has become increasingly sure of the continuity of biological and historical studies, that the story of evolution is in series with that of humanity, and that, if the whole record down to and including Christ is accepted as covering a single process, it discloses a remarkable coherence and can be interpreted continuously in terms of what St. Paul declared to be its end, "the manifestations of the sons of God."[2]

He had already stated in a previous theological work:

> For the most obvious lesson of such study is that the universe is a cosmos, a system of relationships intimately interdependent, a reign of law in which nothing happens by accident and there are no intrusions . . . We must be monists, and take the consequences.[3]

Some men of science, however, are of the opinion that in order to be monists, it is sufficient to present the results of their specialized researches as a more or less coherent symbolic system of verifications made from experiments resting on basic

[1] *Faith and Culture* (New York: Oxford University Press, 1953), pp. 32–33.

[2] *Natural Religion and Christian Theology* (Cambridge: Cambridge University Press, 1953), p. 16.

[3] *The Creator Spirit* (Cambridge: Harvard University Press, 1928), pp. 113–114.

assumptions, and as a result increasing scientific knowledge is manifested in more and more comprehensive theoretical constructions. The theory of "mental constructs" as the expression of the creative activity of the scientific mind has gained prominence, and without exploring detailed analyses of the meaning of mental constructs, it is a moot point whether they are held to refer to an intersubjective agreement among normal minds, or whether they are held to refer to objective structures in the universe itself. It may be affirmed, however, that the drive of the religious sentiment at its deepest is a vindication of an objective world not of our own making, so that the principle of continuity of physical, biological, and historical studies is not merely a continuity of mental concepts but a continuity implied in the very structure of the universe itself. This continuity is stressed by Errol E. Harris:

> The majority of scientists nowadays assume that living matter has arisen from inorganic elements through physiochemical processes of combination, and the continuous evolution of living forms is for the biologist an unquestioned hypothesis. ... The modern conception of nature is thus of a continuous evolutionary process, linking the purely physical with the biological, the biological with the psychological, and the psychological with the social, moral, artistic, and religious experiences of men.[4]

The systematization, the unification, of these evolutionary forms and processes is done through the work of philosophy rather than through the presentation of the achievements of the sciences considered separately. No reconciliation between science and religion may be made merely on a consideration of the sciences in isolation from each other, for the comprehensiveness of the religious and philosophical vision demands a total view—however tentative it may be—of reality considered as a cosmos of evolving forms. This is precisely

4 *Revelation Through Reason* (New Haven: Yale University Press, 1958), p. 65.

where Process philosophies perform their function, and they are much more adequate for this task than philosophies which reduce their application to technical questions of the meaning of verification and the syntactical and logical symbolism utilized to express this meaning. Such linguistic symbolism may result in a formalism without content. The philosophical and religious vision affirms, however, an objective content, which is nothing less than the evolving cosmos existing in its manifold sublimity, immensity, and richness independently of our minds, though including our minds.

Let us consider briefly a few philosophers of Emergent Evolution.[5]

Henri Bergson emphasized "*durée réelle*" as a real inner experience of duration of time and continuity of life. He objected to the tendency of the intellect to take instantaneous snapshots of events, thereby reducing processes of becoming to frozen moments of existential structures at a particular abstract time, *t*. Whether Bergson was correct in thus depreciating the value of intelligence for the sake of intuition is an important debate in Bergsonian philosophical criticism, and we need not enter into this technical controversy here. He did stress "becoming" as the fundamental reality, and it is obvious that Raven's basic assumption of a continuity of developing forms in science may be placed within the larger philosophical doctrine of Becoming as the fundamental view of Reality in Process. Bergson connected real duration with changing reality:

> He who installs himself in becoming sees in duration the very life of things, the fundamental reality. The forms, which the mind isolates and stores up in concepts, are then only snapshots of the changing reality.[6]

[5] For excellent descriptions of evolution from the scientific point of view see many admirable chapters in Harlow Shapley (ed.), *Science Ponders Religion* (New York: Appleton-Century-Crofts, Inc., 1960).

[6] *Creative Evolution* (New York: The Modern Library, 1944), p. 244.

Associated with his doctrine of intuition of processes of becoming is his objection to static philosophy expressed in his shorthand manner: *"Tout est donné."* Everything is given, that is to say, everything is the unfolding in this shadow world of the eternal Platonic ideas. Real novelty is thus denied. Bergson considered this doctrine of unfoldment of pre-existing completed patterns as mechanism in reverse, for it did not provide for spontaneity, growth, development. To him, evolution was the manifestation of the *élan vital*, the vital impetus which drives all living forms in an evolutionary progress, which breaks through the obstacles of matter, which overcomes the restricting bounds of a rigid material determinism to produce the life of the mind, the life of the spirit. Furthermore, for him the ultimate reality is not static, changeless, but the vital impulse in the world, which culminates in the supreme ethical and religious leaders of the race, the great mystics:

> In our eyes, the ultimate end of mysticism is the establishment of a contact, consequently of a partial coincidence, with the creative effort which life itself manifests. This effort is of God, if not God himself. The great mystic is to be conceived as an individual being, capable of transcending the limitations imposed on the species by its material nature, thus continuing and extending the divine action.[7]

It is difficult at this time to recapture the enthusiasm which greeted the evolutionism of Bergson in the early decades of this century. Etienne Gilson's latest work, *The Philosopher and Theology* [8] communicates the ardor with which even young Catholic priests welcomed it as a reply to scientific determinism and materialism, a reply much more adequate than that provided by their own manuals of Scholastic

---

[7] *The Two Sources of Morality and Religion* (New York: Henry Holt and Company, 1935), p. 209.
[8] New York: Random House, 1962.

philosophy. Religious liberals were even more ready to assimilate the *élan vital* to a conception of a struggling God, for if on the one hand Bergson's evolutionism seemed to be the child of a victorious optimism associated with pre-World War I days, on the other hand it provided a thoroughgoing modification of the idea of God so as to do justice to the ineradicable fact of evil in the world, the evil and suffering and anxieties of our world of dictatorships and complacent democracies. This was the concept of a struggling God adopted by John Haynes Holmes and critically elaborated in the writings of Edgar Sheffield Brightman—a concept which some have declared to be the greatest innovation in theology in the twentieth century. Holmes delineates briefly the important changes that such a conception involves:

> Always God has been struggling—falling and beginning again, falling and rising again. A million times has he been halted, turned aside, defeated. But always, by virtue of that essential divinity which makes him God, he has resumed his work, and at last, with the wider knowledge and deeper experience which his very effort has brought him, has achieved the master work of Man. . . . So God has wrestled with his world, and is still wrestling. So God and his world have evolved together, and are still evolving in a mutual process of creation. God is not the source of evolution, or even the guide of evolution. He is Evolution. For God is Life, and life is change and growth. This idea of God seems strange, yet it is only itself an evolution out of well-established ideas which have preceded it. First we had a static idea of *creation*—God and his world, both fixed, immutable. Then we had a mingling of the static and the dynamic in the idea of *evolutionary creation*—a fixed God producing a changing world. Now we have the full dynamic in the idea of *creative evolution*—a changing God fulfilling himself in the changing processes of life.[9]

[9] "A Struggling God," in Joseph Fort Newton (ed.), *My Idea of God* (Boston: Little, Brown and Company, 1926), pp. 117–118.

Though Holmes did not specifically mention his social idealism in this particular instance, it is easy to perceive that his vision of the "struggling God" was imaginatively transformed by his prophetic spirit into the dramatic upsurge of the forces of peace, love, and compassion breaking through the obstructions of a war-torn world to accomplish the work of redemption. Bergson's philosophy of the *élan vital* thus provided direct support for the vision of justice and equality for which Holmes is justly acclaimed, and thereby reached a social application much more inclusive than the French philosopher had ever dreamed. Such an application is indeed an effective reply to the Barthians, who imagine that evolutionary philosophies are out of date in that they are associated with the futilitarian doctrines of the goodness of man and of unending progress—doctrines which they regard with utmost contempt, for they prefer to proclaim the irremediable sinfulness of man to the end of history, and imagine that this is a tribute to a God of Creation. Those who accentuate divine transcendence to the point of denying divine immanence are closer to downright atheism than the so-called atheism of certain tendencies in science and philosophy.

Let us return for a moment to the idea of God as Cosmic Process. There is a trend in some modern philosophies of science which emphasizes process rather than thinghood, which accentuates Becoming to such a degree that Substance— that which becomes—is overlooked. Tillich offers a valuable correction here:

> The problem of substance is not avoided by philosophers of function or process, because questions about that which *has* functions or about that which *is* in process cannot be silenced. The replacement of static notions by dynamic ones does not remove the question of that which makes change possible by not (relatively) changing itself. Substance as a category is

effective in any encounter of mind and reality; it is present whenever one speaks of some*thing*.[10]

Tillich in thus defining substance as that which is in process is very close to Spinoza's conception of God as Substance, especially so as Tillich never uses the expression "Cosmic Mind" for God, an expression found in the writings of such a distinguished philosopher of Personalism as Peter A. Bertocci, for instance. Tillich has flatly denied that God is "a person" and his doctrine of the eternal creativity of God should be assimilated more closely than it has been with evolutionary philosophies. It is interesting to note how similar to Holmes' view of "God fulfilling himself in the changing processes of life" is Tillich:

> God is eternally creative... through himself he creates the world and through the world himself. There is no divine nature which could be abstracted from his eternal creativity.[11]

The intense immanental quality of Tillich's theology is fully apparent here as eternal creativity is linked indissolubly with the world through which God creates himself.

Men of science and process philosophers approach what theologians call creativity in terms of emergent evolution. Emergence is the view which affirms that the accumulation of properties in a particular substance—whether living or non-living—at a particular level, will produce in time and at a certain degree of complexity a new property at a higher level. This higher qualitative level is made up of a complex organization of lower levels, and Professor Paul Weiss of Yale has called this "the layer-cake philosophy," as he is not entirely convinced by it. But for those who are convinced by a philosophy of emergence, it provides rich perspectives from

---

[10] *Systematic Theology* (Chicago: The University of Chicago Press, 1951), Vol. I, p. 197.
[11] *Ibid.* (1957), Vol. II, p. 147.

which to survey the whole fields of science, philosophy, and religion.

Robert Browning in "Abt Vogler" wrote a line that has become the stock illustration for philosophers of emergent evolution. It describes the artistry of the musician: "Out of three sounds he frame[s], not a fourth sound, but a star." Three notes of music heard together are not merely a mechanical addition of three sounds but give us an entirely different quality of music, namely a chord that is a synthesis, an organization of three sounds in a new pattern. A symphony is thus the emergent outcome of all the sounds that make it up, a harmonious combination of all the notes proceeding from the piano, the strings, the woodwinds, the brasses, and the percussion instruments. The composer of a symphony is thus an aesthetic philosopher of emergent evolution.

Among philosophers of emergent evolution are C. Lloyd Morgan, Samuel Alexander, Edmund W. Sinnott, Roy Wood Sellars, Lancelot Law Whyte, Errol E. Harris, Charles P. Conger, Jan Christiaan Smuts, and many others. The assimilation of their views to a theology of emergence has been done with varying degrees of success by Henry Nelson Wieman, Charles Hartshorne, Bernard E. Meland, W. Norman Pittenger, and Pierre Teilhard de Chardin. The powerful system of Paul Tillich has still to be developed into a theology of emergence, but the fundamental premises permitting this articulation are there.

While Bergson emphasized the *élan vital* and the inner intuition of the flow of living forms in a crusade overcoming the downward pull of matter, C. Lloyd Morgan and Samuel Alexander stressed the place of matter in the evolutionary process as the vehicle for the organization of life sustaining higher and higher qualities energized into existence by the Nisus, which they acknowledged to be somewhat similar in function to Bergson's *élan vital*. Alexander's system postulated that the universe of Space-Time had always existed. The stuff of the universe was Space-Time, which emerged into the subatomic particles, then into atoms, complex molecules, cells, and the familiar ladder of evolution up to man himself. For him, the whole universe of emerging forms was the body of God, and the mind of God he assumed to be the quality of Deity to exist in the far distant future. Deity was to be the last emergent of Space-Time, and it is obvious that this is the reverse of the traditional view of God as creator of the world of Space-Time and matter. Alexander's idiosyncratic theology soon found critics among philosophers of religion.[12] He defended himself, however, by a third conception of God, that of the Nisus of Space-Time—a term he borrowed from Spinoza —by which he meant the cosmic Creativity completely immanent within the world of space and time and emergent processes, and activating the emergent ladder from primordial Space-Time to mind and beyond. This is obviously a view of divine immanence which finds a more sympathetic hearing from the exponents of theistic Naturalism than from the defenders of the New Supernaturalism. Alexander, however, made a distinct contribution to religious thought by embracing the religious feeling as described by Rudolf Otto:

> One of the elements of religious feeling is the sense of mystery, of something which may terrify us or may support us in our helplessness, but at any rate which is other than anything we know by our senses or our reflection. And it is natural to believe that there is something real, some feature of actual existence, which calls forth this sentiment in us. Mr. Otto calls this the "numinous" element in the world. . . . In recognizing the existence in real fact of this numinous element in the world, I follow him, and . . . profess myself in this respect an Otto-man.[13]

[12] William Ralph Inge, *God and the Astronomers* (New York: Longmans, Green and Co., 1933), pp. 9–10. See also my book, *God and Space-Time* (New York: Philosophical Library, 1954).

[13] Samuel Alexander *et al.*, *Science and Religion* (New York: Charles Scribner's Sons, 1931), p. 133.

This is a most significant declaration, for it is the first time that a philosophical naturalist had indicated his appreciation for Otto's sense of the numinous, the sense of the Holy. For Alexander religion is the sense of the tremendous and fascinating mystery of the universe that emerges into higher and higher living forms, the highest of which are the ethical and religious leaders of the race who are exemplars of the Nisus of Space-Time. Similarly, the philosopher of emergent Naturalism previously mentioned, Errol E. Harris, is also a disciple of Otto:

> The universe in its ultimate nature remains a mystery, yet a constant lure for further research and a constant stimulus for further reflection. The knowledge of man's insignificance in the face of its awful vastness and the impenetrable enigma of its life and organization is ever foremost in the mind of the true lover of wisdom, who is persistently faced by that *mysterium tremendum et fascinans* which excites the most typically religious emotions.[14]

This orientation of both Alexander and Harris to the sense of the numinous indicates that both naturalistic theists and Christian theists may use Otto's description of a religious sense distinct from the appreciation of the values of truth, goodness, and beauty (though it may well include these), and also distinct from dogmatic formulations, which men of science and philosophers have found too restrictive.

Within the general category of Process philosophy may be placed the writings of Edmund W. Sinnott, for to him process essentially means the activity of a principle of organization:

> If the highest expression of biological goal-seeking is the human spirit, what relation can there be between this and a greater Spirit in the universe? In evolution life has reached

[14] *Op. cit.*, p. 29.

ever higher goals and levels of organization, and has continually opposed the downward and disorganizing tendency of lifeless matter. This suggests that in nature there is a Principle of Organization which, through life, brings order out of chaos, spirit out of matter, and personality out of impersonal stuff. This principle we may identify as an attribute of God.[15]

Much more could be added from the philosophers of physical and biological emergence, and it is clear that each of them has his own particular way of presenting the undeniable fact of cosmic creativity. If the creativity of God is emphasized as a principle of successive emergence of higher qualities and patterns of organization, and if this activity is not limited to the universal temporal process (though it may be difficult to visualize what else God could be doing), then such a conception is easily reconcilable to traditional Christian theism, for it leaves room for divine transcendence beyond the universe. If, however, the creativity of God is envisaged entirely within a spatio-temporal, emergent, universal process, as is done by Alexander, Lloyd Morgan, Smuts, then a philosophical theism of a purely immanental type results, not so easily adaptable to Christian theology. Furthermore, if a philosophical interpretation of emergence stresses it as an immanent force within the levels of matter, so that the emerging qualities are the immanent potentialities within matter, then it is matter that is almost deified and not an *élan vital* or cosmic creativity. The new qualities of life and mind and values are qualities of material organization described as a materialism of levels— which is precisely not a reductive materialism—according to the views of Marvin Farber and Roy Wood Sellars.[16] Such a

[15] *The Biology of the Spirit* (New York: The Viking Press, 1955), p. 122.

[16] Roy Wood Sellars, V. J. McGill, and Marvin Farber, *Philosophy for the Future* (New York: The Macmillan Company, 1949). Note page vi: "The principles of physics and chemistry necessarily apply, but are not by themselves sufficient to the biological level. Thus mechanism, or the theory

stress on evolving matter is a far cry from the creative evolutionism of Bergson, who did not know just what to do with matter. However, it is fully consonant with Tillich's doctrine of God as power of Being. In Tillich's grand conception of the *Logos* as universal structure, there is room for all the physical, chemical, biochemical, psychological, sociological, ethical, and spiritual laws. Wherever there are structures, and especially when structures are considered as objectively existing independently of the mind of man, the operation of structural laws of ever increasing generality may be discovered, and they are all part of the universal *Logos* of Being, whether these patterns of organization be regarded as the manifestation of a transcendental ultimate reality, or the unfoldment of an immanent Creativity, or even the emergence of matter itself in a temporal series of qualitative properties not reducible to mechanism. The Tillichian concept of the *Logos* of Being is broad enough to include a variety of theological and philosophical positions—from Christian theism to a materialism of levels. This is so because the theology of Tillich is fundamentally philosophical in character, and is based on "structures of being":

> Philosophy asks the question of reality as a whole; it asks the question of the structure of being. And it answers in terms of categories, structural laws, and universal concepts. It must answer in ontological terms. Ontology is not a speculative-fantastic attempt to establish a world behind the world; it is an analysis of those structures of being which we encounter in every meeting with reality.[17]

---

that physicochemical explanation is adequate to all levels, is emphatically rejected. The one-floor plan of the classical biological mechanism is thus superseded by a modern structure displaying many diverse stories....The diverse stories, the modern materialist insists, can be easily confirmed by scientific methods. Organized matter reveals integrative levels of organization characterized by distinctive laws."

[17] *Systematic Theology*, Vol. I, p. 20.

And it is readily perceived that Tillich's doctrine of "ultimate concern" is intimately related to his unremitting emphasis on structures of being:

> Theology, when dealing with our ultimate concern, presupposes in every sentence the structure of being, its categories, laws and concepts.[18]

These structures, categories, laws are discovered in all emerging levels and possess their own distinctive properties and qualities. Some may prefer to call the total unity of these structures by James Bissett Pratt's happy phrase: "the Determiner of Destiny." In Tillich's theology, however, the totality and unity of all such structural levels and laws is the *Logos*, and it is fully consonant with Tillich's thought to affirm that the *Logos is Emergence* in its most direct, persistent, and pervasive application from evolving systems of galaxies to the emergence of the religious giant, the founder of a world religion, who is the greatest "whole" produced by the general "holistic" tendency of the universe, so far as we know. The saint and the prophet are culminations of the whole evolutionary process as it has developed on the earth; they are summit characters, to use an expression of Henry Nelson Wieman, and represent the intense and yet harmonious fulfillment of human personality at the highest level. The mystery of the emergence of personality—of the greatest religious personality —is the foundation for traditional Christologies, but it may well be that Smuts has provided the analogue for a completely naturalistic Christology of Holistic evolution:

> Let us not forget that Personality is but a specialized form of Holism, this Personality in all its uniqueness is still but a function of Nature in the wider sense; that in it we see matter itself become somehow aglow and luminous with its own unsuspected fire; that as Personality transforms the material into the spiritual, so regressively a deeper view discloses Per-

[18] *Ibid.*, p. 21.

sonality itself as but a more interior function of that Holism which has been slowly evolving since the beginning of the universe.[19]

A new Personalism of Emergence is thus implicated in Smuts' Holism, and it is regrettable that Personalistic theologies and philosophies have not done justice to it, as they were concerned with idealistic Personalism, which is of an entirely different character. Let us not be concerned at this point, however, with the intellectual battles of philosophers of Idealism and philosophers of Emergence. The sense of the numinous, which is the religious sense, may be summarized as a response of the whole personality to the Whole, which includes the following four elements:

1. The sublimity of the universe of astronomy as described *par excellence* by Harlow Shapley, who is unmistakably right when he enlarges religion beyond the narrow confines of even such a broad formulation as "reverence for life" to reverence for the whole cosmic Process.

2. The emergent or holistic tendency of the cosmic Process presenting a dynamic activity manifested at all levels from the inorganic to the organic and to the mind of man and the "mind" of other intelligent organisms which may exist in other solar systems.

3. The emergence of the religious giants of the race, the seers and prophets who are the greatest "wholes" formed so far as we know in this particular region of the vast cosmic Process. Ethical prophets have emerged from the universe as a culmination of this cosmic Creativity.

4. The universal values that are intensely incarnated in each religious giant, for he is able to achieve a degree of consecration far higher than seems to be possible for the rest of us. He is the supremely dedicated personality because he does

[19] *Holism and Evolution* (New York: The Macmillan Company, 1926), p. 304.

not merely practice justice, or compassion, or outgoing love, or communion with the divine. He *is* the living embodiment of justice or compassion or self-sacrificing love or divine communion in a completely human "incarnation." And he is at the same time an expression of the Creativity of the universe. In him this Creativity becomes luminous and exercises on us its radiance, fascination, ethical demand, the grace of its compassion, and the joy of its salvation.

The religious sense, when intellectualized, must be held to be compounded of these four aspects of cosmic Emergence, for Emergence at all these levels *is* the most emphatic manifestation of Reality. Any one of these aspects when considered by itself is an incomplete apprehension of the religious dimensions of the universe. The sublimity of the universe divorced from the religious giant will yield a cosmic religion which has already been formulated by Einstein and Ernst Haeckel (there is no implication here that they are alike), a noble religion of cosmic grandeur but nevertheless not quite satisfactory. The greatness of the supreme exemplar of religion, when divorced from its evolutionary rootage in the universe, will yield a humanism suspended without ontological reference or a supernaturalism that derives the religious hero from a divine intervention from the mysterious realms of "supranature" or "suprahistory." Such realms, often characterized as "paradoxical" and totally inaccessible to human reason, are wholly unnecessary stumbling blocks for those who take divine immanence seriously. Again, the distinctiveness of the religious giant when regarded merely as a cultural reflection ignores the fact that *emergence* is real, that it *has occurred in history* in a human being manifesting insights into ethical and spiritual values *more profound* than those of his contemporaries. Indeed, they often interpret this greater insight as a threat to their own existence and bring the prophet to his death.

In order to do justice to the universe of science as well as to the intuitions of religion, the religious dimension must include the sublimity of the Universe, its emergent process, its greatest emergent products in the religious giants of this planet, and the universal values they incarnate. These four elements must be held together or else we shall merely be hampered by fragmented views of spirituality or of science. Modern man cannot do with less than this inclusive apprehension of the Whole.

The objection may be raised, however, as to whether this is not a capitulation to the world of emerging forms as given by science. Has religion nothing distinctive to say? Does religion merely "accept the findings of the sciences"? Does religion merely repent in sackcloth and ashes for its ancient superstitions and cruelties in a prescientific age, and in a state of remorse patiently listen to freshman lectures given by scientists on their own specialties? Is the only remaining function of religion to say "Amen" to such lectures? It is at this point that "religion ponders science," or more exactly some naïve, fragmented, subjective interpretations of science by its too ardent, but nevertheless limited, advocates, extremely limited in fields that are not their own. The following are meant as serious questions that imply a distinct lack of vision and understanding on the part of some reconcilers of science and religion.

1. Religion ponders science in wondering whether science can ever be satisfied with a purely subjective interpretation of its experience. All religions of the world are basically ontological in nature in that they affirm an environing reality that is inclusive of both structures of Being and structures of Value. That structures of being and value are discovered in great variety in emerging evolutionary levels does not render these levels less ontological. Let us recall the affirmation of Tillich, who is well aware that the word "metaphysics" is in bad repute—an affirmation which may well be pondered by those who imagine that ontology means some immaterial, etherealized Ghost existing behind the universe:

> Ontology is not a speculative-fantastic attempt to establish a
> world behind the world; it is an analysis of those structures
> of being which we encounter in every meeting with reality.[20]

In other words, ontology has to do with these very structures
discovered by the scientific investigators of the various levels
of the evolutionary process. And yet, philosophers of science
influenced by the Vienna Circle of Positivists tend to the view
that ontology—even an ontology of materialism—is just old-
fashioned metaphysics, and as such, to be dismissed as nonsense. Or a philosophy of science is expressed to the effect that
structures and laws of nature do not really exist but are convenient products of the scientific imagination. For instance,
even such a cautious writer as C. A. Coulson suggests such a
subjective view:

> There is no force of gravitation except in our own minds as
> they try to comprehend the falling stone; there is no electron
> except in our imagination as we seek to understand the be-
> haviour of a wireless valve; there is no radioactive nucleus
> unless it be a creature of our own invention.... What is
> important in science is that it grows by the progressive build-
> ing of what J. B. Conant has called grand conceptual schemes.
> These are the great patterns of science, within which there fit
> together the smaller patterns. As for these patterns, they are
> mental constructs of our own, and their ultimate sanction is
> that they do fit together.[21]

But surely this quotation is influenced by the coherence theory
of truth, and every philosopher knows that this is merely one
theory of truth. The correspondence theory of truth would
affirm that these patterns fit together not simply in the subjective minds of individual men of science, but they do so because they fit together in the first instance in objective reality.

[20] *Systematic Theology*, Vol. I, p. 20.
[21] *Science and Christian Belief* (Chapel Hill: The University of North
Carolina Press, 1955), pp. 35-36.

Are the galaxies of Harlow Shapley merely mental constructs? Are the trillions and quadrillions of miles involved in astronomical distances merely subjective concepts, so that a future space explorer would merely need to travel these enormous distances in *thought*, and not in *reality?* The independent existence of a structured Universe to which our thoughts, concepts, theories, must increasingly conform is a basic presupposition of the common man as well as of the philosophical Realist. There are no doubt many subtle epistemological issues involved in this question that are beyond the limits of this discussion, but the question can never be resolved by denying the objectivity of the universe. This is not to overlook the creative and even aesthetic activity of the mind in formulating a scientific theory—a creative act of the first magnitude ranking with the achievements of the artist and musician. And yet Coulson seems to correct his subjective interpretation by quoting from Whitehead a more realistic view:

> Every such item [of finite knowledge] derives its truth, and its very meaning, from its unanalysed relevance to the background which is the unbounded universe.... Every scrap of our knowledge derives its meaning from the fact that we are factors in the universe, and are dependent on the universe for every detail of our existence.[22]

The view that logical positivism is *the* philosophy of science and that religion must come to terms with it in order to become intellectually respectable is merely a provincial outlook of those who do not know philosophy sufficiently. There is a philosophy of science for every possible ontological position. There is an idealist philosophy of science, and it may be found in the writings of Jeans, Eddington, Blanshard, Bertocci, Brightman. There is a Process philosophy of science, and it may be found in the contributions of the evolutionists mentioned in this chapter. There is a materialist philosophy of

[22] *Ibid.*, p. 45.

science, and it may be found in the works of Donald Williams, Roy Wood Sellars, Marvin Farber, Durant Drake. There is a realist philosophy of science, and it is a vital force in Thomism. Tillich's reply to logical positivism is worth quoting:

> There is always at least one problem about which logical positivism, like all semantic philosophies, must make a decision. What is the relation of signs, symbols, or logical operations to reality? Every answer to this question says something about the structure of being. It is ontological. And a philosophy which is so radically critical of all other philosophies should be sufficiently self-critical to see and to reveal its own ontological assumptions.[23]

Similar important questions that religion may raise to certain philosophers of science are these: Do you dare to believe in the objective reality of your discoveries, or do you think they are merely matters of convenient agreement? After exulting in the mighty efforts of seventeenth-century astronomers who overthrew the old Ptolemaic geocentric conception of the solar system for the Copernican heliocentric view, are you suggesting that whether the earth goes around the sun or the sun around the earth is merely a matter of mathematical convenience and simplicity? Do you dare to believe in evolving Matter? Do you believe in the objective reality of the universe as existing for billions of years before the emergence of life, or do you think that the "universe" is merely a mental process or a universe "of discourse" that will disappear with the death of your consciousness? [24]

    2. Religion ponders science in questioning a reductive

[23] *Systematic Theology*, Vol. I, p. 20.

[24] These questions are not as naive as they appear. See Herbert Feigl, "Matter Still Largely Material," *Philosophy of Science*, Vol. 29, No. 1 (January, 1962), p. 46: "I *grant* the abstract, unvisualizable character of most physical concepts, classical or modern. But I insist that physics deals with happenings in space-time, and that associated with those happenings there are aspects of mass, charge and motion which leave at least *some* characteristics of old-fashioned matter unaltered."

materialism implied in even well-intentioned attempts at reconciliation of science and religion. In some current discussions
it would appear that all that is required to understand religious
experience is some knowledge of the operation of neural processes, of muscular mechanisms, and of electrical waves in the
brain. Let a crucial example bring the issue to a focus, and we
shall choose a recent event rather than one lost in the problems of exegesis of the early Christian centuries. Suppose
Albert Schweitzer at the very time he experienced "reverence
for life" on the Ogowe River had at his side a whole battery
of scientists with equipment so designed that every neural
process, cellular reaction, and electrical wave in his brain could
be recorded at that very moment. Of course, modern science
is not able to carry out this gigantic task, but assume for the
sake of the argument that it can do this complete observation
of the bodily and brain processes of Albert Schweitzer at the
very moment when he experiences "reverence for life." Will
an understanding of all those processes enable us to experience
the full meaning of "reverence for life" for Schweitzer or for
ourselves? I am very much inclined to give a flat denial to
any such possibility, for religious experience must be understood as the reaction of the whole personality, and it is a cardinal principle of emergence that "the whole is more than the
sum of its parts." Emergence really means that a spiritual
capacity has *emerged*—no doubt conditioned by all the biochemical processes of the brain and sustained by the evolutionary ladder that undergirds this living brain—but this spiritual
capacity has its own distinctive quality and is apprehended
only through the spiritual power of the whole person who
reacts to Schweitzer's own experience. Those who are glib
with such phrases as "man is so wired that" indicate that they
have not understood the meaning of emergence, and their re-
ductivist tendencies are merely a measure of their ignorance
of the issues. As well imagine that a knowledge of the number

of vibrations of every note in a symphony will by itself give one the aesthetic experience of hearing the whole symphony!

3. Religion ponders science in asking what precise meaning may be given to the oft-repeated assertion that ethics is rooted in evolution and therefore there is no need of an independent philosophical discipline of ethics that will evaluate human activities. Ethical character and behavior is rooted in the gene constellation of the individual or in the gene pool of the human race. This may be quite acceptable and one might even believe that every ethical and spiritual teaching, every parable of a Buddha was actually an expression of his character, and this character conditioned by a constellation of genes disposed to support this character in the Buddha's cultural environment. But then the total *non sequitur* is made by the advocate of a ridiculously facile reconciliation of science and religion to the effect that we need not be concerned with ethical problems since ethics is rooted in the gene pool, and the gene pool is rooted in the universe, and that is apparently the end of the matter! But it is not the end of the matter, for knowledge of correlations between a constellation of genes and particular ethical dispositions—still in the rudimentary stage of scientific investigation [25]—does not by itself give the observer the significance of the ethical character or the ethical principle involved; nor would it necessarily move the observer to similar ethical behavior.

Again, the meaning of *emergence* has been overlooked, for the determination of an action by ethical principles is an *emergent* capacity of the human mind, which must possess an ethical intuition before it can act accordingly. No doubt the ethical intuition is conditioned by genes, but it needs to be

---

[25] How rudimentary is the present stage of our knowledge may be appreciated from the following: "We have no adequate genetic analysis of a single polygenic trait in man, and one must assume that the characteristics that are particularly important to mankind—the components of character, intelligence, and so forth—are highly polygenic." Ernst Mayr, "Comments on Genetic Evolution," *Daedalus*, Vol. 90, No. 3 (Summer 1961), p. 461.

emphasized that the knowledge of the possibility of this condition is not itself knowledge of the ethical intuition. We are back at the age-old confrontation of ethical problems in terms of persons and their relations and their decisions in situations which involve values. How we react is not a matter of the exceedingly technical problem of relating traits of character to genes, it is solely a matter of our character or lack of it. We react as persons and not as gene pools.

The autonomy of ethics must be vindicated against the naïve assumption of those who simply state there is no problem since "everyone believes in life," and no doubt scientific advances will be used to promote life. Any pseudo-philosopher of science arguing in this way indicates his ignorance of the discipline of ethics and of the insight that distinguishes between various ethical systems, such as the hedonistic, utilitarian, Kantian, self-realization, Christian, Hindu, Buddhist, etc. The insight that attempts to evaluate the contributions of these systems of ethics to individual, social, and international problems is itself an emergent product of human evolution, but it must be grasped in its real *emergent* character, that is to say, with the important recognition that the ethical whole that is the person in society is more than the sum of its parts, however fascinating those parts may be—such as genes—from the point of view of pure science.

At times the dichotomy between facts and values is rejected vehemently, for instance:

> We are to get away from our idiotic schizophrenia that spirit and values lie in one world, and matter and knowledge lie separately and independently in another. That is the great lie, the grave error, of our times.[26]

True, the world of spirit and value and the world of matter belong together in one fundamental emerging reality of vari-

[26] Ralph W. Burhoe, "Salvation in the Twentieth Century," *Science Ponders Religion*, p. 84.

ous levels. But the point is that knowledge of the factuality of the lower levels through scientific methods does not indicate the goals to be achieved by the higher levels, namely, persons. Einstein puts the case persuasively:

> The scientific method can teach us nothing else beyond how facts are related to, and conditioned by, each other. The aspiration toward such objective knowledge belongs to the highest of which man is capable, and you will certainly not suspect me of wishing to belittle the achievements and the heroic efforts of man in this sphere. Yet it is equally clear that knowledge of what *is* does not open the door directly to what *should be*. One can have the clearest and most complete knowledge of what *is*, and yet not be able to deduct from that what should be the *goal* of our human aspirations.[27]

This point is so consistently and so readily overlooked that it must be reinforced by an unusually scrupulous philosopher of science, Henry Margenau:

> In my view ... natural science contains no *normative* principles dealing with ultimate goals; physical reality is the quintessence of cognitive experience and not of values. Its significance is in terms of stable *relations* between phases of experience, and since it draws its power from relations, reality cannot create an *unconditional* "thou shalt." To know physical reality is to know where to look when something is wanted or needed to be seen; it is to be able to cure when a cure is desired, to kill when killing is intended. But natural science will never tell whether it is good or bad to look, to cure, or to kill. It simply lacks the premise of an "ought."[28]

Nevertheless, there is some meaning to the assertion that ethics is rooted in evolution, but not in the sense that we need to go to the ant or the bees or primitive tribes for normative

[27] *Out of My Later Years* (New York: Philosophical Library, 1950), pp. 21–22.
[28] *The Nature of Physical Reality* (New York: McGraw-Hill, 1950), p. 465.

patterns of behavior. Ethics is rooted in evolution in the sense that the evolutionary process is a process of the emergence of values expressed in persons. As previously stated, the supreme persons of the race are the religious giants—saints and prophets —who by their exemplary and self-sacrificing lives produce that impact on our consciousness which leads to a crucial re-examination of our actions and our resolve to do better. The evolutionary process has an ethical claim on us only at its highest level, that of the supreme leaders of the race who incarnate spiritual values so intensely and yet so effortlessly that their spirits smite our spirits, condemn us for our imperfections, and yet sustain our efforts. We may well be filled with wonder at the majestic display of emerging levels of organization within the universe, but this wonder may be changed to fullness of life only through the impact of the highest emerging level, that of the spiritual giant incarnating universal values that feed our souls.

4. Religion ponders science in asking for a more precise meaning of cultural evolution. It is a commonplace that man has evolved a symbolic system of communication in civilization and that his values are expressed and transmitted through this symbolic system much more readily than through genetic evolution. As Julian Huxley has well said:

> This puts mind, in all its aspects, into the business of evolution. Thus, under this new dispensation, beliefs are inevitably brought into being; and once they have been brought into being, they become tools for living. And the same is true of ideals or purposes or scientific theories or religious systems —they are among the emergent properties of the new, human type of organization. They cannot help coming into existence, and then they cannot help becoming operative factors for further change. Thus, once life had become organized in human form it was impelled forward, not merely by the blind forces of natural selection but by mental and spiritual forces as well.

In the light of evolutionary biology man can now see himself as the sole agent of further evolutionary advance on this planet.[29]

Such an interpretation, however, represents a long-range view of the evolutionary process at work at the human level. Some evolutionists have invented the word "ideen" for beliefs and "tools for living," but religion is not satisfied with these sociological abstractions for it has always personified its ideals and values for individual and social living. Religions have possessed the humanistic wisdom of presenting their teachings in "incarnations" of prophets and saints who unify in themselves a harmonious development of their superior spiritual insights. These are heroic founders of religions who dare to challenge what has been regarded as good, what has been sanctified as holy in the culture of their times. Gandhi challenged the evils of a caste-ridden Hinduism with the same directness of ethical intuition with which Jesus castigated the money-changers. And here arises the great tragedy in the history of religions: two ideas of the good in mortal combat, the good imbedded in traditions of the past sincerely defended by those whose vision is limited by the past, and yet challenged by the higher vision of the prophet, a vision that condemns the lesser good as outright evil in comparison with the prophet's inner certitude. And all too often the prophet has been condemned to death by his religious contemporaries, and thus provides the greatest ethical drama presented to our consciousness. This drama is the death of the religious giant at the hands of his contemporaries. And this drama is so intense because at the very moment of his suffering and death, the light of the religious hero shines brilliantly over against the darkness of those good but nevertheless contemptible people who brought him to his destruction. This is good and evil facing each other in implacable opposition. This is the greatest contrast human

[29] *Evolution in Action* (New York: Harper & Brothers, 1953), p. 149.

history can ever give us: on the one hand the religious hero radiating the good, radiating his goodness for all future history; on the other hand, the evil men who brought him to his death are lost in outer darkness and can never be rehabilitated for all future history. Moreover, the greatness of the religious hero shines so brilliantly, so victoriously, that the very instruments of his destruction are sanctified by him. The prison in which Socrates was jailed became the scene of a great painting by David; the place of confinement of Gandhi is sanctified by his presence, and the cross of Jesus "towers over the wrecks of time."

Through the heroic action of the prophet, light is finally separated from darkness, good is finally separated from evil, and this separation is for all future time, for all future history, for all future evolution of mankind for thousands and millions of years. Each spiritual giant effects a momentous separation of a pervasive evil in the lives of his religious contemporaries by his "incarnation" of a higher way of life for which he is prepared to sacrifice himself even unto death. Thus is evil utterly rejected and good finally established in the mental and ethical evolution of humanity, in successive nodal points in the spiritual evolution of mankind, each nodal point being marked by the self-sacrifice of the religious hero, through the dedication of men who are indeed "the wisdom and the power of God. This is a moment of ecstasy in the life of the religious giant. This is a moment of ecstasy in the life of humanity. This is a moment of ecstasy in the life of the emergent Universe itself.

It is this rich heritage that religion provides as the motive power for the transvaluation of values. Such a heritage is much more concrete, much more personal, poignant, and existentially compelling than Julian Huxley's quite correct abstraction: "In the light of evolutionary biology man can now see himself as the sole agent of further evolutionary advance on this planet." So great is the contribution made by the religious hero at the moment of his isolation and death that his experience becomes the source of communion with humanity for all future time. It is the source of the arts, of sculptures, paintings, of oratorios and masses that celebrate the victorious action of the supreme exemplar of religion. And thus does the Emergent Creativity pervade all levels of the universe, sustaining us at every level and enfolding us at the highest level with the grace of its love given through mercy, pity, peace, and love, "the human form divine."

CHAPTER 15

The Meaning of Purpose in Religious Experience

by HOWARD THURMAN

Boston University

PURPOSE MEANS A SENSE of direction; it is the movement of life toward a definite goal or end. We are reminded that all life is goal-seeking. In its simplest manifestations this means that whatever else life is, it is characterized by growth, development, change; and this development or growth is in accordance with a private or particularly individualized scheme or inner code. This binding or shaping characteristic seems to be inherent in life itself. Here I am not referring to choice or deliberation, but rather to a movement within life that manifests itself as actualized potential. It is a kind of unfolding that when observed reveals order, so literal that the term "structural dependability" seems an apt description. It is as if, given a form of life, any form of life, there is in it a potential goal toward which that life moves. When it arrives at such a "fixed" point in its development, it has achieved its end, and the process repeats itself through death and birth or through destruction and fertilization. Any organism seems in itself to be an organized unit showing particular activities, such as main-

266

taining itself, developing and reproducing in one continuous and tight circle. This behavior is in time and is therefore dynamic, making possible variations that show creativity. Purpose in this sense does not involve psychology or metaphysics or religion or even external mechanical manipulation—it is rather what seems to be a characteristic of, or a fundament in, life itself as it unfolds in its environment.

In human life or in personality, purpose takes on a more complex character or meaning. Because man is self-conscious, it is my thought that the tendency to goal-seeking to which reference has been made reaches its apotheosis, for the present, at any rate, in man. His life is grounded in life and life's aliveness. Man is a creature, an organism, a child of nature and a space-binder. His body is a formation which seems to be in and of itself bound by an organized unity characteristic of organisms in general. It is in that sense an actualized potential. It is so sensitively integrated that when any part of it breaks away in independent behavior, the disorder threatens the whole organism, and there seem to be built-in provisions either for handling the unruly member or for protecting the life of the whole from the disruptive influence of a particular part or member of the body.

But man is more than a space-binder. He is also a time-binder. He is not merely a "dynamic pattern in time," but he is also a time-transcender and/or a time-creator or -definer. He functions in time, but he also uses time deliberately as instrumental in his goal-seeking or purposeful activity. It is as a time-binder that the meaning of the term "purpose" finds its significance in my discussion. Purpose in this sense is the capacity to determine, to influence, the future by action, such as choices, decisions in the present. Purpose is that which an individual sets before himself as an object to be attained as a necessity to his own well-being and often the well-being of others.

Personal action is the realization of an intention or a purpose.

In the effort to realize an action we learn what it involves and we learn gradually to make it definite and precise.

There must be continuity in intention.

A long-range purpose has to be realized in stages.

Limitation of purpose must not be confused with a change in purpose.

Science is not science because it is true but because its results are arrived at through the use of a certain technique.

Man has the capacity for such personal action. Such capacity with such results is what I mean when I say that man is a time-binder. This is what religion means when it says that man is created in the image of God.

Such a capacity seems to be what may be called, for lack of a better term, an active dynamic center in man. It is one with his self-consciousness, with his sense of self, with what he means by himself. It is given—and for me it is a part of the "givenness" of God.

It is man's experience that this is the kind of world in which purposes, goals, can be projected, established, and achieved, that effective choice is a part of the formula of his existence. It is well within his resources to marshal the raw materials of his world on behalf of his choice. The responsibility of choice, of purpose, is inescapable. Man discovers that his own personal stability is grounded qualitatively in the same basic structure of dependability as is all of life. But his personal stability is grounded in something that is more, much more than this structure of dependability for his organism and its fulfillment in its environment. Rather is it to be found in an inner quality of well-being, a profound sense of being a part of a larger whole and context of meaning which defines and gives character to his own life and its little purposes.

It is man the time-binder whose fundamental personal stability rests ultimately upon two basic levels of reassurance.

These two levels of reassurance vary in significance in accordance with felt needs and the form that these needs take or assume. The first is the need for a sense of being totally encompassed. It is the realization of a climate that is all-encompassing, of which the individual feels himself a part and yet from which he feels distinctly separate as well. The individual regards himself as being held by or contained in a reality of which he is a part but which at the same time seems independent of him. The emergence of mind makes it possible to distinguish between the self and the not-self. This reality (to refer to the earlier part of my discussion) has as its dominant characteristic a structure of dependability that the mind recognizes as not unlike its own character. Man's experience of this reality is a living, vital thing. His communication with it is so constant that there seems to be literal affinity with it. All the things that are outside of him, the great external world of nature and objects of varied kind, as well as his own body and that strange continuum of his inner world, seem to belong together in some kind of order, some kind of inner relatedness. The result of this affinity is that man knows that there is nothing that will not yield in part or in toto to the persistence of his effort to understand. To understand is the experience of flow—I understand when the wall that separates dissolves—I ask questions about what keeps me from understanding.

Ulysses expresses it:

> I am a part of all that I have met
> Yet all experience is an arch
> Wherethru gleams the untravelled world
> Whose margins fade forever and forever when I move.[1]

It would seem then that there is an all-encompassing reality which is *given*. Man did not create it with his own mind, but he finds it as a literal fact of his world. A sense of fact is a necessity of thought *about*. In the exercise of his affinity with

[1] Tennyson, "Ulysses," lines 18–21.

his world, he learns to understand it, to use it, and to destroy it.
The point is that his experience with this kind of reality is
deeply reassuring, and in it he functions with confidence. He
is in it, a part of it even though in terms of his own sense of
self it is indifferent to him. He sees his life as contained by a
reality beyond him even as this reality contains all else, which
he realizes as being other than himself. He belongs to life, he
is not a thing apart nor a stranger altogether. For many men
this is sufficient for all their days. They would not patronize
this reality by giving it a label or a title nor would they per-
sonalize it in any way. It is often the case that in the contemplation of his experience with this reality, man responds with
a sense of awe and reverence and even with thanksgiving and
praise. This is the significant element in natural religion and
an important aspect of nature mysticism. For me this is not
enough!

It is the second level of reassurance that man, the time-
binder, must have if the deepest and most searching needs of
his spirit are to be met and honored.

A man wants to know what it is after all that he ultimately amounts to. It is here that man seeks personal assurance
and confirmation; it is here that he experiences the satisfaction
of being totally dealt with in a manner that is private, personal, and at the same time social and universal. It is at this
second level that his experience has in it the elements that may
make it religious. This is the region of personal encounter
with the reality that meets the dimensions of the divine. When
Jesus of Nazareth was baptized of John in the Jordan river,
it is recorded that as he came up out of the water, it seemed
to him that the heavens opened and the spirit of God de-
scended upon him like a dove, and he heard the voice of God
saying, "Thou art my son, my beloved. This day have I be-
gotten thee."

It is my position that the critical element in the religious
experience is a personal encounter that the individual has with

"God." It is far from my thought to confine religious experience exclusively to such an encounter, but for me the essence of the meaning of religious experience is that which transpires totally in a man's personality when he feels himself to be in direct touch with the kind of reality that gathers into a single focus all of the values and meanings which the individual at other times has thought, sensed, or felt. Such an experience is possible to man because he is a time-binder. As a time-binder, he is aware that events, experiences in which he may be involved do not ever quite contain all that he is at any particular moment in time. In other words, it is man the time-binder who is at once the observer and the participant in all of his actions or experiences. He seems to stand outside of his experience, to watch himself being molded and shaped by his experience with such intensity that the line between himself and his experience often seems to fade. But there remains always an essential residue which is private and unassailable. The term "religious" may be applied to experiences when they seem to be uniquely vehicular for a communication between the individual and a consciousness that is an infinite expansion of his own consciousness. Therefore it is not the experience per se, that is to say, it is not a certain kind of experience that takes place in a given setting made articulate by particular forms or symbols—it may be, but it does not have to be. The thing that makes any experience a religious experience is the door which the experience opens that makes possible an awareness or encounter between the essential self and a greater expansive living consciousness.

"Religion is a way of living the whole life and consequently as a part of this, a way of thinking the world, and understanding the world.... The world has to be thought religiously."

But this is not enough. The impact of the encounter, despite the element of mystery that is inherent in it, has certain results in the life of the individual. The most significant one for our discussion is the element of purpose. This manifests itself in the first place in the meaning that the individual thinks or feels that life has and that his life has. Even though the result of this search for meaning may be one which causes him to become very conscious of his shortcomings, his inadequacies, or his wrongdoings, these are but meanings in reverse, for it is only because of a certain sense of adequacy that man seems inadequate; only through a sense of strength that he is aware of weakness; only because of a sense of goodness that he is aware of wrongdoing. The point is that man is convinced that his life is involved in purpose. This involvement of his life in purpose is most articulate at such a time because all of the little private purposes, plans, decisions, meanings of his life are so highlighted that their total significance is made clear to him. Sometimes the little purposes are lifted into a dimension that makes him see what they really are as distinguished from what they seemed to have been. Sometimes, in a shattering manner, with transparent honesty he sees that they run counter to what now he recognizes as being his true intent.

I do not wish to indicate or suggest that all of this takes place at a single time, at a particular period or moment in a life, but rather I am describing the essential character of the religious experience whenever and wherever it takes place. The interesting thing to me about the phenomenon of religious experience is that the quality of it may become so pervasive in a man's life that it produces in him a mood or an inner climate out of which more and more he lives his life and does his thinking.

It is with reference to the results of the religious experience that become at the same time tests of its validity that religion experiences its greatest defeats and its greatest glory. For there is no guarantee or protection from self-deception. The quality of humility therefore belongs in all experience and in particular in religious experience, not merely because of a probable feeling of unworthiness in any overwhelming experience of meaning but also because the margin of error is ever present. A man can always be mistaken. Indeed it is possible for a man to live his entire life confident that he has done the right thing in the fulfillment of his private enterprise and to discover just before he dies that his life was a mistake. In addition to this, the mind insists that experience makes sense. Making sense means that there be established some other-than-self reference or criteria for experience by which the experience itself can be validated, checked, proved. So the hound of hell that dogs the footsteps of religious experience is the insistence: Prove it. Prove it. If you can't prove it, how can you know it? Thus religious experience is involved constantly in a dilemma. It must accept the challenge to give empirical validation for its claim, and at the same time it recognizes by its very nature that the integrity, the nitty-gritty, of the experience does not ultimately rest upon any empirical validation. In the last analysis the integrity of the religious experience is the experience itself. In my boyhood there was a spiritual we used to sing, "If Satan says I don't have any grace, I'll take him back to the starting place!"

Here I sense what it means to accept responsibility for my own actions. But a new dimension enters into my responsibility—I am not merely responsible to myself or to my fellows or to some prestige-bearing figure in my world, but I am responsible to God, who is concerned about the kind of human being I am. And this is the primary discovery or disclosure or insight of the religious experience—that I am responsible not only for what I do, for the choices that I make and the motives in me that these choices give expression to, but also for the things that I am willing to back, to support with my life. This is the kind of necessity that is laid upon me. I may fail again and again but always against that failure something wars, something holds. My behavior and the well-spring of my motivation become a lung through which the quality of my religious experience breathes—through which God breathes.

But there is another kind of responsibility that emerges: responsibility for my reactions to the events, the experiences, and the facts of my life. The operation of choice here continues to be crucial. I cannot determine the events, but I can say somewhat concerning my reactions to the experiences.

The entire life of the individual is the validation of the religious experience.

If it is true that the life of the individual is the validation of the religious experience, then we must not be confused by the variety of the interpretations that are given of the experience. For interpretations are always having to do with the element of proof and may not be identified with the experience itself. Interpretations are not explanatory but descriptive. Interpretations are inventions of the mind, necessitous, important inventions, but inventions nevertheless. As inventions they are always after the fact of the experience and are thus somewhat out of date. There is a time interval between the experience and the invention—why theologies must always change, grow, shift! One of the great tensions in religion is always between the invention and the experience. Religious experience is a growing aspect of the religious man's life. It is constantly involving him in growth, in inner conquest of areas of his own life that have not come under his judgment or his scrutiny. The interpretations on the other hand tend to become fixed as ideational patterns of familiarity that often are profoundly resistent to change. Slowly the interpretation becomes a substitute for the living experience, and what was at one time vital and dynamic becomes sterile and static, embalmed in creeds and dogmas that in turn become tests or proofs of religious experience.

I come back now to the heart of the matter. Man, the time-binder, the time-transcender, finds certain events, moments, or experience of his life which are vehicular for providing a vital correspondence with a reality that is infinitely more than anything that he *is* but is essentially related to what he is when stripped to that which is literal and irreducible in him. I am calling this the experience of encounter. It is a form not merely of communication but of communion and fellowship. That which is deepest in him responds to that which is profoundest in life but which seems even to transcend life in all of its particularity. It is knowledge but more than knowledge, because it cannot be contained in any category but is itself categorical. There seems to be a kind of expanding consciousness moving from within the boundaries of the self in one continuous thrust out beyond all the boundaries of the self. The experience has a quality that has the feeling of goodness, of wholeness, of unity. The curious thing is that such terms as goodness, wholeness, unity, in the context of religious experience are not merely value judgments but rather do they seem to be *given* qualitatively in the experience. When the meaning of the experience begins to work itself out in life, the instrument that is used is the value judgment. In the religious experience the individual knows now what his life means and what the purpose of life is. Man, the time-binder in his encounter, finds himself confirmed and affirmed by a reality that uses experience as its vehicle, but relates to all of life in the same way that man relates to his experience. In the presence or midst of this kind of experience, the individual knows that he need not be intimidated or awed by the vicissitudes of life; that in any experience through which he may be going he stands in candidacy for this kind of breakthrough. It robs even the most horrendous experience of its power to create fear and anxiety; he is possessed by the peace of religion, the peace that passeth understanding.

Always man is trying to establish this kind of equanimity for his life. This is the basis of the persistent prayer of his heart and the thing for which he is always seeking. In the history of the race whenever there has arisen in the midst of his fellows anyone who seems to possess this and who can make the way to its possession possible, such a one has been regarded not merely as a fortunate, a good man, but also as a savior.

One of the most striking characteristics of the experience is the way in which it seems to unify all of life. This is not achieved by some external manipulation but is as if the individual becomes a part of all that is when the narrow walls of his own conscious life seem to become enlarged. It is as if his little life becomes the door through which he enters into a larger and fuller dimension of what he has known himself to be all along. The purpose of all spiritual exercise is to aid and abet this development. This is the meaning of worship whenever it is found. It is an attempt to push back the boundaries of the self, to move out beyond the narrow walls that shut one in. If I may, I will illustrate this with a personal experience. Some years ago I was invited to give the address at the Germantown Friends Meeting on a certain Sunday morning. I traveled some eight hundred miles for the occasion. I decided that I would try to enter into the spirit of Quaker worship by trying to experience the depths of dynamic silence and out of that common ground of unity speak to the condition of the meeting. Therefore, I made no formal preparation for the address. At the time of the meeting I entered the meetinghouse with the leader or head of the meeting. We sat together on one of the facing benches. Behind us on a higher level sat a few other people. In front was the full congregation. After a few minutes the quiet began settling in. At first I was beset by a muted panic because I had given no thought to what I was going to say. When this quieted down, it seemed as if the barriers that separated me from the rest of the congregation disappeared and I found myself enveloped in a vast silence and a great stillness. In time a strange thing began happening to me. There came up as if from some depth of my mind one word, then another word. As if transfixed, I watched with a part of my mind the unfolding of a sentence from the Sermon on the Mount. I knew the sentence, but I could not rationalize it; I had to wait for each additional word to emerge. When the quotation or sentence was complete, my mind, released now, pounced upon it and began to think about it in terms of the outline of an address. When I was ready to speak, I leaned forward with my hands on the railing, my right foot extended slightly under the pew, my left foot pushed forward, and I began to rise to my feet, when behind me I heard the voice of a lady in the pew above quoting the very text which was in my mind. After she sat, individuals in different parts of the room took their turns speaking to the subject. At length I was able to have my own say. It seemed that all in that room were sharing deeply in the same kind of transcending experience which greatly confirmed and sustained us all but was at the same time much, much more than any one of us, in and of himself.

What is felt in the religious experience as being true and valid is that the individual is worthful beyond all merit. He seems to be touched at a point in himself beyond all his virtues and beyond his faults. He seems to be regarded as a whole or total or unified being. There is something of such enormous significance in this that the only term that can be used to express it is being cared for, completely and totally understood. After all, this is the meaning of the word love.

Life at its deepest and profoundest seems to be kind and in that sense personal. And this is the claim of religion, that God cares for man and that man is not the creation of some blind impersonal force, but there is purpose, intent, at the heart of reality, which addresses and confirms that which is at the very center and core of personality. There is in the life of man the kind of potential that is actualized at its fullest in the full-orbed sweep of the religious experience. Just as his body is the actualized potential of organism, so his mind and spirit are the same thing in a different dimension and in another universe of discourse. It would seem to follow quite directly that what man as a part of the universe experiences as actualized potential cannot be foreign to that which is characteristic of the universe itself. Man experiences purpose in his own profoundest fulfillment and this provides him with the crucial clue to the understanding not only of his own life but of the world about him. Always he seeks the clue to meaning in all about him, always he seeks a rational active ingredient in all manifestation that will give him understanding of all phenomena. On the basis of this he reads the history of life on the planet and the history of the planet and of the cosmos itself; he understands and relates to the present and predicts the future.

For the religious man the all-encompassing reality which contains and sustains his body is a part of an intent at the very heart of existence. The order within his body gives the content of order to his mind, and the order in his mind makes him seek for order in his world of men and things. He becomes predisposed to harmony, which is the conscious meaning of order—thus he is not only a sharer in values, but is a creator of values. The time and the place of his life on the earth is the time and place of his body, but the meaning, the significance, the purpose of his life is seen in its grandest dimension when he has the experience of being a part of a larger life, a larger consciousness, a larger reality which can only be compassed by the terms "divine, holy, God."

CHAPTER 16

The Essence of Religion and Science

by WINTHROP WADLEIGH*

SO MUCH HAS BEEN written and spoken over the years about the relationship or conflict between science and religion that it is questionable whether a few words from me will make much of a contribution in this field.

Furthermore, I cannot speak with authority, because I am neither a trained theologian nor a trained scientist. I am, however, a lawyer who is theoretically, at least, accustomed to orderly and logical processes of thinking, and I have taken courses in chemistry, physics, mathematics, biology, psychology, and sociology at college. In addition, I was brought up in a deeply religious household and have always been interested in theology. Over the years of my life I have pondered at great length and as deeply as I am capable of about the eternal questions of religion.

It is with this background that I undertake to set forth briefly what I now believe concerning the relationship of science and religion. I use the word *now* advisedly because it may well be that in the future I will be changing some of my

* Attorney at Law, Manchester, New Hampshire.

beliefs about religion and science. For I believe that God gave
us our minds to use, not only in the world of material matters
but also in the spiritual world. Theologians and religious
thinkers as well as scientists must use their minds.

In the twelfth chapter of Mark Jesus made this clear
when he set forth the first and great commandment: "and
thou shalt love the Lord thy God with all thy heart, and with
all thy soul, and with all thy mind and with all thy strength."

Apparently this same commandment in Deuteronomy
6:5 and 30:6 did not use the word *mind* as Jesus did, but this
may have been due to an error or difficulty in translation.

Jesus also said in John 8:32: "And ye shall know the
truth, and the truth shall make you free."

I believe that a real religion must be based on the truth.
If any religious belief or doctrine is shown to be false, it
should be discarded. New beliefs based on the truth should be
added from time to time. For only a religion based on the
truth will endure. A religion not founded on the truth is like
a house built on sand. Consequently the truly religious person
should be searching for the truth unceasingly.

The scientist is also engaged in searching for the truth.
He does so by constantly re-examining and testing what he
believes to be true in the light of new facts, new discoveries,
and new theories that appear on the horizon. If what he believes to be true is shown to be false, he discards the false beliefs and adopts the new ones that he believes to be true. In
this way scientific knowledge has increased tremendously
over the years, and science has become increasingly important
in the world while religion has lost ground.

The approach of the scientist is known as the scientific
attitude. I believe that religious thinkers should be more
scientific in their attitude toward religion so that religion will
have fewer false beliefs and so that more new truths will be
added as time goes on. I believe that religion has lost its appeal
and vitality for a great many people today because the sci-

entific attitude in religion is so infrequently seen. The theme of the hymn "It's the old time religion and it's good enough for me" is far too prevalent in religion.

It is true that to some extent religion has discarded false beliefs and gained new insights over the years. How silly it now seems to us that medieval theologians argued interminably about how many angels could dance on the head of a pin.

Christianity has certainly progressed tremendously from the following acts by our predecessors that were perpetrated in the name of religion:

1. The religious wars between the Catholics and Protestants;

2. The Crusades;

3. The Inquisition, when Christians were burned at the stake by other Christians for their beliefs;

4. The treatment of Jews by Christians;

5. The persecution by other Christians in England and in the United States of the Quakers, who believed and practiced brotherly love.

But changes in religion have usually been accomplished only after bitter denunciation and persecution of those who advocated change. Church leaders and theologians who have resisted changes have not done so with the scientific attitude of searching for the truth. As a result, progress in discarding false doctrines and adopting new truths has been far too slow and too little.

Science has chipped away many false religious beliefs over the years. The statements in the Bible that the earth is flat, that it was created in six days, that it is fixed and the sun moves around it, and many others have been shown by science not to be true.

The scientific doctrine of evolution, so bitterly fought in the past by religious thinkers and theologians, upset many false religious doctrines. In the years ahead many more scientific discoveries may be made that will discredit religious beliefs now held.

But these victories of science in discovering new truths and showing the falsity of certain religious doctrines have not been and will not be defeats for true religion. They have not destroyed or even damaged the essence of real religion. They have only destroyed the false beliefs and doctrines that are the non-essentials of true religion.

What is the essence of real religion? Religion has become so encrusted with dogmas and doctrines over the years that it is difficult for most laymen to know what the real essence is.

The essence of real religion certainly doesn't consist of belief in the virgin birth, the Holy Trinity, miracles, the dogmas of the church, or some outworn creed. These are not the important or vital parts of a real faith.

The fundamental test of a truly religious person is not:

1. How much he goes to church and sings and prays and takes communion, or

2. Whether he believes in the virgin birth, the doctrine of the Trinity, or some outworn creed, or

3. How much he has given to organized charity, or

4. Whether he smokes, drinks, gambles, or swears, or

5. Whether he obeys the Ten Commandments.

All these can be done or not done with the wrong motives and without being truly religious.

The essence of real religion is love—love of God and love of all mankind. The fundamental test of a really religious person is how much does he love God and how much does he love all mankind—not just the nice people of all races, but the humble ones, the unwashed, the poor, the ignorant, and those who are being pushed around by others.

Jesus said so when he said:

> Thou shalt love the Lord thy God with all thy heart, and with all thy soul, and with all thy mind. This is the first

and great commandment. And the second is like unto it, Thou shalt love thy neighbor as thyself. On these two commandments hang all the law and the prophets. . . .

A new commandment I give unto you, That ye love one another; as I have loved you, that ye also love one another. By this shall all men know that ye are my disciples, if ye have love one to another.

Love your enemies, bless them that curse you, do good to them that hate you, and pray for them which despitefully use you, and persecute you.

St. Paul said so in that eloquent passage in First Corinthians 13:

1. Though I speak with the tongues of men and of angels, and have not love, I am become as sounding brass, or a tinkling cymbal.

2. And though I have the gift of prophecy, and understand all mysteries and all knowledge; and though I have all faith, so that I could remove mountains, and have not love, I am nothing.

3. And although I bestow all my goods to feed the poor, and though I give my body to be burned, and have not love, it profiteth me nothing.

13. And now abideth faith, hope, love, these three; but the greatest of these is love.

Albert Schweitzer said so when he said: "The essential element in Christianity as it was preached by Jesus and as it is comprehended by thought, is this, that it is only through love that we can attain to communion with God. All living knowledge of God rests upon this foundation; that we experience Him in our lives as will-to-love."

Jesus says to man: "If you want to be in the spirit of God, you may not think or act otherwise than in love."

Abraham Lincoln, a truly religious person, said so when he said: "When I can find a church which has as its creed only the following—'Love thy God with all thy heart and with all thy soul and with all thy mind and thy neighbor as thyself' I will join that church with all my heart and with all my soul and with all my mind." He never found such a church, so he never became a church member.

Henry Drummond said so when he gave, at Northfield, Massachusetts, in 1887, one of the finest sermons ever given in the English language—"The Greatest Thing in the World" —Christian love.

Henry Hitt Crane, the noted Methodist minister, said so when he affirmed: "Every virtue is vicious unless it is all wrapped around with love."

Ralph W. Sockman, one of the leading Methodist ministers in the United States today, said in a sermon recently: "The need for a new frontier of faith lies beyond social congeniality, beyond nationalism and even beyond the Church. This new frontier should parallel scientific growth, but should be based upon the Christian concept of love and compassion."

I believe that true religion, which has as its essence love of God and love of all mankind as set forth in the above quotations and shown in the illustrations that follow, has nothing to fear from science. It can and will withstand the most rigorous inquiry by anyone searching for the truth with the scientific attitude.

In fact, science has already confirmed in this century by scientific means the importance of love. Here is what a noted scientist, Ashley Montagu, has written about the soundness and importance of love from the standpoint of science:

> The dominant principle which informs all behavior that is biologically healthy is love. Without love there can be no healthy social behavior, co-operation, or security. To love thy neighbor as thyself is not simply good text material for Sunday morning sermons but perfectly sound biology....
>
> Man is born for co-operation, not for competition or conflict. This is a basic discovery of modern science. It confirms a discovery made some two thousand years ago by one

Jesus of Nazareth. In a word: it is the principle of love which embraces all mankind. It is the principle of humanity, of one world, one brotherhood of peoples. . . ."

Man cannot live by bread alone. Physiologically, biologically, psychologically, and socially, he can retain his health and flourish only in love of, and co-operation with his fellow man.

It is only the nonessential and spurious aspects of religion that have anything to fear from the discoveries of science and the scientific attitude.

Some years ago in Manchester, New Hampshire, a mother went in to say good night to her young son. She found him asleep clutching a piece of paper on which was written by him with a childish scrawl:

I love God
I love Mother
I love Father
I love Brother
I love *Every*body

That child was truly religious. He had expressed in the language of a child the essence of religion.

A few years ago an attractive Negro couple came from the South to spend the summer in a small town in New Hampshire. On their first Sunday in the community they attended the local Protestant church. After the service the pastor as usual stood at the exit to greet the congregation as they went out. When the turn of the Negro couple came to shake hands with the pastor, he deliberately turned his back on them and engaged in conversation with others standing nearby. He prolonged the conversation with the others so that it was obvious to everyone there that he was refusing to shake hands with the Negroes.

An uneducated farmer's wife who was standing near saw the whole episode. Grieving in her heart for the snub to the

Negroes, she quietly stepped up to them and invited them to have dinner that noon with her family.

Which of these two do you think was the truly religious person? The pastor who believed in the virgin birth, the Holy Trinity, the miracles, and the Apostle's Creed, or the uneducated farmer's wife who believed and practiced Christian love?

Several years ago in northern New Hampshire a prominent and respected citizen of Manchester went to a group of roadside cabins to obtain lodging for the night. It was rainy and cold and late at night. While he was in the office, arranging for the accommodations, there arrived a nice-looking Jewish couple. The wife was sick with a fever. In spite of their anguished pleas for overnight accommodations or even for a few hours of rest, they were refused because they were Jewish. They had to move on, hoping to find a real Christian somewhere who would take them in.

Yet that cabin owner erroneously believed that he was a truly religious person because he went to church and sang and prayed and took communion.

The truly religious person must be inspired and motivated by love of God and love of all mankind. But something else must be added to this love. His love must be guided by intelligence. For love without intelligence tends to become weakness and sentimentality. Someone has said that nothing is more terrible or terrifying than to see ignorance in action. This may not be as true of ignorance motivated by love, but love guided by intelligence is much greater and more effective than love unguided. It will then bless those who express it and those who receive it.

Science and the scientific attitude can be of tremendous help to religion by increasing the knowledge and wisdom so necessary to guide love. For example, the love of parents for their children, if not guided by intelligence, can ruin the children, and often has. Scientific study of the care and rearing of children has resulted in a body of knowledge that, if used with love, should bring fruitful results.

Science and the scientific attitude can also help religion by exploring, explaining, and knitting together the laws of the spiritual world. For God operates the universe through what we know now as laws. We all are familiar to some extent with natural law in the physical world, such as the laws of physics, chemistry, and biology. We know that if we violate them, the penalty is injury to or death of the body. We know that if we defy the law of gravity by jumping out of a third-story window, the penalty is injury to the body. We know that if we violate the laws of nutrition sufficiently, sooner or later the result is sickness of the body or death.

Some of us, however, do not realize that there are laws in the spiritual world that are even more important. Violation of them results in injury to the soul. The greatest law in the spiritual world is the law of love. Unless we live in accordance with it, we are neither truly religious nor scientifically wise.

The law of love is somewhat analogous to the law of electricity. We don't know what electricity is, but we do know to some extent from scientific investigation how it works. Science has already established that love is inherent in the biological structure of man as a functioning organism. But we need to know more about the law of love and how it works. Various sciences are helping and can help religion by exploring the law of love in its different aspects and ramifications, including the effects of the law of love on the individual and on society.

We do know that hatred, revenge, jealousy, and envy—the opposites of love—injure both our bodies and our souls. We tear ourselves apart by these motives. Most of our problems are created by them and would be solved if they were replaced by love. Science can and does help religion by studying the effects of these motives on the human organism and on society.

Other laws of the spiritual world are set forth in the teachings of Jesus and in other parts of the Bible. One example is the law that an emotion in one person tends to create a similar emotion in others. The Bible expresses it in more colorful language:

"A soft answer turneth away wrath but grievous words stir up anger."

"All they that take the sword shall perish by the sword."

Religion needs the help of science and the scientific attitude to gather together all the known laws of the spiritual world from the Bible and other sources and to explain them in understandable language without the addition of theological speculation. Why so few attempts have been made to do this mystifies me. This is a great project waiting to be undertaken. In undertaking it, science will be serving the best interests of God and mankind as true religion does.

CHAPTER 17

Fellowship of the Spirit*

SARVEPALLI RADHAKRISHNAN**

I

I AM GREATLY HONORED by the invitation to participate in this significant function and give the Address. This is an honor to my country where a process of creation has been at work for many centuries, to which different races have contributed, the Dravidians and the Aryans, the Iranians and the Greeks, the Muslims and the Christians. Adherents of different faiths live there in freedom and fellowship, in spite of occasional conflicts and setbacks.

The donors of this Foundation, I am informed, believe in the fruitful interchange of religious ideas and hope that such an interchange may enrich our lives and pave the way for a fellowship of the spirit.

In the last few decades amazing advances in science and technology have made the world into a neighborhood bound

---

* Condensed from *Fellowship of the Spirit* (Cambridge, Massachusetts: Harvard University Press, 1961). Reprinted with permission from the President and Fellows of Harvard College. Copyright © 1961 by the President and Fellows of Harvard College.
** President of India.

by political ties and economic arrangements, where what happens anywhere affects everywhere. To convert this neighborhood into a world community we need good will and understanding of the basic principles which govern the lives of the different peoples. Religion has been a major factor in the development of the civilizations of the world.

A university is a seat of learning, not a center of worship. It believes in the pursuit of knowledge and not in the establishment of a cult. As university men it is our privilege and honor to seek for truth and in this pursuit we should not be deterred by the fear of what we might find. In many theological institutes both in the East and in the West, students grow up in profound ignorance of other religions, which, if they are presented to them, are done only in gross caricature. They are full of polemics and apologetics. By such a treatment the secret of an alien religion is missed and its genius outraged. By getting the adherents of different religions to work together in a spirit of co-operation and mutual respect, we will promote appreciation of religions at their best.

It is in consistency with the great traditions of this university that the Center should be established here. The education it imparts does not lack in contemporaneity. It carries the spirit of our civilization, which, though rooted in the past, is moving toward a new future. St. Paul in his last letter to his first European converts, the Philippians, written during his captivity and trial, speaks about "forgetting all that is completed and reaching out to things that lie before." It is the great task of universities like this to push forward the frontiers of freedom not only in outer space but in the human soul.

II

The rise of a creature reflecting on himself and his environment is a great development in evolution. Man is said to be the maker of things, *homo faber*. Man is also a pattern-maker. When his cold and hunger are conquered, when his appetites and desires are satisfied he wishes to find out if there is any pattern in things, any purpose to existence, any meaning in life. He cannot be content with formlessness, irrationality, uncertainty, chaos.[1]

When man reflects on the finite and limited character of his existence, he is overcome by fear, which is, as Heidegger says, "more primordial than man himself." Spinoza begins his treatise *On the Improvement of the Understanding* with the words: "I saw that I stood in extreme peril and that I was compelled with all my strength to seek a remedy, however uncertain, as a sick man in the grip of a mortal disease foreseeing inevitable death unless a remedy be applied, is compelled to search with all his strength for that remedy, however uncertain it be, for every hope he has is placed therein." Man asks, Is ultimate nothingness all, or is there any meaning behind it all?

In the words of the Upaniṣad the suffering individual cries out, "Lead me from the unreal to the real. Lead me from darkness to light. Lead me from death to eternal life." Man can step out of the world, and this indicates that he has something of the nontemporal in him. The Buddha believes that there is beyond the world of Karma, of necessity, a world of freedom, of nirvāṇa. Christianity affirms that death is not all. "He is risen." Death has no sting; grave has no victory. In Handel's *Messiah* we read, "Though worms destroy my body yet in my flesh shall I see God."

Man's fear and anguish are the result of the conflict in him. He belongs to two worlds, the spiritual and the natural. Existence is essentially a process in time. It is perched on a

---

[1] Chuangtse, a Chinese philosopher of the fourth century B.C., says: "Joy and anger, sorrow and happiness, worries and fears, come upon us by turns, with ever-changing moods, like music from the hollows, or like mushrooms in the swamp. Day and night they alternate within us, but we cannot tell whence they spring. Alas, alas, would we for a moment lay our finger upon their very cause?"

razor's edge, as it were, which divides being from nonbeing. Human being is involved in nonbeing. We were not: we will not be. What is the nature of being? What is the mystery of nonbeing which surrounds and conditions existence as we know it? Being needs nonbeing for its manifestation. St. Augustine in the first chapter of his *Confessions* asks what his longing for God means. Does it mean that he has found God or has not found God? If he had not found God, he would not know of God since it is God who gives him the yearning for God. If he had found God and known him fully, he would be incapable of yearning since he would be fulfilled and so would not have to struggle and suffer.

Man is a bridge between two worlds. He would cease to be human if he belonged only to one world. Life is a perpetual drama between the visible and the invisible. Man looks to the world of truth, goodness, and beauty not as another world but as the still unrealized good of this world.

There is an inner urge in human nature which impels men to seek in endless ways for something that they do not fully comprehend though they believe it to be the Supreme Reality. Man cannot be happy until he attains the truth.

Everything that lives aims at its own perfection, the blade of grass, the flowering tree, the flying bird, the running deer. While the subhuman species work according to predetermined patterns, man by virtue of his intelligence and capacity for moral choice has to work out his future consciously. The period of involuntary development of minerals, plants, animals has ended with the advent of man. In the depths of his consciousness he feels that he is incomplete, that he has to be surpassed, that he has to enter a larger life of spirit and freedom, that he is still in the making, that he has to make himself. Religion has been the discipline used by man to achieve the goal of spiritual ascent.

The increase of knowledge and the progress of material conditions have led to a weakening of interest in the life of spirit. The scientific temper which has become a part of modern man's mental equipment finds it difficult to accept religious beliefs and dogmas. They seem to obstruct the path to natural truth and moral progress. If we accept religious traditions as unalterable truths we face an unbridgeable chasm between faith and reason.[2] A dogmatic religion obstructs the free flow of ideas and the spirit of inner life.

The movement of Logical Positivism holds that religious truths are not truths because they are not empirically verifiable.

Besides, religion has tolerated barbarism, cruelty, and ignorance. While religious men claim that they are bound by the moral code, while they preach love and brotherhood, they condone wars and persecutions. Man has become man's worst enemy. There is no sense of urgency among religious men to improve the human condition. Men and nations choose evil for the sake of attaining a good cause. We confuse the voice of God with national, racial, and political insanities. Soren Kierkegaard says: "What we have before us is not Christianity but a prodigious illusion, and the people are not pagans but live in the blissful conceit that they are Christians."[3] Lenin once put a question to a bishop: "Bring me one man in the whole of Christendom who lives today as Paul lived and I will have faith." Many people give up religion because they have known too many religious men!

It is one of the major tragedies of the world that the great religions instead of uniting mankind in mutual understanding and good will divide mankind by their dogmatic claims and prejudices. They affirm that religious truth is attained in this

---

[2] An extreme expression of this difficulty is found in Mr. Khrushchev's address to the Central Committee on Atheist Propaganda given on November 10, 1954: "Modern scientific discoveries ... convincingly refute religious dogmas." When Kirsopp Lake's father, who was a physician, was asked what had done the most to relieve human suffering, he answered: "Anaesthesia and the decay of Christian theology."

[3] *Attack upon "Christendom,"* trans. Walter Lowrie (1944), p. 97.

or that special region, by this or that chosen race, condemning others either to borrow from it or else suffer spiritual destitution.

By identifying religion with dogmas and beliefs we fought wars over abstract theological differences. To recover the Holy Tomb the crusaders engaged in bloodshed, cruelty, and treachery. We are familiar with the Presbyterian elder who concluded his argument with a Jesuit by saying, "We must agree to differ. We are both trying to serve the same God—you in your way and I in His." This attitude is not outmoded.

III

The mind of man, proud of its liberation from religion with its legends which ignore the teachings of science, and with its demands which are not consistent with the principles of morals and the needs of humanity, is becoming aware of an emptiness which increasing knowledge and humanitarianism are not able to fill. In our eagerness to throw away the fetters of dogmatic religion we are becoming the victims of an oppressive form of bondage imposed by secularist enlightenment. If millions of our people are in a neurotic condition, if mental hospitals are crowded, if the demand for psychiatrists is on the increase, if a sense of boredom and use of sedatives are the constant companions of many of us it shows that where an ideal or a purpose should be there is only a vacuum.[4] We try to cover up the growing gulf between our inner and outer life by adopting the forms of religion. This is due to the inertia of habit or blind belief which is too lazy to question

[4] Cf. C. G. Jung: "During the last thirty years, people from all over the civilised countries of the world have consulted me. Amongst all my patients in the second half of life—that is to say over thirty-five—there has not been one whose problem in the last resort was not that of finding a religious outlook on life. It is safe to say that every one of them fell ill because he had lost that which the living religions of every age have given their followers and none of them has been really healed who did not regain his religious outlook." *Modern Man in Search of His Soul* (1933).

itself or a kind of utilitarianism which finds adherence to religious organizations useful socially and politically. The paradox of the situation is that we worship God and at the same time doubt his existence. Spiritual life is smothered in all religions by dead forms, making our daily life petty and trivial, breaking up our humanity into different sections, reducing our manhood into a narrow provincialism. We do not become aware of the rule of the one but are kept distracted by the tyranny of the many. We are shut off from the Universal Spirit by a hundred artificial barriers. We must recover the spiritual dimension of life, the lack of which has cramped and darkened the culture of the modern world.

Our difficulties are traceable to the confusion of belief with religious experience. Those who are satisfied with belief live on the surface and do not come to terms with the ultimate mysteries of life and death. Religion is life experienced in its depth.

Logical Positivism is not inconsistent with religion. Though it formally denies the validity of metaphysics it insinuates its own metaphysical views about the world and the individual. Many scientific theories are capable only of indirect verification. Religious theories also are interpretations of experience and not merely speculations. Scientific metaphysicians claim that they start with experience, and their theories are meant to account for the facts observed. We cannot account for the cosmic process with its order and progress if we do not trace it to a Spiritual Reality, a Presence greater than man which governs the whole process. We recognize a First Cause, and from the pattern and purpose of the world admit that it is an expression of Reason. From the intimations of goodness and beauty in the universe we give a more positive content to the Being who is apprehended not only as the source of the world but also its lover. In the heart of man he is felt as the eternal Lord of righteousness. God is wisdom, goodness, and love.

There are some who hold that this spiritual reality is not a mere hypothesis but a felt reality. Job said to God at the end of his long agony: "I have heard of thee by the hearing of the ear, but now mine eye seeth thee." Experience is not limited to what comes to us through science and scientific method. It has many dimensions, moral, aesthetic, and religious. We cannot exclude from the realm of experience the passion for knowledge, the excitement of beauty, the power of goodness, and the sense of the numinous. When it is said that man is made in the image of God, it means that his pure longings are a reflection of a higher reality. There is a spark of the divine in man in the image of God; it means that his pure longings are a reflection of a higher reality. There is a spark of the divine in man with which he has to establish direct contact. Whatever happiness is in the world arises from a wish for the welfare of others; whatever misery is in the world arises from a wish for our own welfare.

Religion is a strenuous endeavor to apprehend truth. Dogmas and rites are intended to awaken in us the spiritual sense, to help us to realize new possibilities of life.

The apprehension of Ultimate Reality is possible only through a life of austerity and self-control. If religion has not saved us from crimes and cruelties, it is because we stop with the observance of rites and acceptance of dogmas and do not work for the purification of the soul, for the transformation of our being. The practice of spiritual exercises, of the vows of poverty, chastity, and obedience, represents the struggle to get beyond the normal sphere of earthly living. The symbol of the Cross in Christianity means getting beyond the frontiers of the sensible world. If we renounce our ego, our nature will become the channel of divine energy, the instrument of divine action. If we are authentically religious, we will bless where others curse, love where others hate, forgive where others condemn, give where others grasp. He who lives in Brahma "shall deceive none, entertain no hatred for any one and never wish to injure any one through anger. He shall have measureless love for all creatures, even as a mother has for her only child whom she protects with her own life." That is the way the Buddha describes *brahma-vihāra*.

If there are quarrels among religions it is because we shun all mystery and express religious truth in intellectual terms. The Supreme Reality cannot be unveiled in propositional forms. We can express it only through imaginative symbols. Disputes about dogmas have led to hysteria among the masses and fanaticism among the leaders. We have to get beyond dogmas if we are to feel the truth in the deeper layers of our consciousness. Religious forms without religious experience do not satisfy man's longing for spiritual fulfillment. True religion means wholehearted commitment and dedication. In moments of devotion and prayer, we offer our whole being to an integrated reality without claiming any reward for ourselves. Religious experience unites rather than divides. In it the sense of separateness is transcended.

The foundation of moral and social progress is the establishment of ties of sympathy with others and of harmony among the contending elements of our own nature. We must foster an inner sense of unity. What is called *Yoga* is the discipline by which we silence the clamor of the senses and forms of intellect and awaken the spiritual in us. Spiritual vision is possible only for those who have understanding, compassion, and love. As we need physical senses for the observation of the outer world we need an inner sense to perceive spiritual realities.

Spiritual perception and intellectual effort are not opposed to each other. Spiritual perception is integral insight. The high degree of intelligence which we have developed in the course of centuries should be used and not scrapped if we are to rid religion of errors and illusions. The wheel of history cannot be turned back or brought to a standstill. We cannot sink into the womb of the unconscious or revert to the irrational. Intellect helps us to discriminate between the authentic and the spurious nonobjective perceptions. Intuition without reason is blind; reason without intuition is ungrounded. Only when they are held in balance does man attain wholeness.

God is the complete response to all the needs of the empirical egos, emotional, intellectual, and spiritual. Religion deals with the whole man. It is not lived in compartments. We have trust which is intellectual, worship which is emotional, and dedication which is volitional. We cannot accept any religious view without inward testimony of spirit at once incommunicable to others and self-evident to the individual. The word "awake" which the Upaniṣads, the Buddha and Jesus use means "experience." Do not go through life sleeping or dreaming. Awakening is personal experience.

We do not wish to eliminate the particular elements in different religions. Beliefs are the codified expressions of experience. Religious traditions, rites, and ceremonies do not grow in a void. They have roots in the soil and they are nourished by the same life-giving and life-sustaining elements. We accept differences and try to understand them. We do not encourage the effort to recast the world in any one image. We do not believe in any religious Esperanto.

Though our thinking is international or global our particular commitments, so long as they are not injurious to human fellowship, should be fostered. Religion is a response to the supersensible reality which we call God of which all men are aware dimly or clearly. We may not all see the same part of the spiritual landscape or see it with equal lucidity. Because the reality is one the responses should have something in common in spite of all diversities. However unique religions may be, there are certain trends which are common to all of them. Besides, they have to reckon today with scientific knowledge, modern criticism, growing conscience, and the emerging unity of the world. As a result they tend to approximate to each other, for all religions are renewing themselves.

. . . .

XV

The Christian religion met its first challenge when it entered the Graeco-Roman world. For centuries the highest minds of the Church applied themselves to this problem, and as a result Christian theology emerged greatly enriched. The second challenge was from the recent developments of science which reveal the universality and unity of the world around us and within us. From this encounter Christian thought was profoundly modified. There is today a truer, deeper intellectual understanding of the Christian faith. The challenge today is from the presence of other religions of which there is greater appreciation and understanding, and great minds of the Christian world are applying themselves to this vital issue. Here in this university some of the great minds were stimulated by the resurgence of the non-Christian religions.

The great philosophers who taught in this university, Josiah Royce, William James, A. N. Whitehead, and W. E. Hocking, were all ecumenical men. They believed in God because of their personal experiences. "If you ask what these experiences are," Wiliam James says, "they are conversations with the unseen, voices and visions, responses to prayer, changes of heart, deliverances from fear, inflowings of help, assurances of support, whenever certain persons set their own internal attitude in certain appropriate ways." [5] In his notes for his famous Gifford Lectures, William James said: "Remember that the whole point lies in really *believing* that through a cer-

[5] *Collected Essays and Reviews* (1920), p. 428.

tain point or part in you, you coalesce and are identical with
the Eternal. This seems to be the saving belief both in Christianity and in Vedāntism." [6]

Josiah Royce places the problem of Christianity in the
relation of each person to the community whose spirit is the
interpreter of his moral experience. Loyalty to the world
community is inseparable from love. "Every one that loveth is
born of God."

When A. N. Whitehead defines religion as "what the
individual does with his solitariness," [7] he makes out that it is
inward experience. We must have the capacity to take our
stand within the self, withdraw serenely into one's incorrupt-
ible depths. Whitehead complains that the interpreters of
Christianity identify the experience with concepts with disastrous results. "You get it in all of the following interpreters
of Christianity from Augustine, even in Francis of Assisi. . . .
Their hearts were right but their heads were wrong. In St.
Francis, for example, it is hardly credible that the two words,
that of grace and mercy and that of eternal damnation, could
exist in one and the same breast. This theological disaster is
what I mean when I speak of the mischief which follows from
banishing novelty, from trying to formulate your truth, from
setting up to declare: 'This is all there is to be known on the
subject and discussion is closed.' " [8]

<hr>

[6] Ralph Barton Perry, *The Thought and Character of William James*
[briefer version (1948)], p. 259. The late Dean Inge said: "What happened
2,000 years ago cannot matter to us now." He commended Plotinus because "his is a deep spiritual religion resting partly on philosophic thought
and partly on intimate personal experience. It stands free of any historical
events in past or future." (*Dean Inge*, by Adam Fox.)

Canon Sheppard in his *The Impatience of a Parson* argues that the idea
that God disclosed himself exclusively to one people and left others in
darkness is an "intolerable idea" (p. 107). Karl Jaspers observes that "in its
motive and in its consequences the claim [to exclusiveness] is catastrophic
for men. We must fight for the truth and for our soul against this fatal
claim." *The Perennial Scope of Philosophy* (1950), p. 88.

[7] *Religion in the Making* (1926), p. 6.

[8] *Dialogues of Alfred North Whitehead*, p. 172.

Professor William Ernest Hocking, who is happily still with us, writes: "The partial de-Christianisation of the West brought about by the various secular movements is destined to work not only to the net advantage of the West but also to that of a reconceived Christianity." [9] He mentions the continuing need for reconception in view of its present unfinishedness and also of the depth and breadth of the religious experience of other lands.[10] "Our Christianity is in need of reconception through a deeper and humbler intercourse with the soul of the East in its age-long acceptance of a searching self-discipline." [11]

XVI

Today when humanity is in grave danger and our civilization is precariously balanced, we must rediscover lost values and recapture reverence and wonder which have fallen victims to the increasing secularization of human life and consciousness. Mankind has always recognized greatness. The sayings and deeds of the great are not mere museum pieces but are answers to the basic questions of mankind.

In every religion we have people who do not believe in provincialism, who emphasize religion as experience to be attained by self-conquest and self-transformation, appreciation of other faiths, and a sense of loyalty to the world community. If man is to achieve wholeness for himself and for the world, if he seeks harmonious living, he must know other religions. We must set aside differences caused by the accidents of geography and history and accept the universal ideas transmitted by a common heritage. It should become as normal for an American or a European student to be familiar with the civilizations of the East, the Chinese, the Japanese, and the Indian

[9] *The Coming World Civilisation* (1956), p. XII.
[10] *Ibid.*, p. 136.
[11] *Op. cit.*, p. 165.

as he is now with the bases of European civilization, in the Greek, the Roman, and the Judaic cultures.

The different religions should be regarded as comrades in a joint enterprise in facing the common problems of the peaceful coexistence of the peoples, international welfare and justice, racial equality and political independence of all peoples.

A study of the different forms of religious life may give us some idea of the deep significance of religion for the life of man. The different religions are to be used as building stones for the development of a human culture in which the adherents of the different religions may be fraternally united as the children of one Supreme. All religions convey to their followers a message of abiding hope. The world will give birth to a new faith which will be but the old faith in another form, the faith of all ages, the potential divinity of man which will work for the supreme purpose written in our hearts and souls, the unity of mankind. It is my hope and prayer that in this Center for the Study of World Religions unbelief shall disappear and superstition shall not enslave the mind and all those who meet here shall recognize that they are brothers, one in spirit and one in fellowship.